Lincoln, the Law, and Presidential Leadership

LINCOLN,
THE LAW, AND
PRESIDENTIAL
LEADERSHIP

Edited by Charles M. Hubbard

Southern Illinois University Press
Carbondale

18 17 16 15   4 3 2 1

Jacket illustration: *A Lincoln Poster*, by Harry Wood, 1970; image
    courtesy of the Abraham Lincoln Library and Museum at Lincoln
    Memorial University, Harrogate, Tennessee

Library of Congress Cataloging-in-Publication Data
Lincoln, the law, and presidential leadership / edited by Charles M.
    Hubbard ; contributions by Burrus Carnahan, Jason R Jividen, Edna
    Greene Medford, Ron Soodalter, Mark E. Steiner, Daniel W. Stowell,
    Natalie Sweet, Frank J. Williams.
    pages cm
Summary: "The essays in this book focus on Lincoln's views on the rule
    of law and the Constitution and expose the difficulty and ambiguity
    associated with the protection of civil rights during the Civil War"—
    Provided by publisher.
Includes bibliographical references and index.
ISBN 978-0-8093-3454-4 (hardback)
ISBN 0-8093-3454-2 (cloth)
ISBN 978-0-8093-3455-1 (e-book)
1. Lincoln, Abraham, 1809–1865 2. Lawyers—Illinois—Biography.
    3. Presidents—United States—Biography. 4. Presidents—United
    States—History 5. Rule of law—United States—History.
    6. Constitutional law—United States—History. I. Hubbard, Charles
    M., 1939– editor.
KF368.L52L56 2015
973.7092—dc23
[B]   2015010066

To R. Gerald McMurtry, whose love of all things
Lincoln inspired generations of Lincoln scholars

CONTENTS

ACKNOWLEDGMENTS

Several years ago, Lincoln Memorial University began a lecture series named for the legendary Lincoln scholar R. Gerald McMurtry, who taught and served as the dean of Lincolniana from 1937 to 1956. Professor McMurtry devoted his professional life to the study of Abraham Lincoln, and the university honors his contributions and legacy with the lecture series. Since the lectures began, prestigious and recognized Lincoln scholars from around the world have lectured on a variety of Lincoln-related topics. The lectures focus on Lincoln's leadership and the influence of the law on his actions as president. The idea to publish these essays developed from the earliest lectures and the stimulating and provocative discussions that followed. The lecture series and these essays were made possible through the generous support of the McMurtry family and Lincoln Memorial University.

I wish to acknowledge my sincere gratitude to the scholars who contributed essays to this volume. All of them took the task seriously and invested themselves in this undertaking. Each essay stands on its own, reflecting the unique approach of its contributor, and can be read independently. It was my pleasure to work with these highly respected academics, and I hope they all enjoyed exploring Lincoln and the law as much as I did.

I am indeed grateful to Sara Gabbard, who first suggested pulling all these ideas together, and to Sylvia Frank Rodrigue of Southern Illinois University Press for her patient guidance through the process. Christian Samito deserves our thanks for reading the early drafts and offering constructive suggestions that were helpful in clarifying certain legal terminology. I appreciate Professor

Sheila Clyburn, who read the manuscript in draft form and offered valuable editorial and formatting recommendations.

I am indebted to Michelle Ganz, the archivist at the Abraham Lincoln Library and Museum, for her assistance in locating, identifying, and obtaining appropriate permissions for the illustrations included in this volume. Thanks are due Elizabeth Yagodzinski, professor of information systems, who provided timely technical assistance while I assembled all the moving parts of this project.

Finally, I thank my colleagues in the History Department at Lincoln Memorial for their support and encouragement throughout this undertaking. I am indebted to Dr. Debra Salata for reading parts of the manuscript and correcting a number of my mistakes. I am particularly grateful to Michael Toomey, who listens patiently to my numerous theories and ideas and always reminds me to return to the point.

Charles M. Hubbard
Signal Mountain, Tennessee
Spring 2015

INTRODUCTION

Charles M. Hubbard

This collection of essays examines the influence of the law on Lincoln's presidential leadership. The essays included in this book are written by scholars from various backgrounds and academic disciplines, who use different perspectives, methodologies, and writing styles to explore the dimensions of Abraham Lincoln's complex leadership style. Although the approaches differ, each essay emphasizes the connection between Lincoln's respect for the law and the responsibility of presidential leadership, and all in specific ways expand our understanding of Lincoln's vision for a united nation grounded on the Constitution.

Lincoln believed the law provided the foundation for social order and justice, and in his view, those who practiced law or held public office were obligated to be honest and faithful to the people. The following Lincoln quotation reflects his conviction:

> There is a vague popular belief that lawyers are necessarily dishonest. I say vague, because when we consider to what extent confidence and honors are reposed in and conferred upon lawyers by the people, it appears improbable that their impression of dishonesty is very distinct and vivid. Yet the impression is common, almost universal. Let no young man choosing the law for a calling for a moment yield to the popular belief—resolve to be honest at all events; and if in your own judgment you cannot be an honest lawyer, resolve to be honest without being a lawyer. Choose some other occupation, rather than one in the choosing of which you do, in advance, consent to be a knave.[1]

As a young man, Abraham Lincoln felt called to be an honest lawyer, as this fragment suggests. He probably wrote this note in 1858 when preparing to speak to a group of law students. Lincoln read and studied the law on his own, and after passing the bar, he practiced the profession for more than twenty-five years. He progressed in his career from a small-town, rural lawyer traveling the frontier circuit in central Illinois to an accomplished attorney representing the interests of some of the largest and most successful corporations in the Midwest. It is difficult to identify specific life experiences particularly in Lincoln's law practice that shaped his views on presidential responsibility. However, it is certainly possible to assess his actions as president and identify within the decision-making process Lincoln's commitment to law and order and the principles of the Constitution. As Daniel W. Stowell points out in his chapter, Lincoln's relationship as president with his cabinet and other advisors was informed by a "lawyerly" approach.[2]

Lincoln believed in the rule of law as the fundamental principle regulating civil society. He understood that in a democracy, the laws are made and implemented by the people's elected representatives. As a young adult, he discovered a passion for politics. After all, the politicians made the laws that provided the order and structure necessary for a functioning civil society. Furthermore, because the people entrusted their representatives with extraordinary power, they expected lawyers and politicians to be honest and genuinely concerned for the greater good. The influence of the law on his decisions is evident in his efforts to develop legal arguments to sustain his actions.

Lincoln generally left the making of new laws, particularly domestic legislation, to the people's representatives in Congress. Nevertheless, as president, he advanced the evolution and interpretation of the law. For example, during the Civil War, Lincoln found it necessary to codify his orders to the army regulating the treatment of civilians and prisoners of war. As Burrus M. Carnahan reminds us in his essay, Lincoln's requirement to produce a "law of war" had profound domestic and international implications. Lincoln felt compelled to identify a solid legal foundation for his presidential policies and actions. During his presidency, Lincoln continued the indirect practice of law through interpretation and implementation. Throughout his professional life, Lincoln relied on the law and practiced it with an energy that to some seemed almost an obsession.[3]

Lincoln's energy translated into his support of the Whig political party. When the party broke up in the early 1850s over the issue of slavery, Lincoln gravitated to the newly emerging Republican Party. In 1860, the Republicans nominated him to run for president. The country was profoundly divided over the issue of slavery, and the presidential campaign debates further divided the country along sectional lines. Underlying the passionate debate over the future of slavery was a more fundamental question involving the structure of the federal system. The relationship between the states and the federal government would soon be called into question by secession.[4]

Lincoln's election as the sixteenth president of the United States put in motion a series of events that ultimately led to secession and the greatest constitutional crisis in American history. After Lincoln took the oath of office to "preserve, protect and defend the Constitution,"[5] the crisis escalated into civil war. Secession threatened the integrity of the Union and the governing institutions established by the Constitution. The challenge for the incoming president was to preserve the constitutional guarantees for loyal Americans while prosecuting a war against the rebellious portion of the population. To accomplish and balance these seemingly impossible tasks simultaneously, Lincoln needed all of his remarkable legal and political skills. Moreover, it is difficult to imagine that his decisions were not informed by a belief in the righteousness of the Union cause and a sense of his moral and ethical responsibility to maintain democracy.

Lincoln's respect for the rule of law both restrained and expanded his power as president. This apparent paradox is expressed by Edna Greene Medford, who shows how Lincoln's respect for the Constitution, which protected slavery where it existed, encumbered Lincoln's drive toward emancipation and black freedom. Ultimately, Lincoln issued the presidential Emancipation Proclamation as a necessity of war to avoid the constitutional restraints. Frank J. Williams explains how Lincoln managed to emancipate slaves and prosecute the war by using his emergency war powers. He describes how Lincoln expanded presidential authority using the provisions of the emergency war powers granted by the Constitution to limit habeas corpus and other constitutionally guaranteed civil rights.

Despite Lincoln's strict interpretation of the Constitution, he found it necessary to use the previously undefined emergency war powers provided to the president to subdue the rebellion. Lincoln believed, as did most Whigs of the nineteenth century, that the Constitution represented the supreme law of the land, and that without adherence to its principles, national unity could not long endure. His views on the Constitution and its connection to representative government are the focus of my essay. In Lincoln's view, if secession succeeded, it would undermine the basic principle of majority rule and democratic government by the people. The rebellion threatened not only national unity but also the larger concept of republican government. Lincoln resorted to the use of force to protect the Constitution, reduce the rebellion, and resolve the slavery issue permanently.

One of the most frustrating and troublesome legal and constitutional issues confronting Lincoln was the inadequate language in the Constitution defining US citizenship. The emergence of the politically influential, nativist American Party in the 1850s called attention to the citizenship status of recent European immigrants. The citizenship status of free black people in America remained unresolved, particularly in light of the Supreme Court decision in *Dred Scott v. Sandford*. Mark E. Steiner addresses the specific legal dilemma that these issues posed for Lincoln before and after his election as president. Lincoln rejected the idea that there were different levels of citizenship between native and foreign-born Americans. The Constitution protected the rights of all American citizens, regardless of ethnic origin or race. Steiner explains how Lincoln navigates through this difficult and controversial political and legal difficulty.

The Civil War tended to blur the lines between civil and military law. When Lincoln was president, he acted as a court of last resort for both military and civilian courts. Lincoln was a compassionate leader and believed that the law provided sufficient remedies to maintain law and order and administer justice. The Constitution provides the president with the "power of the presidential pardon." Lincoln frequently used that power to balance the unique demands for social and military justice during the Civil War. His compassionate nature notwithstanding, he held those guilty of crimes accountable to the law. Ron Soodalter reminds us that as president, Lincoln reviewed and heard arguments on behalf of numerous petitioners for pardons. Ultimately, the president based his decision on the reasonable and fair application of the law. Soodalter believes that Lincoln viewed some crimes, including the slave trade, as so horrific that justice demanded the harshest punishment. However, in the appropriate circumstances, particularly in the military courts, Lincoln used the presidential pardon to achieve a just and compassionate result.

Lincoln's experience as a trial lawyer gave him a highly developed sense of the rules of evidence. Natalie Sweet describes Lincoln's awareness and sensitivity to this legal precedent when he responded to political and racially motivated accusations against members of the White House staff. Lincoln relied in an informal way on his legal experience to ascertain the validity of accusations against individuals. When the Potter Committee leveled unsubstantiated charges of treason and collaboration against government employees, including servants working in Lincoln's White House, Lincoln required proof before taking action. Sweet explores the motives behind these allegations and Lincoln's politically sensitive, yet ethical, response.

In the final essay, Jason R. Jividen expands on Lincoln's lasting contribution to the American experience. Lincoln continues to mold our understanding of equality and liberty. Jividen concludes that many presidents following Lincoln, whether Democrats or Republicans, liberals or conservative, have appealed to the image of Lincoln and referred to him in their public rhetoric. Jividen argues that acknowledging the universally accepted principles of Lincoln will help us better understand the sixteenth president and the genuine and lasting results of Lincoln's commitment to American republicanism.

Abraham Lincoln is recognized as America's quintessential leader, and these essays clearly demonstrate the influence of law on his presidential leadership. His was one of the "hinge" presidencies of American history.[6] Although Lincoln left the majority of domestic issues to Congress, he nevertheless presided over the sweeping legislative agenda that transformed the nation. He put in motion the amendments to the Constitution that forever charged the federal government with protecting personal freedom and equality. The country that emerged from the crucible of Civil War was reshaped in no small measure by his dynamic and pragmatic leadership. Lincoln exhibited a confidence that transformed those around him, and they accepted the revolutionary changes that reshaped and reunited the nation and its people.

Notes

1. Abraham Lincoln, Notes for a Law Lecture, [July 1, 1850?], in *The Collected Works of Abraham Lincoln*, ed. Roy P. Basler et al. (New Brunswick, NJ: Rutgers University Press, 1953), 2:82.

2. Mark E. Steiner, *An Honest Calling: The Law Practice of Abraham Lincoln* (DeKalb: Northern Illinois University Press, 2006), 6.

3. Douglas L. Wilson and Rodney O. Davis, eds., *Herndon's Informants: Letters, Interviews, and Statements about Lincoln* (Urbana: University of Illinois Press, 1997), 173.

4. Phillip Shaw Paludan, *The Presidency of Abraham Lincoln* (Lawrence: University Press of Kansas, 1994), 15.

5. US Const. art. II, § 1, cl. 8.

6. Allen Guelzo, "Afterword," in *Lincoln and Leadership*, ed. Randall M. Miller (New York: Fordham University Press, 2012), 97.

Abraham Lincoln, the lawyer, in a campaign photograph while running for the US presidency, 1860. Courtesy of the Library of Congress, LC-USZ62-7728B.

ABRAHAM LINCOLN: LAWYER, LEADER, PRESIDENT

Daniel W. Stowell

Abraham Lincoln brought to the most challenging presidency in American history a particular set of leadership skills that he had developed over his quarter-century legal career in central Illinois. His experiences as a lawyer framed the ways in which he approached the personalities and leadership challenges he encountered as president. As president-elect, Abraham Lincoln assembled a cabinet of seven men, nearly all of whom were attorneys or had legal training. The dictates of political patronage meant that Lincoln had to balance within his cabinet appointments the various geographic and ideological constituencies that had elected him. As president, he presided over this talented but quarrelsome "law firm." Though their effectiveness as a group has been overstated, and despite their persistent jealousies and disagreements among themselves, the members of Lincoln's cabinet generally managed their various departments effectively and gave him needed advice.[1]

Generals and politicians formed a sort of "bar association" for Lincoln the president, and as in Illinois, he patiently worked with them all without regard to political affiliation. Lincoln's clientele as president included the entire nation, just as his law practice drew clients from a broad and diverse cross section of antebellum Illinois. Contentious and litigious, Lincoln's neighbors, clients, and legal adversaries in the quarter century before 1860 had given him an advanced education in both human nature and political culture that served him well as president. He had excelled as an advocate before a jury, and he used those persuasive skills in keeping the fractious Northern states together to fight a war for the survival of the Union. His law practice developed within

Abraham Lincoln a commitment to the rule of law, a command of persuasive speech, and a method for approaching conflicts that aided him in presidential decision-making. Representing clients facing an array of economic, legal, and personal problems developed Lincoln's empathy for fellow human beings. This ability served him well as president, as he encountered enslaved African Americans, grieving parents, wounded soldiers, imprisoned Southerners, desperate widows, impatient newspaper editors, nervous governors, and many others.

Abraham Lincoln practiced law for nearly twenty-five years in the courts of central Illinois. From his admission to the bar in 1836 to his inauguration as president in 1861, the law was Lincoln's occupation and professional identity. Over the course of his career, Lincoln remained a general practice attorney. He neither specialized in one area of the law nor sought other legal offices, such as state's attorney or judge. He was persuasive both in front of a jury of farmers and townspeople and before a bench of appellate judges, and his extensive legal practice in central Illinois aided his political ambitions.[2]

Lincoln's early interest in the law may have come from attending local justice of the peace courts in Indiana or in New Salem, Illinois. While serving as the captain of a company of volunteers in the Black Hawk War (1832), Lincoln met John Todd Stuart, a first cousin of Lincoln's future wife, Mary Todd. When Lincoln returned from his brief military service, he campaigned for a seat in the state legislature. Although he lost, he ran again in 1834 and won the first of four successive terms in the Illinois General Assembly. In the state legislature, Lincoln was instrumental in lobbying for the relocation of the state capital from Vandalia to the more centrally located Springfield, a decision with important implications for his legal career. Lincoln considered his education "defective," but at Stuart's urging, he began reading law books while living in New Salem and serving in the state legislature.[3]

In March 1836, the clerk of the Sangamon County Circuit Court wrote in the court record that Abraham Lincoln was "a man of good moral character," one of the first steps in being admitted to the bar. On September 9, 1836, the Illinois Supreme Court in Vandalia admitted Lincoln to the practice of law. Lincoln moved to Springfield and became Stuart's junior partner in the spring of 1837. Aristocratic and college educated, Stuart, who was only fifteen months older than Lincoln, had already established himself as an attorney in the growing town of Springfield. At the time, Springfield had about nineteen hundred inhabitants, rivaling Chicago in population, and was the governmental seat of Sangamon County. On April 15, 1837, the new firm of Stuart & Lincoln first announced in the local newspaper that they would "practice, conjointly, in the Courts of this Judicial Circuit." The two men shared a passion for politics that included support for fellow Kentuckian Henry Clay, whose American System called for internal improvements, a Bank of the United States, a high tariff, and the sale of public lands to generate revenue and unify the nation. Stuart and Lincoln also had served together in the Illinois House of Representatives from 1834 to 1836.[4]

From the beginning of his career, Lincoln was captivated by the order that the law represented and believed that "reverence for the laws" should become the "*political religion* of the nation." It should be "taught in schools, in seminaries, and in colleges; let it be written in Primmers, spelling books, and in Almanacs; let it be preached from the pulpit, proclaimed in legislative halls, and enforced in courts of justice," he said. This reverence for the rule of law led Lincoln to view secession in 1861 as "the essence of anarchy."[5] When Springfield became the state capital in 1839, both the Illinois Supreme Court and the federal courts moved there. On December 3, 1839, the clerk of the US District Court entered Abraham Lincoln's name on the roll of attorneys qualified to practice before the federal courts in Illinois.[6]

Migrants to the territory and the state of Illinois generally settled in the area from the south northward, initially settling along major rivers and gradually moving inland to the vast prairie areas. Many of the earliest settlers of Illinois came from the upland Southern states of Virginia, North Carolina, Tennessee, and Kentucky, and they settled in the southern portions of the state. Settlers from the Middle Atlantic and Midwest states of Maryland, New Jersey, Pennsylvania, Ohio, and Indiana settled in the central and northern portions of Illinois. Later, emigrants from New England and New York settled in the northern third of the state. European immigrants from Ireland, Germany, and England also settled in Illinois, but most remained close to the regional economic centers of St. Louis and Chicago. Each group of settlers brought its own preconceptions on race, slavery, and politics to the state.

These waves of settlement created distinct, though overlapping, cultural and political regions within the state by the 1850s. An upland Southern culture and Democratic politics dominated in the southern quarter of the state and northwestward through the Sangamon River area and across the Illinois River. In the northern third of Illinois, New England culture and Republican politics dominated, while the culture of the north-central region most displayed the influence of settlers from the Middle Atlantic states and the other states of the Old Northwest.[7] While none of these regions had sharp boundaries, the settlement patterns influenced both the politics and the economy of the state. Equally important for Abraham Lincoln, the settlement of Illinois by this diverse population gave him acquaintance with a wide array of individuals.

Throughout Lincoln's life in Illinois, Democratic politicians had routinely controlled all branches of state government. Democrats held a majority in the state legislature from the 1830s through the 1850s. State voters elected only Democratic governors, with the exception of Democrat-turned-Whig Joseph Duncan in 1834, until former Democrat William H. Bissell united Republicans and anti-Nebraska Democrats to win the gubernatorial election in 1856. Because either the Democratic legislature or the electorate chose justices for the Illinois Supreme Court and judges for the circuit courts, most of these jurists were also Democrats. The delegation representing Illinois in the US House of Representatives had a majority of Democrats throughout the period, except from 1854 to 1856, when five Republicans and four Democrats represented Illinois. Because the Democratic majority in the state legislature selected US Senators, Illinois had only Democratic senators until the election in 1855 of anti-Nebraska Democrat Lyman Trumbull, who soon became a Republican.

The shortage of coin currency meant that Illinoisans often used promissory notes to make purchases and pay debts. Because creditors often lacked currency as well, they sometimes transferred promissory notes owed to them to their own creditors to settle debts. These webs of credit structured the antebellum economy as much as trade networks and other relationships. When individual transactions failed, they often generated more litigation. The printing and circulation of bank notes that varied in value by public and private banks exacerbated the instability of economic transactions. This land-rich, cash-poor society in which Lincoln practiced law produced a particular constellation of legal actions. Breach-of-contract and debt cases for failure to pay promissory notes, foreclosures of mortgages when land secured the debt, disputes over the division of land when someone died, and conflicts over land ownership comprised a large portion of Lincoln's legal cases. County sheriffs often sold land at auction to satisfy court judgments, when the losing party had no other assets. As a loyal Whig, Lincoln had supported a tariff, a national bank, and a uniform national currency throughout his career, in part because he witnessed the effects of economic chaos in the courtroom.[8]

For clients or even opponents in dire economic straits, Lincoln counseled patience and compromise. In February 1850, Lincoln wrote to his client Abraham

Bale that Virgil Hickox was planning to meet Bale "to settle the difficulty about the wheat." Lincoln urged Bale, "I sincerely hope you will settle it. I think you <u>can</u> if you <u>will</u>, for I have always found Mr. Hickox a fair man in his dealings. If you settle, I will charge nothing for what I have done, and thank you to boot. By settling, you will most likely get your money sooner; and with much less trouble & expense." The parties settled the dispute six weeks later.[9]

In this and many other cases, Lincoln followed his own advice to law students: "Discourage litigation. Persuade your neighbors to compromise whenever you can. Point out to them how the <u>nominal</u> winner is often a <u>real</u> loser, in fees, expenses, and waste of time. As a peace-maker, the lawyer has a superior opertunity of being a good man. There will still be business enough."[10]

Fluctuations in the antebellum economy also affected the types of cases that Lincoln and his partners handled. Lincoln was personally acquainted with the damage a failed economic opportunity could inflict. The failure of the Berry-Lincoln store in New Salem left Lincoln saddled with what he called a "national debt" that took him several years to pay off.[11] The nationwide Panic of 1837 left the economy of Illinois depressed and many people in desperate straits. During the brief tenure of federal bankruptcy legislation in 1842 and 1843, the partnership of Logan and Lincoln represented more than seventy applicants for bankruptcy in the federal court. Two decades later, the Panic of 1857 likewise disrupted the economy, prevented debtors from paying their creditors, and produced a flurry of lawsuits. In these periods of economic depression, courts had difficulty collecting judgments from financially ruined defendants. Lincoln's experiences with such defendants helped him identify with their difficulties as an attorney and later as president, strengthening his reputation as a "man of the people."[12]

Like most other attorneys in frontier Illinois, the partnership of Stuart & Lincoln represented clients in a variety of civil and criminal lawsuits. In 1838, Lincoln handled most of the firm's business because Stuart was campaigning against Democrat Stephen A. Douglas for a seat in Congress. Stuart won, and when he left for Washington, DC, in November 1839, Lincoln continued the practice alone. Earlier in 1839, the state legislature had shifted Sangamon County from the First Judicial Circuit to the newly created Eighth Judicial Circuit, and Lincoln began to travel to the courts of the new circuit. When Stuart decided early in February 1841 to run for reelection to Congress, it became clear to Lincoln that his partner's political ambitions prevented him from being a mentor.

In April 1841, Stuart and Lincoln dissolved their partnership, and Lincoln became the junior partner of Stephen T. Logan. Many regarded Logan, who had already served as a circuit court judge, as one of the best attorneys in the state. Nine years older than Lincoln, Logan offered him an expanded practice before the Illinois Supreme Court and in the federal courts. As president, Lincoln later remembered that Logan was "almost a father to me."[13]

When Logan decided to practice law with his son, he and Lincoln dissolved their partnership in December 1844. As an established lawyer, Lincoln selected William H. Herndon to become his junior partner. Herndon was almost a decade younger than Lincoln, had attended Illinois College in Jacksonville for one year, and had read law in the Logan & Lincoln law office. The Illinois Supreme Court admitted him to the practice of law on December 9, 1844. When asked later why Lincoln had chosen him, Herndon replied, "I don't know and no one else does."[14] As the junior partner, Herndon kept up the law office, conducted legal research, and represented clients in the courts in Springfield and in nearby counties. Intensely political, Herndon held radical abolitionist beliefs, which Lincoln dared not share. The partnership of Lincoln & Herndon continued until Lincoln's death.[15]

Throughout all three partnerships, Lincoln helped to resolve a wide variety of legal conflicts, including broken contracts, land titles, slander, divorce, dower, estate partitions, mortgage foreclosures, larceny, and murder. The majority of Lincoln's cases involved the collection of debts. Lincoln and his partners frequently represented local merchants such as Jacob Bunn, James Bell, and Robert Allen in lawsuits to collect unpaid debts. They also represented private individuals suing to collect debts. The legal actions of assumpsit (breach of a contract, such as a promissory note) and debt accounted for more than one-third of Lincoln's cases. In addition, many other types of cases were essentially the collection of a debt. Lincoln's practice included many legal actions of foreclosure of mortgage, sale of real estate to pay debts, petition and summons, mechanic's lien, bankruptcy, and settlement of partnerships, all designed to settle some form of debt.[16]

Several Kentuckians accused Abraham Lincoln of keeping profits that rightfully belonged to his father-in-law, Robert Todd's, estate. While Lincoln had a deserved reputation for patience with those who attacked him politically or even personally, he would not disregard attacks on his integrity. Todd had been a partner in a company at the time of his death, and in the spring of

1853, the remaining partners accused Lincoln of defrauding the company by collecting debts owed to it in Illinois and keeping the money. They filed the case in Kentucky, and an attorney there wrote to Lincoln informing him of the case. Lincoln immediately replied, "I find it difficult to suppress my indignation towards those who have got up this claim against me." He insisted in his answer to the bill of complaint filed against him that the court should require his accusers to file a bill of particulars that stated the names and addresses of those from whom he allegedly received payment of debts owed to the company. Lincoln insisted that "if they will name any living accessable man, as one of whom I have received their money, I will, <u>by that man</u> disprove the charge."[17]

Four months later, Lincoln complained that "this matter harrasses my feelings a good deal" and asked the attorney in Kentucky to get the court to command the plaintiffs to submit a bill of particulars so that Lincoln could defend himself against specific charges.[18] After he received specific charges in mid-September 1853, Lincoln quickly arranged to take depositions to disprove the allegations. Lincoln filed these depositions as evidence, and the plaintiffs dismissed their case in February 1854. It is important to note that although the surviving partners impugned Lincoln's honor as a man and an attorney, he responded strictly within the legal system. Lincoln expected vindication from the court.

Widely known and respected for his integrity, Lincoln and his partners received requests from attorneys in all parts of the state to argue the appeals of their cases to the Illinois Supreme Court in Springfield. Lincoln and his successive law partners represented clients in more than four hundred cases before the state's highest court. In nearly half of those cases, they had not been involved in the circuit court from which the case was appealed. Springfield was also the location for federal courts in Illinois until 1855, when a second federal court opened in Chicago. Lincoln and his partners handled more than 340 cases in the US Circuit and District Courts. In 1842, Lincoln wrote to a fellow attorney in Mount Sterling that he and Logan would be "willing to attend to any business in the Supreme Court you may send us." On the matter of fees, he wrote, "We believe we are never accused of being very unreasonable in this particular; and we would always be easily satisfied, provided we could see the money—but whatever fees we earn at a distance, if not paid <u>before</u>, we have noticed, we never hear of after the work is done. We therefore, are growing a little sensitive on that point."[19]

Although he was active in the federal courts and the Illinois Supreme Court, most of Lincoln's law practice consisted of thousands of cases in the county circuit courts of central Illinois, especially that of his home county of Sangamon. These county circuit courts, the primary trial courts in Illinois, were divided into a series of ever-shifting circuits, over which a supreme court justice or a circuit judge presided. Lincoln and his partners handled more than twenty-four hundred cases in the Sangamon County Circuit Court. In other county circuit courts beyond Sangamon, Lincoln represented clients in hundreds of additional cases.

From 1839 through 1861, Lincoln practiced in the courts of the Eighth Judicial Circuit and occasionally in counties that neighbored that circuit. The circuit varied from six to fifteen counties, depending on a variety of factors, including population changes, the creation of new counties, and who presided over the circuit courts. Twice yearly, Lincoln left Springfield for a two- or three-month journey around the circuit, often accompanied by the judge and the state's attorney. Lincoln traveled by horseback or buggy along frequently difficult roads and over open prairies, fording swollen streams in the spring and staying at a colorful array of private homes and crude inns. Most of the county seats on the circuit were small villages of a few hundred residents with unpaved streets, although their populations swelled during court week. In some county seats, Lincoln established informal partnerships with local attorneys, such as that in Danville with Ward Hill Lamon, with whom he worked frequently in the Vermilion County Circuit Court.

During the 1840s, Lincoln's legal career followed the seasons of the courts, occasionally interrupted by intensive political activity on behalf of the Whig Party. In a typical year, Lincoln argued appeals before the Illinois Supreme Court in January, February, and early March. In mid-March, the spring term of the Sangamon County Circuit Court convened as the first court on the Eighth Judicial Circuit. In April, May, and early June, Lincoln followed the spring term of the other county circuit courts on the Eighth Circuit in eastern and central Illinois. In June, the federal courts convened in Springfield, followed by the summer term of the Sangamon County Circuit Court in July. In August, the fall terms of the county circuit courts began again with Sangamon County. Lincoln then traveled to the various county seats of the Eighth Judicial Circuit from September to November. In December, the Illinois Supreme Court began its session in Springfield and the federal courts convened for a second term.[20]

Judge Samuel H. Treat presided over the courts of the Eighth Judicial Circuit from 1839 until 1848, first as a circuit judge, then as a justice of the Illinois Supreme Court. Unlike most antebellum Illinois attorneys, who practiced in their home courts and perhaps a few neighboring counties, Lincoln often accompanied Judge Treat and State's Attorney David B. Campbell around the entire circuit. Judge Treat was a native of New York, a Democrat, a devout Episcopalian, and two years younger than Lincoln. In spite of their differences, the two men developed a mutual respect for one another and frequently enjoyed a game of chess together at Treat's office in Springfield. In the courts of the Eighth Judicial Circuit, in the Illinois Supreme Court, and after 1855 in the federal courts in Springfield, Treat presided over more than one thousand cases in which Lincoln was an attorney.[21]

Lincoln served a single term in Congress from 1847 to 1849. While in Washington, he argued one case before the US Supreme Court. Presiding over the court was Chief Justice Roger B. Taney, who a dozen years later administered the oath of office to President Abraham Lincoln. During the 1850s, Lincoln served as an attorney of record in four other cases before the US Supreme Court but did not offer oral arguments. When he returned to Springfield in 1849, he resumed his law practice with Herndon.[22]

Lincoln's growing reputation as an attorney led younger men to seek his advice or ask to read law with him. He routinely refused requests to read law because he was away on the circuit too often, but he freely offered advice. In 1858, he urged a prospective lawyer to read several standard works, "get a license, and go to the practice, and still keep reading." It was a formula that had worked for him, and Lincoln continued to keep learning throughout his legal career. In 1860, he explained to another aspiring law student, "Work, work, work, is the main thing." He also habitually assisted younger lawyers in the courtroom by offering advice on their cases.[23]

From March 1849 through the end of Lincoln's legal career, Judge David Davis presided over the courts of the Eighth Judicial Circuit, and Lincoln frequently traveled the circuit with Davis. A native of Maryland and six years younger than Lincoln, Davis had settled in Bloomington, Illinois, in 1835. He was an active Whig and served in the state legislature and as a delegate to the 1847 Constitutional Convention. While on the circuit, the rotund judge and the tall, lanky lawyer shared travel, meals, and lodging in farmhouses and village taverns. "In my opinion," Davis later recalled, "I think Mr Lincoln was happy—as happy as *he* could be, when on this circuit—and happy no other place. This was his place of Enjoyment."[24] By the mid-1850s, the expanding network of railroads in Illinois began to revolutionize circuit travel by allowing Judge Davis and attorneys like Lincoln to travel more quickly to individual courts and return home between court sessions. Although circuit-riding attorneys in the 1850s enjoyed improved transportation and accommodations, the mix of legal issues remained much the same as in earlier years.[25]

On the circuit, Lincoln handled cases with local attorneys without regard to their political affiliation. He often served with and against the same attorney in different cases at the same term of court. For example, he served as co-counsel with Edward D. Baker, a Springfield attorney and the namesake of his second child, in 56 cases, but he opposed Baker in 128 cases. In Danville, Illinois, he formed a sort of informal partnership with Ward Hill Lamon in the early 1850s, and the two men worked together in more than 150 cases and advertised together in the Danville newspaper. Occasionally while on the circuit, Judge Davis asked Lincoln to serve as a temporary judge for a few hours or days. Because the attorneys trying the cases had to approve of the substitution, Davis's choice of Lincoln and a handful of other attorneys for this duty reflected their status among their peers. Lincoln served as a temporary judge in more than 320 cases, but in more than two-thirds, he merely continued the case until the next term of that court or made a procedural ruling.[26]

As Lincoln's reputation grew and credit and trade networks expanded, clients from major commercial cities retained him to collect debts from individuals and companies in Illinois. In at least seventy-six cases, Lincoln and his partners represented out-of-state creditors, from whom Illinois residents had purchased goods or land. In 1858, the St. Louis wholesale firm of S. C. Davis & Company retained Lincoln & Herndon to collect debts from local merchants in Illinois. The partnership filed twenty-five suits for the St. Louis company in the federal courts in Illinois between 1858 and 1861. Clients from Philadelphia, Boston, and New York also hired Lincoln and his partners to represent their interests in the courts of Illinois.[27]

It was through his participation in thousands of individual cases that Lincoln earned his living as an attorney. He typically received $5 or $10 for ordinary circuit court cases and might command several hundred dollars for important federal and Illinois Supreme Court cases. In rare instances, he received more than $1,000 for his legal services, and in the case of *Illinois Central Railroad v.*

McLean County, Illinois and Parke, he received $5,000 from the Illinois Central Railroad, although he had to sue the railroad to obtain the balance of his fee. In his partnerships with Stuart and with Herndon, Lincoln and his partner equally divided all of the fees they received for legal work. In his partnership with Logan, Lincoln received a smaller percentage of the fees that either he or his partner earned. Because he did not hold elective office for most of his legal career or engage in other business activities, as many lawyers did, Lincoln earned nearly all of his income practicing law in the courts of central Illinois. Generally, he earned small fees from many cases, rather than large fees from a few cases.[28]

Disputes arising from the financing, construction, and operation of railroads generated nearly two hundred cases for the partnership of Lincoln & Herndon. While they frequently represented railroads, especially the Illinois Central Railroad, they nearly as often represented clients who were suing railroads. Although litigation involving railroads was a new class of business for lawyer Lincoln, he continued to handle a wide array of cases throughout his career.[29]

Traveling to a dozen or more county seats expanded Lincoln's law practice and enhanced his political contacts. Throughout his career, Lincoln interacted with Illinoisans of all sorts. The lawyers and judges were an interesting mix of characters, but the litigants added even more variety. On the circuit, Lincoln developed relationships with Whig and Republican leaders and voters and honed his oratorical skills in both courtroom and political speeches. The passage of the Kansas-Nebraska Act in 1854 rekindled Lincoln's interest in politics, and throughout the 1850s, he balanced an extensive law practice with active involvement in Whig and later Republican politics.[30]

Although he had been unsuccessful in his bid to replace Stephen A. Douglas in the US Senate in 1858, Lincoln gained a national reputation in his oratorical contest with "the Little Giant." That reputation, his moderate stance against slavery, and the vital support of several members of the Illinois bar allowed him to win the Republican nomination in Chicago. Fellow attorneys including Judge David Davis, Jesse Fell, and Leonard Swett of Bloomington; Ward Hill Lamon of Danville; Norman Judd of Chicago; Henry Clay Whitney of Champaign; and William Butler, former partner Stephen T. Logan, and current partner William H. Herndon, all of Springfield, campaigned assiduously to ensure that the nomination went to Lincoln.[31] Elected president in November 1860 over his long-term opponent and fellow Illinois attorney Stephen A. Douglas and two other candidates, Lincoln took office in March 1861, leaving behind him a substantial and varied law practice. Ahead of him lay the most serious legal and constitutional crisis in the nation's short history.

A vital part of Lincoln's skill as a leader consisted not only in his communication skills but also in his ability to know when not to speak, when to keep silent. From his election on November 6, 1860, until his inauguration four months later, president-elect Abraham Lincoln steadfastly refused to make any public pronouncements regarding his position on the secession crisis that was removing one state after another from the Union. On December 15, he wrote a "strictly confidential" letter to John A. Gilmer, a former Whig from North Carolina who had served in the 30th Congress with Lincoln. Although he was "greatly disinclined to write a letter" in response to Gilmer's inquiry, Lincoln feared that Gilmer might "misconstrue my silence." Lincoln refused to "shift the ground upon which I have been elected" and asked if Gilmer and other Southerners had read the Republican platform or Lincoln's speeches. Lincoln continued:

> If not, what reason have I to expect that any additional production of mine would meet a better fate? It would make me appear as if I repented for the crime of having been elected, and was anxious to apologize and beg forgiveness. To so represent me, would be the principal use made of any letter I might now thrust upon the public. My old record cannot be so used; and that is precisely the reason that some new declaration is so much sought.[32]

By his silence, Lincoln refused to give his critics any more statements that they could twist to misrepresent him. A few days later, Lincoln invited Gilmer to visit him in Springfield; if they could reach agreement, Lincoln would ask Gilmer to join his cabinet as a Southern Unionist.

Lincoln's response to fellow congressman and Whig lawyer Gilmer echoed a lesson he had learned more than a decade earlier as a lawyer. In February 1848, Congressman Lincoln had written from Washington to a Whig ally and fellow attorney in Illinois, "In law it is good policy to never <u>plead</u> what you <u>need</u> not, lest you oblige yourself to <u>prove</u> what you <u>can</u> not. Reflect on this well before you proceed."[33] Lincoln learned the dangers of saying too much as an attorney, and the lesson proved valuable in his political career as well.

As president, Abraham Lincoln presided over a cabinet consisting almost entirely of lawyers. Lincoln scholars have long pointed out that Secretary of State William H. Seward and Secretary of War Edwin M. Stanton were lawyers, and one would expect his attorneys general, Edward Bates and then James Speed, to have been lawyers. In addition, all three secretaries of the treasury, Salmon P. Chase, William P. Fessenden, and Hugh McCullough; both secretaries of the interior, Caleb B. Smith and John P. Usher; and both postmasters general, Montgomery Blair and William Dennison, were also attorneys. Although Secretary of the Navy Gideon Welles was a publisher, he had studied law as a young man. Only Simon Cameron, Lincoln's secretary of war for ten months at the beginning of his administration, had no legal training.

A quarter century earlier, just as Abraham Lincoln was beginning his dual career in law and politics, Alexis de Tocqueville had observed in his classic analysis, *Democracy in America*, that lawyers "form the highest political class." Because attorneys were the only "enlightened class which the people does not mistrust," they were often elected to political offices. "They fill the legislative assemblies," de Tocqueville continued, "and they conduct the administration; they consequently exercise a powerful influence upon the formation of the law, and upon its execution." In notes for a speech prepared in the 1850s, Lincoln himself acknowledged the dominance of attorneys in public life while referring to the "vague popular belief that lawyers are necessarily dishonest." He insisted that the public's impression was only "<u>vague</u>" because the extent to which "<u>confidence</u>, and <u>honors</u>, are reposed in, and conferred upon lawyers by the people" makes it "improbable that their <u>impression</u> of dishonesty, is very distinct and vivid."[34]

The presence of so many attorneys as counselors and, more important, Lincoln's own experience as a lawyer deeply influenced his presidency. Not only was he acutely aware of, and committed to, the constitutional limitations on his power, but also he was confident enough in a room—or a city—full of lawyers to stand on his own interpretation of the Constitution to guide his actions. From his inauguration on March 4, 1861, until Congress assembled on July 4, Lincoln took many extraordinary actions to respond to the disintegration of the Union. On his own authority, he summoned state militias into federal service, expanded the navy, raised funds to pay and equip the army and navy, suspended the writ of habeas corpus in certain areas, and authorized a blockade of Southern ports. In his address to Congress, when it assembled on

July 4, Lincoln reported, "These measures, whether strictly legal or not, were ventured upon under what appeared to be a popular demand and a public necessity, trusting then, as now, that Congress would readily ratify them. It is believed that nothing has been done beyond the constitutional competency of Congress." Lincoln concluded his address in a third-person reference to himself: "In full view of his great responsibility, he has, so far, done what he has deemed his duty." And he challenged Congress, "You will now, according to your own judgment, perform yours."[35] The Republican-dominated Congress quickly approved Lincoln's emergency actions.

Further evidence of his constitutional confidence lay in Lincoln's response to Supreme Court Chief Justice Roger B. Taney's writ of habeas corpus for John Merryman. Military authorities in Baltimore arrested Maryland planter John Merryman in May 1861 for "acts of treason" against the United States and held him at Fort McHenry. The following day, Taney issued a writ of habeas corpus to bring Merryman before him. The commanding officer refused to produce Merryman because Lincoln had authorized the officer to suspend the writ of habeas corpus. Taney issued his decision in the case of *Ex parte Merryman* and insisted that the president, "under the constitution of the United States, cannot suspend the privilege of the writ of habeas corpus, nor authorize a military officer to do so." In sum, Lincoln had acted unconstitutionally. Though not dismissive of the chief justice's opinion, Lincoln clearly disagreed. His most important public response came in the same message to Congress on July 4, 1861, in which he explained his other extraordinary actions in the first weeks of the rebellion: "To state the question more directly, are all the laws, *but one*, to go unexecuted, and the government itself go to pieces, lest that one be violated?" Lincoln thought not.[36]

Likewise, in July 1862, the president notified allies in Congress that he would veto a confiscation bill if they did not modify it, because it caused the forfeiture of property beyond the life of the party guilty of treason. This provision conflicted with the Constitution's prohibition against "corruption of blood," through which a traitor's family was prevented from inheriting the traitor's property. "With great respect," Lincoln wrote to a Congress filled with many attorneys, "I am constrained to say I think this feature of the act is unconstitutional." The president signed what became known as the Second Confiscation Act, but only after insisting that Congress pass an explanatory resolution to address the constitutional issue.[37]

President Lincoln also worked closely with Secretary of the Treasury Salmon P. Chase to urge Congress to establish a stable national currency. It was a "duty of the national government," Lincoln wrote in a June 1862 veto message, "to secure to the people a sound circulating medium." During his administration, he signed legislation that established a national banking system, high tariffs, an income tax, and a national currency unredeemable in specie ("greenbacks"). His career as an attorney in the developing economy of Illinois convinced him of the need to implement the Whig economic policies, though they were often couched in the language of wartime necessity.[38]

As the head of a sort of "law firm cabinet," Lincoln often asked for written opinions from his cabinet officers on important questions. His request took the form of interrogatories that lawyers might pose to witnesses. Immediately after his inauguration, Lincoln received a letter explaining that Major Robert Anderson's small command could hold out for only a few weeks in Fort Sumter in the harbor of Charleston, South Carolina, without further supplies. On learning of the details, Lincoln queried his cabinet, "Assuming it to be possible to now provision Fort-Sumpter, under all the circumstances, is it wise to attempt it? Please give me your opinion, in writing, on this question."[39] All of the cabinet members except Postmaster General Montgomery Blair initially favored surrendering the fort, and Secretary of State William Seward asserted that an expedition to supply the fort would "provoke combat, and probably initiate a civil war."[40] Ultimately, two other cabinet members joined Blair in recommending that the president send only provisions to Fort Sumter, but Confederates in South Carolina attacked the fort before the supplies arrived and forced Major Anderson to surrender.

When a flamboyant US naval officer seized Confederate emissaries from a British vessel in November 1861, he triggered a diplomatic crisis that threatened war with Great Britain. Although Lincoln was initially delighted with this blow to Confederate diplomatic efforts, his joy soon turned to concern when the British demanded an apology and the release of the prisoners. When Lincoln met with his cabinet on Christmas Day 1861, Seward had begun to prepare a response that explained how the seizure had violated international law and why the prisoners must be released. As the meeting closed, Lincoln said to Seward, "Governor Seward, you will go on, of course, preparing your answer, which . . . will state the reasons why they ought to be given up. Now, I have a mind to try my hand at stating the reasons why they ought *not* to be given up. We will compare the points on each side." On the following day, Seward asked about Lincoln's brief, and Lincoln replied, "I found I could not make an argument that would satisfy my own mind, and that proved to me your ground was the right one."[41] The Lincoln administration quietly released the prisoners, and the crisis passed. Lincoln often used writing as a way to clarify his thoughts on certain subjects. In other cases, he sometimes wrote an angry letter to vent his feelings and then never sent the letter.[42]

One year later, President Lincoln and his cabinet faced the sensitive political and constitutional question of statehood for West Virginia. In his first message to Congress, Lincoln explained, "What is now combatted is the principle that secession is *consistent* with the Constitution—is *lawful*, and *peaceful*. It is not contended that there is any express law for it; and nothing should ever be implied as law which leads to unjust or absurd consequences."[43] According to the Constitution, the creation of a new state from a part of an existing state required the permission of that state. Since the majority of Virginia was effectively out of the Union, how could it approve the formation of West Virginia? The Senate passed a statehood bill for West Virginia in July 1862, and the House of Representatives passed the act on December 10 and forwarded it to the president for his signature. On December 23, Lincoln requested of his cabinet, "I respectfully ask of each of you, an opinion in writing, on the following questions, to wit: 1st. Is the said Act constitutional? 2nd. Is the said Act expedient?"[44]

Lincoln received the written opinions of six of his cabinet attorneys: Seward, Chase, and Stanton favored the act, and Welles, Blair, and Bates opposed it. Lincoln broke the tie with his own written opinion. Admitting that the consent of the legislature of Virginia was "constitutionally necessary to the bill for the admission of West Virginia becoming a law," Lincoln then considered whether the legislature that had approved the creation of West Virginia was a legitimate body. Employing his lawyerly ability to split hairs, Lincoln insisted that a legislature was elected, not by the majority of qualified voters, but by the majority of qualified voters who chose to vote. Voters in secessionist Virginia had chosen not to vote, and therefore the body that approved the creation of West Virginia *was* the legislature of Virginia, although it represented only a small portion of the voters. Lincoln then asked the incisive question, "Can this government stand, if it indulges constitutional constructions by which men in open rebellion against it, are to be accounted, man for man, the equals of those who maintain their loyalty to it?"[45] Lincoln thought not.

Having satisfied himself that the act was constitutional, Lincoln then considered whether it was expedient. "More than on anything else," Lincoln determined, "it depends on whether the admission or rejection of the new state would under all the circumstances tend the more strongly to the restoration of the national authority throughout the Union." West Virginians had been true to the Union during the war, and their support needed to be recognized. Lincoln admitted:

> The division of a State is dreaded as a precedent. But a measure made expedient by a war, is no precedent for times of peace. It is said that the admission of West-Virginia, is secession, and tolerated only because it is our secession. Well, if we call it by that name, there is still difference enough between secession against the constitution, and secession in favor of the constitution.

"I believe," he concluded simply, "the admission of West-Virginia into the Union is expedient."[46] In this brief opinion, one can see the mind of both Lincoln the lawyer and Lincoln the politician at work. On December 31, 1862, Lincoln signed the act making West Virginia the thirty-fifth state in the Union.[47]

On April 12, 1864, Confederate troops under Major General Nathan Bedford Forrest defeated the Union garrison at Fort Pillow, forty miles north of Memphis on the Mississippi River. The Union force at the fort consisted of some six hundred men, including both white and African American soldiers. After Forrest's troops overran the fort, they shot many of the Union soldiers after they had surrendered. On May 3, Lincoln addressed his cabinet:

> It is now quite certain that a large number of our colored soldiers, with their white officers, were by the rebel force, massacred after they had surrendered, at the recent capture of Fort Pillow. So much is known, though the evidence is not yet quite ready to be laid before me. Meanwhile, I will thank you to prepare, and give me in writing, your opinion as to what course the Government should take in the case.[48]

At the cabinet meeting that followed, each cabinet member read his opinion to the others.[49] Initially, Seward, Stanton, Chase, and Usher favored man-for-man retaliation by executing Confederate prisoners of war. Welles, Blair, and Bates favored declaring the Confederate officers outlaws who, if captured, would stand trial for murder. Lincoln initially considered setting Confederate prisoners of war aside for retaliation unless the Confederate government agreed to treat African American soldiers as prisoners of war rather than insurgent slaves. He later told Frederick Douglass, however, that with retaliation, "if once begun, there was no telling where it would end."[50]

In these examples, and other instances during his presidency, Lincoln turned to his "law firm cabinet" for advice in the form of briefs on specific military, diplomatic, constitutional, and political questions. By weighing his cabinet members' opinions and sometimes writing his own, he availed himself of their best advice, yet determined his own policies.

Lincoln's experiences as a lawyer prepared him to contend with a variety of strong personalities. Two examples from his presidency will perhaps suffice to demonstrate both his decisiveness and his deft handling of sensitive, egotistical, and arrogant personalities. Throughout the first three years of Lincoln's presidency, Secretary of State William H. Seward and Secretary of the Treasury Salmon P. Chase were adversaries, both ideologically and temperamentally. Seward began his tenure as secretary of state arrogantly believing that he would run the administration while Lincoln served as a figurehead. In a remarkable memorandum that he submitted to the president in April 1861, Seward boldly asserted that the administration had neither a foreign nor a domestic policy. He also suggested that the president designate some cabinet member—read William H. Seward—to direct the foreign policy of the nation energetically. Despite the presumptuous and offensive tone of this memorandum, Lincoln responded kindly but firmly. He insisted that his administration had implemented several policies. Whatever policy was adopted, Lincoln declared, "I must do it."[51]

Likewise, Secretary of the Treasury Salmon P. Chase considered himself superior to the president. A favorite of Radical Republicans, Chase was intensely ambitious and despised Seward. In the fall of 1862, he convinced Radical Republicans in Congress that Seward exercised undue conservative influence over Lincoln, who, Chase claimed, ignored the advice of other cabinet members and deferred to Seward. In mid-December, Republican Senators voted to request a reorganization of the cabinet without Seward. Like Seward's brash memo, this demand also threatened the president's control over his own administration. Seward quietly offered his resignation, and Lincoln met with many of the senators in the White House to listen to their grievances. He invited them back the next night to meet with him and the entire cabinet except Seward. After several secretaries testified that there had been full and free consultation on all important matters, Chase had to admit reluctantly that they were right. Many of the Republican senators were furious with Chase, who failed to repeat his criticisms of Seward in the presence of the president and the rest of the cabinet.

The following day, a humiliated Chase visited the president to tender his written resignation. "Where is it?" Lincoln asked. "Let me have it." Lincoln snatched the paper from Chase, who was now reluctant to release it. Lincoln exulted, "This . . . cuts the Gordian knot. I can dispose of this subject now without difficulty. I see my way clear." Dismissing Chase, Lincoln wrote to both Seward and Chase that the "public interest" required that they both remain at their posts. Shortly afterward, Lincoln told a visiting senator, "I can ride on now, I've got a pumpkin in each end of my bag!"[52] By obtaining the resignations of both Seward and Chase, he could reject both and reassert his control over both his cabinet and the executive branch in relation to Congress.

Lincoln's long-suffering relationship with Major General George B. McClellan as commander of the Army of the Potomac is well known, but Lincoln's relationships with several of his other leading generals were challenging as well. In the first years of the war, General Joseph Hooker gained renown as an aggressive fighter, in marked contrast to the overly cautious McClellan. However, Hooker also achieved notoriety as an insubordinate grouser who once told a newspaper reporter that the nation needed a dictator. After the disastrous Battle of Fredericksburg ruined General Ambrose Burnside's reputation for leadership, Lincoln turned to Hooker to command the Army of the Potomac. In a letter of appointment, Lincoln both praised and warned Hooker:

> I have placed you at the head of the Army of the Potomac. Of course I have done this upon what appear to me to be sufficient reasons. And yet I think it best for you to know that there are some things in regard to which, I am not quite satisfied with you. I believe you to be a brave and a skilful soldier, which, of course, I like. I also believe you do not mix politics with your profession, in which you are right. You have confidence in yourself, which is a valuable, if not an indispensable quality. You are ambitious,

which, within reasonable bounds, does good rather than harm. . . .
I have heard, in such way as to believe it, of your recently saying
that both the Army and the Government needed a Dictator. Of
course it was not for this, but in spite of it, that I have given you
the command. Only those generals who gain successes, can set up
dictators. What I now ask of you is military success, and I will risk
the dictatorship.[53]

Although it was a masterful letter, Hooker seemed to miss the point. "That
is just such a letter as a father might write to his son," Hooker proudly told
a reporter. "It is a beautiful letter, and, although I think he was harder on
me than I deserved, I will say that I love the man who wrote it."[54] Hooker
managed to restore order and morale to the Army of the Potomac, but he
soon proved as inept against Confederate general Robert E. Lee as others had
before him.

Abraham Lincoln learned many valuable leadership lessons from his quarter-century legal career. First and foremost, he learned much about human
nature. His law practice introduced him to thousands of people in central
Illinois and beyond—litigants, juries, witnesses, attorneys, judges, and spec-
tators. They came from a variety of backgrounds and conditions, and Lincoln
studied them all. Many of the burdensome politicians, military officers, cler-
gymen, inventors, office seekers, and supplicants whom he met as president
reminded him of people he had known in Illinois, and they often elicited
one of his famous stories. Second, the law allowed him to hone his oratorical
abilities and encouraged precision in written communication. As president,
Lincoln wrote carefully for both the eye and the ear. He recognized that the
men and women before him on any given occasion were only a small portion
of his real audience; the majority read his words in a newspaper or heard
someone else read them. Third, Lincoln's law practice developed his incisive
powers of analysis, permitting him to focus on the central aspect of a case, a
political issue, or a military strategy. Finally, twenty-five years in the court-
rooms of central Illinois committed Lincoln firmly to the concept of ordered
liberty in a democratic republic. It was this tenacious commitment to both
the Declaration of Independence and the Constitution that allowed Abraham
Lincoln to wield broad powers without becoming dictatorial and to persevere
in the struggle to maintain the constitutional order of the Union in the face
of civil war.

Notes

1. Doris Kearns Goodwin, *Team of Rivals: The Political Genius of Abraham Lincoln* (New York: Simon and Schuster, 2005), 318–19. For the limitations of this approach, see James Oakes, "What's So Special about a Team of Rivals?," *New York Times*, November 19, 2008, A43.

2. Daniel W. Stowell et al., eds., *The Papers of Abraham Lincoln: Legal Documents and Cases* (Charlottesville: University of Virginia Press, 2008), 1: xxix–xlii; Mark E. Steiner, *An Honest Calling: The Law Practice of Abraham Lincoln* (DeKalb: Northern Illinois University Press, 2006); Brian Dirck, *Lincoln the Lawyer* (Urbana: University of Illinois Press, 2007).

3. Charles Lanman to Abraham Lincoln, August 1858, in *The Collected Works of Abraham Lincoln*, ed. Roy P. Basler et al. (New Brunswick, NJ: Rutgers University Press, 1953), 2:459; Steiner, *Honest Calling*, 26–54.

4. Order, March 24, 1836, Sangamon County Circuit Court admitted Lincoln to bar (N05067), in *The Law Practice of Abraham Lincoln*, 2nd ed., ed. Martha L. Benner, Cullom Davis, et al. (Springfield: Illinois Historic Preservation Agency, 2009), http://www.lawpracticeofabrahamlincoln.org; *Sangamo Journal* (Springfield, IL), April 15, 1837, 3:2.

5. Lincoln, Address before the Young Men's Lyceum of Springfield, Illinois, January 27, 1838, *Collected Works*, 1:112; First Inaugural Address, March 4, 1861, ibid., 4:268; Phillip S. Paludan, "The American Civil War Considered as a Crisis in Law and Order," *American Historical Review* 77 (October 1972): 1013–34.

6. Paul Simon, *Lincoln's Preparation for Greatness: The Illinois Legislative Years* (Urbana: University of Illinois Press, 1971); Roll of Attorneys, December 3, 1839, U.S. District Court Admitted Lincoln to Bar (N05931), *Law Practice of Abraham Lincoln*.

7. Douglas K. Meyer, *Making the Heartland Quilt: A Geographical History of Settlement and Migration in Early-Nineteenth-Century Illinois* (Carbondale: Southern Illinois University Press, 2000).

8. Steiner, *Honest Calling*, 55–61; Dirck, *Lincoln the Lawyer*, 54–75.

9. Abraham Lincoln to Abraham Bale, February 22, 1850, *Papers of Abraham Lincoln*, 1:5; Judge's Docket, April 1850, *Bale v. Wright & Hickox* (L00153), *Law Practice of Abraham Lincoln*.

10. Abraham Lincoln, Notes for a Law Lecture, c. 1859, *Papers of Abraham Lincoln*, 1:12–13; Mark E. Steiner, "The Lawyer as Peacemaker: Law and Community in Abraham Lincoln's Slander Cases," *Journal of the Abraham Lincoln Association* 16 (Summer 1995): 1–22.

11. Kenneth J. Winkle, *The Young Eagle: The Rise of Abraham Lincoln* (Dallas: Taylor, 2001), 97–100.

12. Edward J. Balleisen, *Navigating Failure: Bankruptcy and Commercial Society in Antebellum America* (Chapel Hill: University of North Carolina Press, 2001); Charles Warren, *Bankruptcy in United States History* (Cambridge, MA: Harvard University Press, 1935), 60–79.

13. Stephen T. Logan to Abraham Lincoln, 13 January 1862, Box 187, Record Group 56, General Records of the Department of the Treasury, Entry 210, Part II, Records of Various Divisions within the Office of the Secretary of the Treasury, Records of the Division of Appointments, Correspondence of the Division, Applications and Recommendations for Positions in the Washington, D.C. Offices of the Treasury Department, 1830–1910, National Archives and Records Administration, College Park, MD.

14. William H. Herndon to Jesse Weik, February 24, 1887, Herndon-Weik Collection, Library of Congress, Washington, DC.

15. David Donald, *Lincoln's Herndon: A Biography* (New York: Knopf, 1948); David Herbert Donald, *"We Are Lincoln Men": Abraham Lincoln and His Friends* (New York: Simon and Schuster, 2003), 65–92.

16. Roger D. Billings Jr., "A. Lincoln, Debtor-Creditor Lawyer," *Journal of Illinois History* 8 (Summer 2005): 82–102.

17. Abraham Lincoln to George B. Kinkead, May 27, 1853, *Papers of Abraham Lincoln*, 2:361–62; "*Oldham & Hemingway v. Lincoln et al.* (1853–1854)," ibid., 2:355–72.

18. Abraham Lincoln to George B. Kinkead, September 13, 1853, ibid., 2:365–66; "*Oldham & Hemingway v. Lincoln et al.* (1853–1854)," ibid., 2:355–72.

19. Abraham Lincoln to James S. Irwin, November 2, 1842, *Collected Works*, 1:304.

20. See "A Term in the Sangamon County Circuit Court (Spring 1842)" and "A Tour of Two Circuits with Lincoln (Spring 1842)," *Papers of Abraham Lincoln*, 1:131–238.

21. Daniel W. Stowell, *Samuel H. Treat, Prairie Justice* (Springfield: Illinois Historic Preservation Agency, 2005).

22. Chris DeRose, *Congressman Lincoln: The Making of America's Greatest President* (New York: Simon and Schuster, 2013); "Lewis for the use of Longworth v. Lewis (1845–1849)," *Papers of Abraham Lincoln*, 1:399–431.

23. Abraham Lincoln to James T. Thornton, December 2, 1858, *Papers of Abraham Lincoln*, 1:14; Abraham Lincoln to John M. Brockman, September 25, 1860, ibid., 1:20.

24. David Davis, Interview with William H. Herndon, September 20, 1866, in *Herndon's Informants: Letters, Interviews, and Statements about Abraham Lincoln*, ed. Douglas L. Wilson and Rodney O. Davis (Urbana: University of Illinois Press, 1998), 349.

25. Willard L. King, *Lincoln's Manager: David Davis* (Cambridge, MA: Harvard University Press, 1960); "A Tour of the Circuit with Lincoln (Spring 1852)," *Papers of Abraham Lincoln*, 211–304.

26. "The Law Practice of Abraham Lincoln: A Statistical Portrait," *Law Practice of Abraham Lincoln*; "Lincoln as a Court Official (1838–1860)," *Papers of Abraham Lincoln*, 4:279–86.

27. "*S. C. Davis & Company v. Lowry & Randle* (1857–1858)," ibid., 4:49–63.

28. Harry E. Pratt, *The Personal Finances of Abraham Lincoln* (Springfield, IL: Abraham Lincoln Association, 1943), 25–57; "*Illinois Central Railroad v. McLean County, Illinois, and Parke / Lincoln v. Illinois Central Railroad* (1853–1857)," *Papers of Abraham Lincoln*, 2:373–415.

29. "*Barret v. Alton & Sangamon Railroad* (1851–1852)," *Papers of Abraham Lincoln*, 2:172–210; "*People ex rel. Moulton v. Brough et al.* (1854)," ibid., 2:430–59; "*Allen v. Illinois Central Railroad et al. / Allen v. Illinois Central Railroad* (1854–1859)," ibid., 3:1–23; "*Clark and Morrison v. Page et al. / Bacon v. Ohio & Mississippi Railroad* (1855–1859)," ibid., 3:149–92; "*Eads & Nelson v. Ohio & Mississippi Railroad* (1855–1858)," ibid., 3:205–24; "*Hurd et al. v. Rock Island Bridge Company* (1856–1857)," ibid., 3:308–83.

30. Guy C. Fraker, *Lincoln's Ladder to the Presidency: The Eighth Judicial Circuit* (Carbondale: Southern Illinois University Press, 2012), 168–217.

31. Ibid., 227–33.

32. Abraham Lincoln to John A. Gilmer, December 15, 1860, *Collected Works*, 4:151–53; Harold Holzer, *Lincoln, President-Elect: Abraham Lincoln and the Great Secession Winter, 1860–1861* (New York: Simon and Schuster, 2008), 167–68; Daniel W. Crofts, "A Reluctant Unionist: John A. Gilmer and Lincoln's Cabinet," *Civil War History* 24 (September 1978): 225–49.

33. Abraham Lincoln to Usher F. Linder, February 20, 1848, *Papers of Abraham Lincoln*, 1:4.

34. Alexis de Tocqueville, *Democracy in America*, trans. Henry Reeve, 3rd American ed. (New York: George Adlard, 1839), 277–78; Lincoln, Notes for a Law Lecture, c. 1859, *Collected Works*, 10:20.

35. Lincoln, Message to Congress in Special Session, July 4, 1861, *Collected Works*, 4:429, 440.

36. *Ex parte Merryman* (1861) 17 Fed. Cases 144–146; Lincoln, Message to Congress in Special Session, July 4, 1861, *Collected Works*, 4:440; Brian McGinty, *Lincoln and the Court* (Cambridge, MA: Harvard University Press, 2008), 72–83; Jonathan W. White, *Abraham Lincoln and Treason in the Civil War: The Trials of John Merryman* (Baton Rouge: Louisiana State University Press, 2011).

37. Lincoln to the Senate and House of Representatives, July 17, 1862, *Collected Works*, 5:331.

38. Lincoln to the U.S. Senate, June 26, 1862, *Collected Works*, 5:282; Gabor S. Boritt, *Lincoln and the Economics of the American Dream* (Memphis, TN: Memphis State University Press, 1978), 197–210; Heather Cox Richardson, *The Greatest Nation of the Earth: Republican Economic Policies during the Civil War* (Cambridge, MA: Harvard University Press, 1997), 66–102.

39. Abraham Lincoln to William H. Seward, March 15, 1861, *Collected Works*, 4:284–85. Lincoln's secretaries sent copies of this letter to the other members of the cabinet.

40. William H. Seward to Abraham Lincoln, March 15, 1861, Abraham Lincoln Papers, Library of Congress, Washington, DC.

41. Frederick W. Seward, *Reminiscences of a War-Time Statesman and Diplomat, 1830–1915* (New York: G. P. Putnam's Sons, 1916), 189–90.

42. Michael Burlingame, *The Inner World of Abraham Lincoln* (Urbana: University of Illinois Press, 1994), 189–90.

43. Lincoln, Message to Congress in Special Session, July 4, 1861, *Collected Works*, 4:435.

44. Lincoln to Members of the Cabinet, December 23, 1862, ibid., 6:17.

45. Lincoln, Opinion on the Admission of West Virginia into the Union, December 31, 1862, ibid., 6:27.

46. Ibid., 6:27–28.

47. Michael P. Riccards, "Lincoln and the Political Question: The Creation of the State of West Virginia," *Presidential Studies Quarterly* 27 (Summer 1997); David R. Zimring, "'Secession in Favor of the Constitution': How West Virginia Justified Separate Statehood during the Civil War," *West Virginia History* 3 (Fall 2009):23–51.

48. Lincoln to Members of the Cabinet, May 3, 1864, *Collected Works*, 7:328.

49. See Edward Bates to Abraham Lincoln, May 4, 1864; William H. Seward to Abraham Lincoln, May 5, 1864; Edwin M. Stanton to Abraham Lincoln, May 5, 1864; Gideon Welles to Abraham Lincoln, May 5, 1864; Montgomery Blair to Abraham Lincoln, May 6, 1864; Salmon P. Chase to Abraham Lincoln, May 6, 1864; and John P. Usher to Abraham Lincoln, May 6, 1864, all in Abraham Lincoln Papers, Library of Congress.

50. Frederick Douglass, *The Life and Times of Frederick Douglass* (Hartford, CT: Park Publishing, 1882), 423.

51. William H. Seward to Abraham Lincoln, April 1, 1861, Abraham Lincoln Papers; Abraham Lincoln to William H. Seward, April 1, 1861, *Collected Works*, 4:317.

52. Gideon Welles, *Diary of Gideon Welles, Secretary of the Navy under Lincoln and Johnson* (Boston: Houghton Mifflin, 1911), 1:201–2; Abraham Lincoln to William H. Seward and Salmon P. Chase, December 20, 1862, *Collected Works*, 6:12–13; Frederick W. Seward, *Seward at Washington as Senator and Secretary of State* (New York: Derby and Miller, 1891), 148.

53. Abraham Lincoln to Joseph Hooker, January 26, 1863, *Collected Works*, 6:78–79.

54. Noah Brooks, *Washington in Lincoln's Time* (New York: Century Co., 1895), 53.

LINCOLN AND CITIZENSHIP

Mark E. Steiner

This essay marks the beginning of a project that explores Abraham Lincoln's views on citizenship regarding both European immigrants and African Americans. Citizenship itself was a developing concept in antebellum America.[1] In 1862, Edward Bates, Lincoln's attorney general, lamented the lack of a "clear and satisfactory definition of the phrase *Citizen of the United States*."[2] At its most basic level, though, citizenship was about membership in a political community. Lincoln believed that all (male) European immigrants belonged to this community; he thought that the Declaration of Independence provided basic values that defined what it meant to be an American and that unified all those who believed in its ideals. Moreover, Lincoln long associated immigration with economic growth.[3] He thus rejected the anti-immigrant nativism common in the antebellum North.

Lincoln, for most of his adult life, could not imagine African Americans belonging to this political community. His understanding of the Declaration of Independence led him to antislavery convictions, but those antislavery convictions only went so far. In his debates with Stephen Douglas, Lincoln acknowledged the natural rights of black people, while rejecting civil rights such as voting or jury duty. By the end of the Civil War, however, Lincoln's position had changed.

ETHNICITY AND CITIZENSHIP

Abraham Lincoln believed in American exceptionalism.[4] America, said Lincoln, was the "last best hope of earth."[5] The principles announced in the Declaration of Independence were what gave "hope to the world for all future time." Lincoln said he had "never had a feeling politically that did not spring from the

Come and Join Us Brothers, *circa 1864. Published by the Supervisory Committee for Recruiting Colored Regiments. African American men enlisted in the military, believing that their service would earn them the right of citizenship. Lincoln eventually agreed. Courtesy of The Abraham Lincoln Library and Museum at Lincoln Memorial University, Harrogate, Tennessee.*

sentiments embodied in the Declaration of Independence." The Declaration promised "that in due time the weights should be lifted from the shoulders of all men, and that all should have an equal chance."[6]

Unlike those white Anglo-Saxon Protestants who believed that the foundation of American greatness was white Anglo-Saxon Protestants, Lincoln believed American greatness grew from the principles of the Declaration. Lincoln did not believe in "ethno-nationalism" because ethnicity did not matter to him.[7] Any European immigrant who came to the United States because of the promise of the Declaration was already sufficiently "Americanized." Lincoln never worried about whether immigrants would assimilate, because belief in the principles of the Declaration would unify all Americans, native and foreign-born. The Declaration was the "electric cord" that linked all men together. Lincoln explained:

> We have besides these men—descended by blood from our ancestors—among us perhaps half our people who are not descendants at all of these men, they are men who have come from Europe—German, Irish, French and Scandinavian—men that have come from Europe themselves, or whose ancestors have come hither and settled here, finding themselves our equals in all things. If they look back through this history to trace their connection with those days by blood, they find they have none, they cannot carry themselves back into that glorious epoch and make themselves feel that they are part of us, but when they look through that old Declaration of Independence they find that those old men say that "We hold these truths to be self-evident, that all men are created equal," and then they feel that moral sentiment taught in that day evidences their relation to those men, that it is the father of all moral principle in them, and that they have a right to claim it as though they were blood of the blood, and flesh of the flesh of the men who wrote that Declaration, and so they are. That is the electric cord in that Declaration that links the hearts of patriotic and liberty-loving men together, that will link those patriotic hearts as long as the love of freedom exists in the minds of men throughout the world.[8]

Lincoln believed that Europeans would be attracted to America's promise of an "equal chance" given to all. He welcomed all immigrants from Europe, making no distinctions between those who were of Anglo-Saxon stock and those who were not. In this respect, he differed from many in the Whig Party, some in the Republican Party, and everyone in the Know-Nothing Party. During the debates with Stephen Douglas over slavery in the territories, Lincoln presented his vision of "free soil, free labor, free men":

> I am still in favor of our new Territories being in such a condition that white men may find a home—may find some spot where they can better their condition—where they can settle upon new soil and better their condition in life. I am in favor of this not merely, (I must say it here as I have elsewhere,) for our own people who are born amongst us, but as an outlet for free white people everywhere, the world over—in which Hans and Baptiste and Patrick, and all other men from all the world, may find new homes and better their conditions in life.[9]

Lincoln flatly rejected the nativism of the northeastern Whigs in the 1840s and of the Know-Nothings in the 1850s.[10] The Know-Nothing Party, which had a dramatic rise and fall in the mid-1850s, was antislavery, anti-Catholic, and anti-immigrant. In Illinois, the party's platform called for modifying naturalization laws by extending the residency requirement and repealing any state law that permitted resident aliens to vote, resisting "the corrupting influences and aggressive policy of the Roman Church" and restoring the Missouri Compromise to keep slavery out of the territories.[11] Lincoln was unable to understand how a party could be both antislavery and anti-immigrant. He said of the Know-Nothings, "Of their principles I think little better than I do of those of the slavery extensionists. Indeed I do not perceive how any one professing to be sensitive to the wrongs of the negroes, can join in a league to degrade a class of white men."[12] In an 1855 letter, he stated:

> I am not a Know-Nothing. That is certain. How could I be? How can any one who abhors the oppression of negroes, be in favor of degrading classes of white people? Our progress in degeneracy appears to me to be pretty rapid. As a nation, we began by declaring that "all men are created equal." We now practically read it "all men are created equal, except negroes." When the Know-Nothings get control, it will read "all men are created equal, except negroes, and foreigners, and catholics." When it comes to this I should prefer emigrating to some country where they make no pretence of loving liberty—to Russia, for instance, where despotism can be taken pure, and without the base alloy of hypocracy.[13]

A contemporary remembered Lincoln opposing the Know-Nothing platform of "circumscribing the Election franchise—universal suffrage" because "he wanted to lift men up & give 'Em a chance."[14]

Lincoln helped draft an antinativist plank at an 1855 meeting of antislavery newspaper editors in Decatur, which Lincoln attended as an informal guest. The meeting was designed to launch a new party in Illinois. When the antinativist plank introduced by German editor George Schneider met with opposition, Lincoln said, "The resolution . . . is nothing new. It is already contained in the Declaration of Independence." The plank called for maintaining "naturalization laws as they are, believing as we do, that we should welcome the exiles and emigrants from the Old World, to homes of enterprise and of freedom in the New."[15] When the Illinois Republican Party formally began at the Bloomington convention in May 1856, the Decatur plank formed the basis of an antinativist resolution: "That the spirit of our institutions, as well as the constitution of our country guarantee the liberty of conscience as well as political freedom, and that we will proscribe no one, by legislation or otherwise, on account of religious opinions, or in consequence of place of birth."[16] Lincoln associated America with freedom and Europe with despotism. European immigrants were fleeing from "tyranny" and to "freedom." In an 1861 address to Germans in Cincinnati, Lincoln said:

> In regard to the Germans and foreigners, I esteem them no better than other people, nor any worse. It is not my nature, when I see a people borne down by the weight of their shackles—the oppression of tyranny—to make their life more bitter by heaping upon them greater burdens; but rather would I do all in my power to raise the yoke, than to add anything that would tend to crush them. Inasmuch as our country is extensive and new, and the countries of Europe are densely populated, if there are any abroad who desire to make this the land of their adoption, it is not in my heart to throw aught in their way, to prevent them from coming to the United States.[17]

While Lincoln publicly welcomed "Hans and Baptiste and Patrick," he harbored some suspicion about "Patrick."[18] Irish voters generally supported the Democratic Party; Lincoln once alluded to Irish immigrants as "those adopted citizens, whose votes have given Judge Douglas all his consequence."[19] During the 1858 Senate campaign, he privately expressed concerns about "fraudulent votes" from "Celtic gentlemen." Lincoln feared that the Democrats would transport "into the doubtful districts numbers of men who are legal voters in all respects except residence and who will swear to residence and thus put it beyond our power to exclude them."[20] That Irish immigrants engaged in voter fraud was a common belief of the opponents of the Democratic Party.[21] When Lincoln publicly made the charge that "Irishmen had been imported expressly to vote him down," the local Democratic newspaper retorted, "Doubtless Mr. Lincoln entertains a holy horror of all Irishmen and other adopted citizens who have sufficient self-respect to believe themselves superior to the negro."[22]

Lincoln was particularly solicitous toward German immigrants. Germans were the largest immigrant group in the Republican Party. One of the reasons Republican politicians in the Midwest disavowed anti-immigrant policies was to garner votes from Germans.[23] During the 1858 senate campaign, Lincoln called for German speakers to be sent across the state and helped arranged the publication of his speeches in German. He warned Gustave Koerner, a German immigrant and Republican politician, that the party was "in great danger" in Madison County and asked if Koerner, the newspaper editor Theodore Canisius, "and some other influential Germans set a plan on foot that shall gain us accession from the Germans, and see that, at the election, none are cheated in their ballots."[24] Before the 1860 presidential campaign, Lincoln bought a printing press for Canisius to start a German paper in Springfield that "in political sentiment" was to adhere to the "Philadelphia and Illinois Republican platforms."[25]

It is helpful to review Lincoln's record on both voting rights and naturalization. When Abraham Lincoln announced his candidacy for the Illinois legislature in 1836, he said that he believed that "the privileges of the government" should go to those who assisted "in bearing its burthens." Those entitled to vote would be "all whites" who paid taxes or were in the militia. Lincoln's position actually would have restricted the franchise in Illinois. The Illinois Constitution of 1818 granted suffrage to "all white male inhabitants above the age of 21 years" who had resided in the state for six months. It did not require paying taxes or serving in the militia. The 1818 Constitution did not even require a voter be a citizen of the United States. Lincoln did not address residency or citizenship as qualifications; however, he did require potential voters to pay property taxes or be in the militia. The militia consisted of all "able-bodied" white males between the ages of eighteen and forty-five.[26] While David Donald concluded that Lincoln "shared the standard Whig belief that property holding ought to be a prerequisite for voting," Lincoln's inclusion of those who "bear arms" meant that more than just owning property qualified white males to vote.[27] Those over forty-five who did not own property would have been denied the right to vote.

The Illinois provision that allowed resident aliens to vote was unusual. The extension of suffrage to resident aliens had been more common in the early republic. Alexander Keyssar, in his history of voting rights, explained that "the line separating citizens from aliens was not clearly or consistently drawn"; in many jurisdictions, foreign-born men who were not yet naturalized but otherwise met property, taxpaying, and residency requirements were able to vote.[28] Illinois was the only new state admitted between 1800 and 1840 that allowed noncitizens to vote. The Illinois Supreme Court noted in 1840 that "each state has the undoubted right to prescribe the qualifications of its own voters. And it is equally clear, that the act of naturalization does not confer on the individual naturalized, the right to exercise the elective franchise."[29] Illinois did change its qualifications for voting in its 1848 Constitution. Non-naturalized aliens were no longer eligible to vote, as suffrage was limited to "every white male citizen above the age of 21 years." The residency period was changed from six months to one year.[30]

The battle over universal white male suffrage was already over by the time Lincoln called for its limitation in 1836. The Age of Jackson saw the expansion of suffrage for white males as property and taxpaying requirements were reduced or eliminated.[31] The New York Constitutional Convention of 1821 was a sign of things to come. James Kent, jurist and Whig, refused to "bow before the idol of universal suffrage" and defended the freehold requirement. Kent asserted that the "extreme democratic principle" invariably produced "corruption, injustice, violence, and tyranny." Martin Van Buren succeeded in broadening white suffrage with a constitutional provision that merely required white males to have paid any tax on real or personal property; however, the state's constitution also restricted black suffrage by requiring that a "man of color" possess a "freehold estate of the value of two hundred and fifty dollars."[32] In 1840, Lincoln, the Whig politician, attacked then-president Van Buren's record, "especially his votes in the New York Convention in allowing Free Negroes the right of suffrage." The newspaper account of the speech left it at that, but it appears that Lincoln was criticizing Van Buren for leaving black New Yorkers with any voting rights at all.[33]

Lincoln's 1836 announcement of his candidacy was the last time he publicly favored restrictions on suffrage for white males. In the 1840s, Whigs sought a broader appeal, capitulating on property requirements; Lincoln reflected this shift in Whig "democratization."[34] Lincoln took the more liberal side on another suffrage issue—immigrant voting rights. The 1840s and 1850s saw a dramatic increase in the number of immigrants from Ireland and Germany. From 1840 to 1860, more than four million immigrants, mostly from Ireland and Germany, came to America. In the ten years between 1845 and 1854, three million immigrants arrived to a country of only twenty million—the largest influx of immigrants in American history, in proportion to the total population.[35] Nativist organizations pressed for restrictions on the voting rights of immigrants.[36] The Whigs appeared split on this issue, with those in the Northeast generally pressing for further restrictions and those in the Midwest generally opposed.

After riots erupted in Philadelphia between Catholics and Protestants, Lincoln and his fellow Springfield Whigs met in June 1844 to answer charges by Democrats that Whigs were responsible for the riots because of their "supposed hostility" to "foreigners and Catholics." The assembled Whigs passed several resolutions, denying they were anti-immigrant or anti-Catholic:

> Resolved, That in admitting the foreigner to the rights of citizenship, he should be put to some reasonable test of his fidelity to our country and its institutions; and that he should first dwell among us a reasonable time to become generally acquainted with the nature of those institutions; and that, consistent with these requisites, naturalization laws, should be so framed, as to render admission to citizenship under them, as convenient, cheap, and expeditious as possible. Resolved, That we will now, and at all times, oppose as best we may, all attempts to either destroy the naturalization laws or to so alter them, as to render admission under them, less convenient, less cheap, or less expeditious than it now is. Resolved, That the guarantee of the rights of conscience, as found in our Constitution, is most sacred and inviolable, and one that belongs no less to the Catholic, than to the Protestant; and that all attempts to abridge or interfere with these rights, either of Catholic or Protestant, directly or indirectly, have our decided disapprobation, and shall ever have our most effective opposition.[37]

What was significant about these resolutions was that they clearly rejected nativist proposals to increase the residency period for citizenship. (The American Republican Party in June 1843 had proposed replacing the five-year residency period with one of twenty-one years.)[38] The writer for the *Illinois State Register*, the Democratic newspaper in Springfield, noted, "Mr. Lincoln expressed the kindest, and most benevolent feelings towards foreigners; they were, I doubt not, the sincere and honest sentiments of *his heart*; but they were not those of *his party*."[39]

William H. Herndon, Lincoln's law partner, remembered a case he was handling in the Illinois Supreme Court about "lessening & narrowing the right of suffrage." The case was probably *Moody v. Peake*, which was an 1851 Sangamon County case that was to decide whether a resident alien could vote in a city election. Herndon, who was the city attorney for Springfield at the time, asked Lincoln to assist him on the appeal. Lincoln refused, saying, "I am opposed to the limitation—the lessening of the right of suffrage—am in favor of its Extension—Enlargement—want to lift men up and broaden them—don't intend by no act of mine to crush or contract."[40] The Illinois Supreme Court dismissed the appeal.

Lincoln, in an unsigned 1856 editorial published in a Galena newspaper, took the time to answer an article published in a Democratic newspaper that had asserted that "foreigners, who have not been naturalized, according to the laws of the United States, even though they resided here previous to the adoption of our new Constitution, cannot legally vote for Presidential electors." "This is a grave error," Lincoln wrote. "Our Legislature has directed, that unnaturalized foreigners, who were here before the adoption of our late State Constitution, shall in common with others, vote for and appoint Presidential Electors." Lincoln was on the side of these "unnaturalized foreigners," stating, "Let not this class of foreigners be alarmed. Our Legislature has directed that they may vote for Electors; and the U.S. Constitution has expressly authorized the Legislature to make that direction." He then concluded by implying the Democrats were anti-immigrant: "But, what's in the wind? Why are Mr. Buchanan's friends anxious to deprive foreigners of their votes? We pause for an answer."[41]

Massachusetts was a stronghold of the short-lived Know-Nothing Party, which swept state elections in 1854. The Know-Nothing governor, Henry J. Gardner, proposed a twenty-one-year waiting period *after naturalization* before immigrants could vote. This proposal, along with a literacy test for voting, passed the legislature in 1855. Under Massachusetts law, it had to pass two successive legislatures before it would be put before the electorate. In 1856, the legislature instead substituted a fourteen-year period. In the 1857 legislature, now dominated by Republicans, a two-year waiting period before naturalized citizens could vote was substituted for the fourteen-year period. The two-year period passed again in 1858. The measure was then placed before the voters for approval.

Lincoln was one of many western Republicans who opposed the two-year period, worried that the provision would hinder their ability to appeal to immigrant voters, particularly Germans.[42] In April, Lincoln prepared a resolution for the Illinois Republican Party condemning the Massachusetts legislature for approving the two-year period. Lyman Trumbull suggested, "It would be better to select some act of our adversaries, rather than of our own friends, upon which to base a protest against any distinction between native and naturalized citizens, as to the right of suffrage."[43]

After the provision in Massachusetts passed, Theodore Canisius asked Lincoln if he supported it. Lincoln conceded that Massachusetts had the perfect right to pass such a provision: "Massachusetts is a sovereign and independent state; and it is no privilege of mine to scold her for what she does." Lincoln was more than willing to state his opposition to such a provision in Illinois, "or in any other place, where I have a right to oppose it." He explained:

> Understanding the spirit of our institutions to aim at the elevation of men, I am opposed to whatever tends to degrade them. I have some little notoriety for commiserating the oppressed condition of the negro; and I should be strangely inconsistent if I could favor any project for curtailing the existing rights of white men, even though born in different lands, and speaking different languages from myself.

Canisius published the letter in both the German-language *Illinois Staats-Anzeiger* and the *Illinois State Journal.*[44]

Lincoln understood that such nativist appeals were politically damaging in the Midwest. In an 1859 letter, he decried Republicans' tendency to include issues that were popular in that state but a "firebrand" elsewhere. He included the "movement against foreigners" in Massachusetts as an example. He lamented that "Massachusetts republicans should have looked beyond their noses; and then they could not have failed to see that tilting against foreigners would ruin us in the whole North-West." The "movement against foreigners" was an "apple of discord."[45] The Republican Party platform in 1860 included a plank that repudiated the Massachusetts residency provision. It stated that the Republican Party was "opposed to any change in our naturalization laws, or any state legislation by which the rights of citizenship hitherto accorded by emigrants from foreign lands shall be abridged or impaired; and in favor of giving a full and efficient protection to the rights of all classes of citizens, whether native or naturalized, both at home and abroad."[46]

Lincoln continued to strongly support European immigration as president.[47] In his 1863 Annual Message to Congress, he asked it to consider "the expediency of establishing a system for the encouragement of immigration." He continued to link immigration with economic development, referring to immigration as "this source of national wealth and strength." The nation faced a "great deficiency of laborers in every field of industry" while "tens of thousands of persons" thronged to American consulates offering to emigrate to the United States if they received assistance in transportation. Lincoln suggested that "essential, but very cheap, assistance" would allow this much-needed immigration.[48]

Congress responded to Lincoln's call the following summer, passing an immigration bill on July 4, 1864. The legislation established the nation's first "commissioner of immigration," permitted immigrants' labor contracts to be garnished up to "12 months of wages" to pay for "the expenses of their emigration," and promised that military service would not be "compulsively enrolled" unless an immigrant had renounced his oath to his country of birth and declared his intent to become a citizen of the United States. The commissioner of immigration was charged with helping immigrants obtain the "cheapest and most expeditious manner to place of their destination."[49]

Lincoln returned to the subject of immigration in his Annual Message to Congress in 1864. Immigration was "one of the principal replenishing streams which are appointed by Providence to repair the ravages of internal war, and its wastes of national strength and health," he said. To ensure the "flow of that stream in its present fullness," the government had to make it clear that it would not impose "involuntary military service" on immigrants "who came from other lands to cast their lot in our country." Lincoln also asked Congress to do something to prevent the "practice of frauds against immigrants."[50] Congress did not heed that call.

RACE AND CITIZENSHIP

Lincoln opposed civil rights for black Northerners in the debates with Stephen Douglas. In the very first debate, Douglas charged that Lincoln and the Republican Party supported citizenship for African Americans. Douglas thundered:

> If you desire negro citizenship, if you desire to allow them to come into the State and settle with the white man, if you desire them to vote on an equality with yourselves, and to make them eligible to office, to serve on juries, and to adjudge your rights, then support Mr. Lincoln

and the Black Republican party, who are in favor of the citizenship
of the negro. For one, I am opposed to negro citizenship in any and
every form. I believe this government was made on the white basis.
I believe it was made by white men, for the benefit of white men and
their posterity for ever, and I am in favour of confining citizenship to
white men, men of European birth and descent, instead of conferring
it upon negroes, Indians and other inferior races.[51]

Douglas went out of his way to proclaim all nonwhites as inferior: "I am not only
opposed to negro equality, but I am opposed to Indian equality. I am opposed
to putting the coolies, now importing into this country, on an equality with
us, or putting the Chinese or any other inferior race on an equality with us."[52]

   Lincoln gave his infamous answer to Douglas at the beginning of the fourth
debate, which was held at Charleston. There, Lincoln made it clear he did not
support civil rights for African Americans:

> I will say then that I am not, nor ever have been in favor of bringing
> about in any way the social and political equality of the white and
> black races,—that I am not nor ever have been in favor of making
> voters or jurors of negroes, nor of qualifying them to hold office, nor
> to intermarry with white people; and I will say in addition to this
> that there is a physical difference between the white and black races
> which I believe will for ever forbid the two races living together on
> terms of social and political equality. And inasmuch as they cannot
> so live, while they do remain together there must be the position of
> superior and inferior, and I as much as any other man am in favor of
> having the superior position assigned to the white race.[53]

   Lincoln was hardly breaking new ground when he rejected civil rights for
black people in Illinois—the state with the most racist laws in the antebellum
North.[54] Lincoln had supported these laws. In his first term in the Illinois
legislature, Lincoln voted for a resolution that "the elective franchise should be
kept pure from contamination by the admission of colored votes."[55] In 1858, he
refused to sign a petition circulated by black abolitionist H. Ford Douglas that
called for the repeal of the Illinois law that prohibited blacks from testifying
in court against whites.[56] In 1854, he explained why he thought the two races
could not live together as equals.

What next? Free them, and make them politically and socially, our
equals? My own feelings will not admit of this; and if mine would,
we well know that those of the great mass of white people will not.
Whether this feeling accords with justice and sound judgment, is not
the sole question, if indeed, it is any part of it. A universal feeling,
whether well or ill-founded, can not be safely disregarded. We can
not, then, make them equals.[57]

According to Eric Foner, Lincoln thus represented "the mainstream of white
northern opinion, by now convinced that slavery posed a threat to 'free society,'
but still convinced of the inherent inferiority of African Americans."[58] Lincoln
confessed in this same speech, "If all earthly power were given me, I should
not know what to do, as to the existing institution. My first impulse would be
to free all the slaves, and send them to Liberia,—to their own native land."[59]
Lincoln had long favored colonization.[60] His public support for colonization
ended only with the Emancipation Proclamation.

Where Lincoln and Douglas differed was the meaning of the Declaration
of Independence's statement that "all men are created equal." Douglas mocked
Lincoln's belief that the founders meant this statement to be literally true.
Douglas initially argued that when the signers "declared all men to have been
created equal—that they were speaking of British subjects on this continent
being equal to British subjects born and residing in Great Britain." Lincoln
lambasted this notion that the Declaration was so limited, declaiming, "What
a mere wreck—mangled ruin—it makes of our once glorious Declaration."
Lincoln pointed out that Douglas's formulation excluded a good number of
European immigrants: "Why, according to this, not only negroes but white people outside of Great Britain and America are not spoken of in that instrument.
The English, Irish and Scotch, along with white Americans, were included to
be sure, but the French, Germans and other white people of the world are all
gone to pot along with the Judge's inferior races."[61] Douglas did not directly
answer Lincoln's criticism; however, he quit making that particular argument.
The signers of the Declaration, Douglas now asserted, were not referring to "the
negro whatever when they declared all men to be created equal. They desired
to express by that phrase, white men, men of European birth and European
descent, and had no reference either to the negro, the savage Indians, the
Fejee, the Malay, or any other inferior and degraded race, when they spoke
of the equality of men."[62] Lincoln understood that natural rights were truly

universal: "Every man, black, white or yellow, has a mouth to be fed and two hands with which to feed it—and that bread should be allowed to go to that mouth without controversy."[63]

Throughout the debates with Stephen Douglas, Lincoln made clear his opposition to slavery:

> There is no reason in the world why the negro is not entitled to all the natural rights enumerated in the Declaration of Independence, the right to life, liberty and the pursuit of happiness. I hold that he is as much entitled to these as the white man. I agree with Judge Douglas he is not my equal in many respects—certainly not in color, perhaps not in moral or intellectual endowment. But in the right to eat the bread, without leave of anybody else, which his own hand earns, he is my equal and the equal of Judge Douglas, and the equal of every living man.[64]

Throughout the 1850s, Lincoln consistently separated a black man's entitlement to natural rights and his entitlement to civil, or citizenship, rights.[65]

Lincoln changed his mind on black Americans and civil rights. Strangely, the first inkling that he had done so came in his First Inaugural Address. After Lincoln conceded the North's obligation to enforce the Fugitive Slave Act, he took a surprising turn. Lincoln not only cautioned that every safeguard should be taken to ensure that "a free man" was not wrongfully enslaved but also suggested that he was entitled to the privileges and immunities of citizenship.

> In any law upon this subject ought not all the safeguards of liberty known in civilized and humane jurisprudence to be introduced, so that a free man be not in any case surrendered as a slave? And might it not be well at the same time to provide by law for the enforcement of that clause in the Constitution which guarantees that "the citizens of each State shall be entitled to all privileges and immunities of citizens in the several States"?[66]

Herman Belz has noted that Lincoln "advanced a civil rights proposal that was deeply offensive to southern and border state opinion." Lincoln's proposal struck at "the inequality of the races, the fundamental principle on which slavery rested."[67]

Ultimately, the service of black troops changed Lincoln's mind about black citizenship, as it did for many white Northerners. Military service had been associated with citizenship since the American Revolution.[68] Recall that in 1836, Lincoln called for voting rights for those who served in the militia. But serving in the militia had been a white privilege. The federal militia law enrolled "each and every free able-bodied white male citizen."[69] Similarly, Illinois limited the militia to "free white male inhabitants."[70]

When Lincoln issued the Emancipation Proclamation on January 1, 1863, he included a provision that was not contained in the preliminary proclamation of September 1862: the recruitment of black troops. The proclamation stated that "such persons of suitable condition, will be received into the armed service of the United States to garrison forts, positions, stations, and other places, and to man vessels of all sorts."[71]

Lincoln had initially opposed the use of black troops. In August 1862, a "deputation of Western gentlemen" offered two regiments of black soldiers from Indiana, but Lincoln demurred. He stated that he could not lose the border states, and "to arm the negroes would turn 50,000 bayonets from the loyal Border States against us that were for us." He "would employ all colored men offered as laborers, but would not promise to make soldiers of them."[72] When Frederick Douglass pressed Lincoln on his tardiness in using black soldiers, Lincoln responded that "the measure could not have been more successfully adopted at the beginning of the war; that the wisdom of making colored men soldiers was still doubted: that their enlistment was a serious offense to popular prejudice."[73] In addition to political considerations, Lincoln privately had opposed arming black men because he believed they would quickly surrender or retreat: "But I am not so sure we could do much with the blacks. If we were to arm them, I fear that in a few weeks the arms would be in the hands of the rebels; and indeed thus far we have not had arms enough to equip our white troops."[74] Lincoln thus assumed that black men lacked courage; they did not possess the same manly virtues as white men.

Frederick Douglass clearly understood the opportunity that military service could provide: "The opportunity is given us to be men." In a July 1863 speech to promote "colored enlistments," Douglass said:

> With one courageous resolution we may blot out the hand-writing
> of ages against us. Once let the black man get upon his person the
> brass letters U. S., let him get an eagle on his button, and a musket

on his shoulder, and bullets in his pocket, and there is no power on earth or under the earth which can deny that he has earned the right of citizenship in the United States.

Douglass told his audience, "Nothing can be more plain, nothing more certain than that the speediest and best possible way open to us to manhood, equal rights and elevation, is that we enter this service."[75] Douglass understood that masculinity, military service, and citizenship were all interconnected. Service in the military proved one's manhood, which in turn proved one's entitlement to citizenship.[76] One month later, Lincoln made a similar argument to skeptical whites about the "promise of freedom" for black troops: "But negroes, like other people, act upon motives. Why should they do any thing for us, if we will do nothing for them? If they stake their lives for us, they must be prompted by the strongest motive—even the promise of freedom. And the promise being made, must be kept."[77]

Robert Hamilton, in the *Weekly Anglo-African*, asked, "What better field to claim our rights than the field of battle."[78] This connection was also made in an address "from the colored citizens of Norfolk" published in June 1865. The committee asked that "a Christian and enlightened people shall, at once, concede to us the full enjoyment of those privileges of full citizenship," pointing out that "over 200,000 colored men have taken up arms on behalf of the Union . . . on a hundred well fought fields, have fully proved their patriotism and possession of all *the manly qualities* that adorn the soldier."[79]

In a January 1865 letter from the "colored citizens of Nashville" to the Union convention, this connection between service and citizenship was again noted. These petitioners declared, "We know the burdens of citizenship, and are ready to bear them." In fact, they had assumed the obligations of citizenship before obtaining its privileges:

> Near 200,000 of our brethren are to-day performing military duty
> in the ranks of the Union army. Thousands of them have already
> died in battle, or perished by a cruel martyrdom for the sake of the
> Union, and we are ready and willing to sacrifice more. But what
> higher order of citizen is there than the soldier? or who has a greater
> trust confided to his hands? If we are called on to do military duty
> against the rebel armies in the field, why should we be denied the
> privilege of voting against rebel citizens at the ballot-box? The latter
> is as necessary to save the Government as the former.[80]

Lincoln overcame his initial reluctance to use black troops. In a March 26, 1863, letter to Andrew Johnson, Lincoln said, "The colored population is the great available and yet unavailed of, force for restoring the Union. The bare sight of fifty thousand armed, and drilled black soldiers on the banks of the Mississippi, would end the rebellion at once."[81]

The bravery of black troops was soon in evidence. Lincoln answered a critic of both emancipation and the use of black troops in an August 1863 letter. Lincoln noted that some of his generals believed "purely as military opinions" that "the emancipation policy, and the use of colored troops, constitute the heaviest blow yet dealt to the rebellion; and that, at least one of those important successes, could not have been achieved when it was, but for the aid of black soldiers." Lincoln further argued that "negroes, like other people, act upon motives." If black men were to "stake their lives for us, they must be prompted by the strongest motive—even the promise of freedom. And the promise being made, must be kept." Peace would come, and black soldiers who had fought gallantly and white Northerners who had opposed their service would look back differently on the Civil War: "And then, there will be some black men who can remember that, with silent tongue, and clenched teeth, and steady eye, and well-poised bayonet, they have helped mankind on to this great consummation; while, I fear, there will be some white ones, unable to forget that, with malignant heart, and deceitful speech, they have strove to hinder it."[82]

In March 1864, Lincoln wrote to Michael Hahn, the newly elected governor of Louisiana, suggesting that the new constitution include black suffrage:

> Now you are about to have a Convention which, among other things, will probably define the elective franchise. I barely suggest for your private consideration, whether some of the colored people may not be let in—as, for instance, the very intelligent, and especially those who have fought gallantly in our ranks. They would probably help, in some trying time to come, to keep the jewel of liberty within the family of freedom.[83]

The Louisiana Constitution failed to provide suffrage to African Americans; it instead deferred to the legislature.

In Lincoln's last public address, he noted this situation: "It is also unsatisfactory to some that the elective franchise is not given to the colored man. I would myself prefer that it were now conferred on the very intelligent, and on those who serve our cause as soldiers."⁸⁴ When Lincoln spoke those words, John Wilkes Booth, who was in the crowd that day, turned to a friend and said, "That means nigger citizenship. Now, by God, I will put him through. That will be the last speech he will ever make."⁸⁵

Notes

1. James H. Kettner, *The Development of American Citizenship, 1608–1870* (Chapel Hill: University of North Carolina Press, 1978); William J. Novak, "The Legal Transformation of Citizenship in Nineteenth-Century America," in *The Democratic Experiment: New Directions in American Political History*, ed. Meg Jacobs, William J. Novak, and Julian E. Zelizer (Princeton, NJ: Princeton University Press, 2003), 85–119; Rogers Smith, *Civic Ideals: Conflicting Visions of Citizenship in U.S. History* (New Haven, CT: Yale University Press, 1997).

2. Opinion of Attorney General Bates on Citizenship (Washington, DC: Government Printing Office 1863), 3.

3. G. S. Boritt, *Lincoln and the Economics of the American Dream* (Memphis, TN: Memphis State University Press, 1978), 27, 98, 141, 221.

4. Richard J. Carwardine, *Lincoln: Profiles in Power* (Edinburgh: Pearson Education, 2003), 23.

5. Abraham Lincoln, Annual Message to Congress, December 1, 1862, in *The Collected Works of Abraham Lincoln*, ed. Roy P. Basler et al. (New Brunswick, NJ: Rutgers University Press, 1953), 5:537.

6. Lincoln, Speech in Independence Hall, Philadelphia, Pennsylvania, February 22, 1861, *Collected Works*, 4:240–41.

7. Eric Kaufmann, "American Exceptionalism Reconsidered: Anglo-Saxon Ethnogenesis in the 'Universal' Nation, 1776–1850," *Journal of American Studies* 33 (1999): 437–57.

8. Lincoln, Speech at Chicago, July 10, 1858, *Collected Works*, 2:249–500.

9. Lincoln, Seventh and Last Debate with Stephen A. Douglas at Alton, Illinois, October 15, 1858, *Collected Works*, 3:312.

10. See Bruce Levine, "'The Vital Element of the Republican Party': Antislavery, Nativism, and Abraham Lincoln," *Journal of the Civil War Era* 1 (2011), 488–93.

11. John P. Senning, "The Know Nothing Movement in Illinois, 1854–1856," *Illinois State Historical Society Journal* 7 (1914): 27–29. For a good overview of Know-Nothing beliefs, see Tyler Anbinder, *Nativism and Slavery: The Northern Know Nothings and the Politics of the 1850s* (New York: Oxford University Press, 1994), 103–26.

12. Lincoln to Owen Lovejoy, August 11, 1855, *Collected Works*, 2:316.

13. Lincoln to Joshua F. Speed, August 24, 1855, ibid., 2:323.

14. Douglas L. Wilson and Rodney O. Davis, eds., *Herndon's Informants: Letters, Interviews, and Statements about Abraham Lincoln* (Urbana: University of Illinois Press, 1997), 705.

15. Michael Burlingame, *Abraham Lincoln: A Life* (Baltimore: Johns Hopkins University Press, 2008), 1:412–13.

16. Official Record of Convention, reprinted in *Transactions of the McLean County Historical Society*, ed. Ezra Prince (Bloomington, IL: Pantagraph Printing, 1900), 3:161.

17. Lincoln, Speech to Germans at Cincinnati, Ohio, February 12, 1861, *Collected Works*, 4:202.

18. See Kevin Kenny, "Abraham Lincoln and the American Irish," *American Journal of Irish Studies* 10 (2013), 48.

19. Lincoln, Speech to the Springfield Scott Club, August 14, 1852, *Collected Works*, 2:143.

20. Lincoln to Norman B. Judd, October 20, 1858, *Collected Works*, 3:330.

21. Anbinder, *Nativism and Slavery*, 257–59.

22. Lincoln, Speech at Meredosia, Illinois, October 18, 1858, *Collected Works*, 3:329.

23. Alison Clark Efford, *German Immigrants, Race, and Citizenship in the Civil War Era* (Cambridge: Cambridge University Press, 2013), 69.

24. Lincoln to Gustave P. Koerner, July 15, 1858, *Collected Works*, 2:502; Lincoln to Gustave P. Koerner, August 6, 1858, ibid., 2:537–38; Lincoln to Norman P. Judd, September 23, 1858, ibid., 3:202; Lincoln to Gustave P. Koerner, July 25, 1858, ibid. 2:524.

25. Contract with Theodore Canisius, May 30, 1859, ibid., 3:383.

26. Ill. Const. of 1818, art. II, sec. 27, and art. V, § 1.

27. David Donald, *Lincoln* (New York: Simon and Schuster, 1996), 59.

28. Alexander Keyssar, *The Right to Vote: The Contested History of Democracy in the United States* (New York: Basic Books, 2000), 32.

29. *Spragins v. Houghton*, 3 Ill. (2 Scam.) 377 (1840).

30. Ill. Const. of 1848, art. VI, § 1.

31. Keyssar, *Right to Vote*, 22–42; Sean Wilentz, *The Rise of American Democracy: Jefferson to Lincoln* (New York: W. W. Norton, 2005), 201–2.

32. *Reports of the Proceedings and Debates of the Convention of 1821, Assembled for the Purpose of Amending the Constitution of the State of New York* (Albany: E. & E. Hosford, 1821), 219; N.Y. Const. of 1821, art. II, § 1.

33. Lincoln, Speech at Tremont, Illinois, May 2, 1840, *Collected Works*, 1:210.

34. Keyssar, *Right to Vote*, 32–34.

35. Maldwyn Allen Jones, *American Immigration*, 2nd ed. (Chicago: University of Chicago Press, 1992), 79.

36. Keyssar, *Right to Vote*, 67–69.

37. Speech and Resolutions Concerning Philadelphia Riots, June 12, 1844, *Collected Works*, 1:337–38.

38. Anbinder, *Nativism and Slavery*, 11.

39. Speech and Resolutions Concerning Philadelphia Riots, *Collected Works*, 1:338.

40. Wilson and Davis, *Herndon's Informants*, 705; *Moody v. Peake* (1851) case file, "Law Practice of Abraham Lincoln," http://www.lawpracticeof abrahamlincoln.org.

41. Lincoln, Editorial on the Right of Foreigners to Vote, July 23, 1856, *Collected Works*, 2:335–36.

42. Eric Foner, *Free Soil, Free Labor, Free Men: The Ideology of the Republican Party before the Civil War* (New York: Oxford University Press, 1995), 250–52.

43. Lincoln to Gustave P. Koerner, April 11, 1859, *Collected Works*, 3:376.

44. Lincoln to Theodore Canisius, May 17, 1859, ibid., 3:380.

45. Lincoln to Schuyler Colfax, July 6, 1859, *Collected Works*, 3:390–91.

46. Republican platform adopted by the National Republican Convention, May 17, 1860, reprinted in *A Political Text-Book for 1860*, comp. Horace Greeley and John F. Cleveland (New York: Tribune Association, 1860), 27.

47. See Boritt, *Lincoln and the Economics*, 221–23; Jason H. Silverman, "One of the Principal Replenishing Streams": Lincoln and his Evolving Relationship with Immigrants and Ethnic Groups, *Lincoln Herald* 114 (Fall 2012): 173–74.

48. Lincoln, Annual Message to Congress, December 8, 1863, *Collected Works*, 7:40.

49. An Act to Encourage Immigration, 38th Cong., 1st Sess., July 4, 1864, Ch. 246, *U.S. Statutes at Large*, vol. 13.

50. Lincoln, Annual Message to Congress, December 6, 1864, *Collected Works*, 8:141.

51. Lincoln, First Debate with Stephen A. Douglas at Ottawa, Illinois, August 21, 1858, ibid., 3:9.

52. Stephen A. Douglas, "Speech at Springfield," July 17, 1858, in *The Political Debates between Abraham Lincoln and Stephen A. Douglas*, ed. George Haven Putnam (New York: G. P. Putnam's Sons, 1912), 144.

53. Lincoln, Fourth Debate with Stephen A. Douglas at Charleston, Illinois, September 18, 1858, *Collected Works*, 3:145–46.

54. Eugene H. Berwanger, *The Frontier against Slavery: Western Anti-Negro Prejudice and the Slavery Extension Controversy* (Champaign: University of Illinois Press, 2002), 48–51; Leon F. Litwack, *North of Slavery: The Negro in the Free States, 1790–1860* (Chicago: University of Chicago Press, 1962), 69–71, 93, 278.

55. Kenneth J. Winkle, *The Young Eagle: The Rise of Abraham Lincoln* (Dallas: Taylor Publishing, 2001), 253.

56. Matthew Norman, "The Other Lincoln-Douglas Debate: The Race Issue in a Comparative Context," *Journal of the Abraham Lincoln Association* 31, no. 1 (2010): 2.

57. Lincoln, Speech at Peoria, Illinois, October 16, 1854, *Collected Works*, 2:256.

58. Eric Foner, "The Ideology of the Republican Party," in *The Birth of the Grand Old Party: The Republicans' First Generation*, ed. Robert Engs and Randall Miller (Philadelphia: University of Pennsylvania Press, 2002), 9–10.

59. Lincoln, Speech at Peoria, Illinois, October 16, 1854, *Collected Works*, 2:256.

60. See Richard Blackett, "Lincoln and Colonization," *OAH Magazine of History* 21 (October 2007): 19–22; Eric Foner, "Lincoln and Colonization," in *Our Lincoln: New Perspectives on Lincoln and His World*, ed. Eric Foner (New York: Norton, 2008), 135–66; Phillip Shaw Paludan, "Lincoln and Colonization: Policy or Propaganda?," *Journal of the Abraham Lincoln Association* 25 (2004): 23–37; Michael Vorenberg, "Abraham Lincoln and the Politics of Black Colonization," *Journal of the Abraham Lincoln Association* 14 (Summer 1993): 23–45.

61. Lincoln, Speech at Springfield, Illinois, June 26, 1857, *Collected Works*, 2:407.

62. Douglas, Third Debate with Stephen A. Douglas at Jonesboro, Illinois, September 15, 1858, ibid., 3:113.

63. Lincoln, Speech at Hartford, Connecticut, March 5, 1860, ibid., 4:9.

64. Lincoln, First Debate with Stephen A. Douglas at Ottawa, Illinois, August 21, 1858, ibid., 3:16.

65. Joseph R. Fornieri, "Lincoln on Black Citizenship," in *Constitutionalism in the Approach and Aftermath of the Civil War*, ed. Paul D. Moreno and Johnathan O'Neill (New York: Fordham University Press, 2013), 55–80; James Oakes, "Natural Rights, Citizenship Rights, States' Rights, and Black Rights: Another Look at Lincoln and Race," in *Our Lincoln: New Perspectives on Lincoln and His World*, ed. Eric Foner (New York: W. W. Norton, 2008), 109–34; Michael Vorenberg, "Abraham Lincoln's 'Fellow Citizens'—Before and After Emancipation," in *Lincoln's Proclamation: Emancipation Reconsidered*, ed. William A. Blair and Karen Fisher Younger (Chapel Hill: University of North Carolina Press, 2009), 151–67.

66. Lincoln, First Inaugural Address, March 4, 1861, *Collected Works*, 4:264.

67. Herman Belz, "Lincoln's Construction of the Executive Power in the Secession Crisis," *Journal of the Abraham Lincoln Association* 27, no. 1 (2006): 34–35; see also Fornieri, "Lincoln on Black Citizenship," 75–77.

68. Herman Belz, *A New Birth of Freedom: The Republican Party and Freedmen's Rights, 1861–1866* (New York: Fordham University Press, 2000), 17–31; Gregory T. Knouff, "White Men in Arms: Concepts of Citizenship and Masculinity in

Revolutionary America" in *Representing Masculinity: Male Citizenship in Modern Western Culture*, ed. Stefan Dudink, Karen Hagemann, and Anna Clark (New York: Palgrave Macmillan, 2007), 25–40.

69. An Act More Effectually to Provide for the National Defence by Establishing an Uniform Militia throughout the United States, 2nd Cong., 1st Sess., May 8, 1792, Ch. 33, *U.S. Statutes at Large*, vol. 1.

70. *Revised Statutes of Illinois* (1845), 356.

71. Lincoln, Emancipation Proclamation, January 1, 1863, *Collected Works*, 6:30.

72. Lincoln, Remarks to Deputation of Western Gentlemen, August 4, 1862, ibid., 5:356–57.

73. Frederick Douglass, *Life and Times of Frederick Douglass*, reprinted in *Frederick Douglass: Autobiographies*, ed. Henry Louis Gates Jr. (New York: Library of America, 1994), 786.

74. Lincoln, Reply to Emancipation Memorial Presented by Chicago Christians of All Denominations, September 13, 1862, *Collected Works*, 5:423.

75. *Addresses of the Hon. W. D. Kelley, Miss Anna E. Dickinson, and Mr. Frederick Douglass, at a Mass Meeting, Held at National Hall, Philadelphia, July 6, 1863, for the Promotion of Colored Enlistments* (Philadelphia, 1863), 5, 7.

76. See Jim Cullen, "'I's a Man Now': Gender and African American Men," in *Divided Houses: Gender and the Civil War*, ed. Catherine Clinton and Nina Silber (Oxford: Oxford University Press, 1992), 76–96; John David Smith, *Lincoln and the U.S. Colored Troops* (Carbondale: Southern Illinois University Press, 2013), 113–14.

77. Lincoln to James C. Conkling, August 26, 1863, *Collected Works*, 6:406–10.

78. Robert Hamilton, *Weekly Anglo-African*, January 17, 1863, quoted in Joseph P. Reidy, "The African American Struggle for Citizenship Rights in the Northern United States during the Civil War," in *Civil War Citizens: Race, Ethnicity, and Identity in America's Bloodiest Conflict*, ed. Susannah J. Ural (New York: New York University Press, 2010), 221.

79. *Address from the Colored Citizens of Norfolk Va., to the People of the United States* (New Bedford: E. Anthony & Sons, 1865), 1–2.

80. Andrew Tait et al. to Union Convention of Tennessee, January 9, 1865, reprinted in *Freedom: A Documentary History of Emancipation, 1861–1867*, ser. 2, *The Black Military Experience*, ed. Ira Berlin, Joseph P. Reidy, and Leslie S. Rowland (Cambridge: Cambridge University Press, 1982), 812.

81. Lincoln to Andrew Johnson, March 26, 1863, *Collected Works*, 6:149–50.

82. Lincoln to James C. Conkling, August 26, 1863, ibid., 6:406–10.

83. Lincoln to Michael Hahn, March 13, 1864, ibid., 7:244.

84. Lincoln, Last Public Address, April 11, 1865, ibid., 8:403.

85. Burlingame, *Abraham Lincoln*, 2:803.

Abraham Lincoln, two weeks prior to the final Lincoln-Douglas debate. A short time earlier, Lincoln had pronounced that "a house divided against itself cannot stand." Courtesy of the Library of Congress, LC-USZ62-16377.

LINCOLN'S DIVIDED HOUSE: THE CONSTITUTION AND THE UNION

Charles M. Hubbard

On March 4, 1861, Abraham Lincoln was sworn in as the sixteenth president of the United States and was immediately confronted with the greatest constitutional crisis in American history. The crisis developed when the Southern slave states decided to secede from the Union. Lincoln believed it was his responsibility to maintain national unity and representative government to the best of his ability and, as he had sworn when he took the presidential oath of office, to "preserve, protect and defend the Constitution of the United States."[1]

Lincoln thought, as did the Founding Fathers, that the Constitution was a unifying document. The men who drafted the Constitution believed that republican government required popular and widespread support from the population. The Constitution of the United States reflected the necessity of national unity to sustain a nation grounded on democratic principles.

Lincoln understood that the immediate threat to the Constitution and the nation came from slavery. That "peculiar institution" was the wedge that divided the American people. Ultimately, slavery had to be eliminated if the American people were to be united in their support for the Constitution and popular government. Despite Lincoln's belief that slavery was morally wrong, he realized that the institution had coexisted with popular government for more than seventy years and was protected by the Constitution. Slavery posed a real threat to the continuation of a united nation. However, Lincoln recognized that secession, even though it was provoked by slavery, was a larger and more urgent threat to democracy and majority rule than slavery.

In 1858, Abraham Lincoln accepted the nomination of the Republican Party in Illinois to run for the US Senate. In his acceptance speech, he addressed the slavery issue that was dividing the country:

> In *my* opinion, it *will* not cease, until a *crisis* shall have been reached, and passed. "A house divided against itself cannot stand." I believe this government cannot endure, permanently half *slave* and half *free*. I do not expect the Union to be *dissolved*—I do not expect the house to *fall*—but I *do* expect it will cease to be divided. It will become *all* one thing, or *all* the other.[2]

This was certainly a radical statement in the context of the political environment of the 1850s. More than any other issue, different opinions over slavery undermined the political alliances that supported the Whig Party. The Kansas-Nebraska Act of 1854 provoked passionate debate over the extension of slavery into the territories and abolished the Missouri Compromise. The Supreme Court's controversial decision in *Dred Scott v. Sandford* focused further attention on the "peculiar institution." It is reasonable to believe that because the audience was a friendly Republican group, Lincoln wanted to see how his fellow Republicans would respond to his position on slavery and its expansion into the territories. Lincoln expected a passionate debate with Stephen Douglas, and possibly he saw an opportunity for a preemptive strike against Douglas and his popular sovereignty doctrine. In a more indirect way, Lincoln was affirming his belief in a unified country that could not continue permanently divided. His remarks on that occasion revealed his views on national unity as much as they did his feelings about slavery.[3]

Lincoln could be assured that at least some in the crowd shared his sentiments, certainly with regard to slavery. Antislavery sentiment had grown steadily during the 1840s, and during the 1850s, it radicalized into the abolitionist movement. By the time Lincoln delivered his "House Divided" speech in 1858, many Americans viewed slavery as an evil plague that would eventually destroy the nation. As the abolitionists became more vocal and politically active, so did the proslavery faction. Slaveholders had a vested interest in expanding and maintaining the institution. The house was indeed divided over this contentious issue.[4]

Lincoln's remarks to the friendly Republican audience were a response, at least in part, to the 1856 decision by the Supreme Court in *Dred Scott v. Sandford*, more commonly known as the *Dred Scott* case. Chief Justice Roger

Taney, in his majority opinion, went beyond the basic question before the court and determined that Dred Scott was a slave and not a citizen, and therefore he was not entitled to the protection of the law. Slaves were property according to Taney's ruling and could be transported anywhere in the country, including the territories. Further, slaves were considered property for which their owners were entitled to the protection of the law.[5] The court's decision effectively negated the Missouri Compromise of 1820 and most of the provisions of the Compromise of 1850.[6] The decision confirmed that slavery was constitutional and legal throughout the country. Lincoln disagreed with the Supreme Court ruling, but he respected the court's authority and believed the appropriate response was to bring another case to the Supreme Court that would reverse the *Dred Scott* decision, at least to the extent of confirming federal authority over slavery in the territories.[7]

The *Dred Scott* case was fraught with political implications dating back to 1852, when the Missouri Supreme Court first rendered its decision. James Buchanan, a Democrat running for president, went so far as to pressure Chief Justice Roger Taney, also a Democrat appointed by Andrew Jackson, to delay issuing his opinion until after the 1856 election. This opinion reflected the court's proslavery bias as well as the political influence of the Democrats on the Taney court. The ruling focused national attention on the slavery issue, further dividing the country, as Lincoln pointed out later in his "House Divided" speech.[8]

After securing the Republican nomination to run for the Senate, Lincoln expected the forthcoming political debate with his opponent Stephen Douglas to place the question of the expansion of slavery into the territories squarely in front of the people of Illinois. Lincoln had repeatedly acknowledged his hatred of the institution of slavery, but his commitment to the rule of law prevented him from any formal association with the radical abolitionist movement. Lincoln wanted to project an image of a moderate Republican opposed to the expansion of slavery, while allowing it to continue where it already existed.

In the debates that followed, it was slavery that called attention to the fundamental problems associated with democracy in a federal republic. In a federal system, the power to govern was diffused and divided between local governments and the central government. Could the three branches of the federal government, as provided by the Constitution, resolve the question of slavery, yet again through compromise? Further, was it a local matter or one to be decided at the national level, particularly as it applied in the territories? Throughout the history of the republic, numerous compromises on slavery had been suggested and tried. However, none of the compromises that were put into place completely resolved the problem or completely resolved the fundamental difficulties presented by federalism.

The contentious issue was acknowledged at the very beginning of the republic, when the Northwest Ordinance prohibited slavery in the territories north of the Ohio River, and later, as an accommodation to the slave states, the framers of the Constitution provided that three-fifths of slaves could be counted for purposes of determining the number of representatives to the House of Representatives. In effect, this meant that slaves were equal to three-fifths of a person. Subsequently, as new territory was added, further compromise was necessary to maintain a balance between free states and slave states. The result was the Compromise of 1820 and later the Compromise of 1850. None of these accommodations or compromises were completely satisfactory to either side, and by 1858, passions were running high and the public demanded a definitive resolution of the problem. It was in this highly charged atmosphere that Chief Justice Roger Taney issued his opinion in the *Dred Scott* case in 1856, further inflaming abolitionists.

For the American system of government to function, the people had to unite in their support of the government, and that meant overcoming or at least compromising on their differences. The Founders wanted the Constitution to unify the new nation, while providing opportunities for expansion and annexation. The government they created with the Constitution provided opportunities for the people to voice their opinions from differing points of view. However, the government they created also required allegiance and acquiescence by the people to the laws of the land, meaning the Constitution.

The Constitution, through the diffusion of power among the branches of the federal government, as well as local governments, provided the means to accommodate differing public opinions. Despite this apparent contradiction, the founders saw the Constitution as a document unifying the American people. The men who drafted the Constitution were aware of the remarkably diverse cultural differences existing within the American population in the late eighteenth century and expected the country as it grew to remain diverse. Through a series of complicated negotiations and compromises, they produced a remarkable framework for governing a federal republic that protected individual rights and unified the population. The concept of a government responsible to the people was the unifying principle that the Founders placed in the Constitution.

For decades, most Americans on both sides of the slavery divide accepted the institution and its right to exist. Even most of those who were morally opposed were indifferent toward and tolerant of slavery where it existed. In fact, the Constitution not only allowed slavery but also provided the basic foundation for the protection of the institution in its Tenth Amendment, which gave states the authority to regulate and protect slavery: "The powers not delegated to the United States by the Constitution, nor prohibited by it to the states, are reserved to the states respectively, or to the people."

The Constitution did not specifically mention slavery, as the Founders had deliberately avoided using the word. Lincoln claimed that by allowing slavery, the Founders had placed a "rot" in the document that would eventually destroy the Union and the Constitution if not removed.[9]

During the antebellum period, each state decided whether slavery was legal in that particular state. What about the territories expected to become states at some point? Was it the responsibility of the federal government to regulate and govern the territories before they were admitted as states to the Union? If so, should the federal government allow slavery within its jurisdiction? The Supreme Court in the *Dred Scott* case effectively ruled that slavery was legal throughout the country, including the territories. Abraham Lincoln and Stephen Douglas vigorously debated the issue during their campaign for the Senate in 1858. Lincoln's position and that of Douglas identified slavery as the issue that would, two years later, define the presidential election of 1860.

The American people and their political parties struggled to identify candidates that represented their positions. The 1860 presidential election provided an opportunity for the people to express their opinions on the slavery issue. In the Northern free states, there was an enthusiastic and vocal abolitionist minority. In the slave states of the Deep South, a radical minority inflamed the passions of both the slaveholders and nonslaveholders. Both the Democratic and Republican Parties were further divided into factions. The newly formed Republican Party included German immigrants, former Whig protectionists, moderates with strong nationalistic tendencies, and abolitionists. The Democratic Party separated along geographic lines into Northern and Southern Whigs. As the election grew closer, the Southern wing of the Democratic Party split into three separate factions. Eventually, the national Democratic Party fractured, resulting in the nomination of three candidates to run against Lincoln in the general election. The Republicans managed to remain a united but sectional party, with little or no support in the slave states.

Despite the widening divide within American society over the slavery issue, Lincoln continued to believe that the overwhelming majority of Americans were united in their belief in the principles enumerated in the Declaration of Independence. The Founders of the country had soon discovered that a unified nation was necessary to protect those inalienable rights. The Constitution was therefore, among other things, designed as a unifying document. It created governing institutions that unified the nation into a federal republic. Lincoln certainly realized that the Constitution was more than a symbol of union—it was essential to the preservation of the United States. Lincoln viewed the Constitution and the Union as inextricably linked. He remarked to George Thompson and a group of antislavery visitors to the White House on April 7, 1864, "The paramount idea of the Constitution is the preservation of the Union. It may not be specified in so many words, but that this was the idea of its founders is evident; for, without the Union, the Constitution would be worthless."[10] Lincoln viewed the Constitution and the rule of law that it sustained as necessary to maintaining sufficient unity and harmony within society to ensure the perpetuation of the Union. As Lincoln approached the presidential election of 1860, the house was clearly divided against itself and quite possibly could not stand.

A very fragile coalition of Republicans managed to elect Abraham Lincoln president. Lincoln was the consummate politician and strongly believed in party unity. For Lincoln, it was political parties that provided opportunities for the people to voice their opinions on the great issues of the day. As president, he used political patronage and some controversial cabinet appointments to unite the Republican Party, but even his remarkable leadership skills could not overcome the proslavery secessionists. It was Lincoln's hope, at the start of his presidency, that the people's elected officials could hold the country together. He believed that both proslavery and antislavery Americans were united in their acceptance of the principles enumerated in the Declaration of Independence and codified in the Constitution. Ultimately, he believed the people would not allow the slavery issue alone to destroy the country. In fact, on December 22, 1860, shortly after he was elected president, he wrote to Alexander Stephens, who later became vice president of the Confederacy:

> Do the people of the South really entertain fears that a Republican
> administration would, *directly, or indirectly*, interfere with their
> slaves, or with them, about their slaves? If they do, I wish to assure
> you, as once a friend, and still, I hope, not an enemy, that there is
> no cause for such fears.

The South would be in no more danger in this respect, than it was in the days of Washington. I suppose, however, this does not meet the case. You think slavery is *right* and ought to be extended; while we think it is *wrong* and ought to be restricted. That I suppose is the rub. It certainly is the only substantial difference between us.[11]

Lincoln made repeated efforts to reassure Southerners that slavery was not threatened where it existed and that their intention to break up the Union was unnecessary.

Shortly after Abraham Lincoln's election, the Southern slave states, led by South Carolina, chose to secede from the Union and created a slaveholders' republic called the Confederate States of America. The secession of the Southern states created the greatest constitutional crisis in American history. Southerners believed that President Lincoln and the so-called "Black Republicans" threatened the future of slavery and much of their cultural and economic identity. It was Lincoln's election and the perceived threat he posed to slavery that provoked Southerners to withdraw from the Union. However, for Lincoln, the breakup of the Union identified a larger threat than the continuation of slavery, not only for Americans but for all mankind. That threat was whether a "government of the people, by the people, and for the people" could endure.[12] Secession in Lincoln's view was a clear and fundamental threat to democracy.

Paradoxically, the potential threat to democracy lies within the strength of the system. Majority control of the system and, more precisely, the institutions of the government are both its strength and its major weakness. Democracy's strength is found in the unity and with it the power of the majority. The problem for democracy generally develops when the majority refuses to accommodate and protect the rights of the minority. The problem is further exacerbated when the minority refuses to accept the will of the majority. The refusal of a large and reasonably united minority to accept the will of the majority provoked the secession crisis of 1860–61 in the United States.

This frustrating dilemma and potential flaw continued to plague advocates of self-determination who were grounded on a democratic system of majority rule. The concept of tyranny by the majority was generally associated with Alexis de Tocqueville, the early nineteenth-century French political philosopher and historian. Tocqueville traveled extensively in the United States and observed American democracy. In general, he admired the concept of representative government and majority rule but recognized the threats inherent in the American political system.[13]

Remarkably, the problems associated with democratic rule were not lost on those who drafted the Constitution of the United States. In the late eighteenth century, John Adams identified the problem and pointed out several ways that the Founders of the United States sought to address and eliminate the potential breakdown of democratic rule. This issue was also discussed by James Madison in "The Federalist, No. 10," in which Madison recognized that "the superior force of an interested and overbearing majority" might encroach on the personal liberties and freedoms of the minority. Just before the presidential election of 1860, the British political thinker John Stuart Mill argued for a limited representative government instead of pure democracy in his book *On Liberty*.[14]

Lincoln, in his Cooper Union address, referred to the comments of the Founders when calling for unity and respect for the Constitution. After all, as John Adams had pointed out during the early stages of the debate in Philadelphia, the Constitution provided a number of remedies designed to avoid the potential pitfalls of tyrannical rule by the majority, such as limits on the branches of government such as the separation of powers, supermajority rules of the legislature, and the Bill of Rights, to name a few. All these, argued Adams and other supporters of American constitutional government, would enable the United States of America to have democracy with adequate protection for personal liberty and freedom for all citizens, including dissenting minorities. Lincoln agreed with Adams and appreciated the need to protect the rights of minorities. Moreover, Lincoln understood that the Constitution, because of its checks and balances, protected minority rights, including protections for private property ownership.[15]

Despite these protections, by 1860, a large and determined minority felt threatened by the majority and decided to break up the Union of states. Lincoln was careful in his First Inaugural Address to explain that no constitutionally protected civil rights were being infringed upon, and therefore there was no legitimate justification for breaking up the Union.[16] The secession crisis not only was a threat to the country but also potentially signaled the end of American democracy. To resolve this crisis, Lincoln needed to effectively convince Americans, both North and South, that secession was a threat to democracy and, moreover, that the system was sufficient to resolve any problems or issues while remaining a unified nation.

Abraham Lincoln certainly possessed the persuasive skills to motivate the people to save the Union and democracy without resorting to violence. No other president, except possibly Thomas Jefferson, was such an acknowledged literary genius and communicator. Lincoln was arguably the best of America's wordsmiths, and his words, as much as anything about him, justified Edwin Stanton's comment upon Lincoln's death that "now he belongs to the ages."[17] With this lamentation, Stanton made Lincoln's words an integral part of American political rhetoric for the ages. Among America's most famous speeches, Lincoln's Gettysburg Address has been considered by most historians and political philosophers as the supreme statement of the meaning of American democracy and civil society. With these now familiar words, Lincoln eloquently expressed the conviction of Americans: "Four score and seven years ago our fathers brought forth, upon this continent, a new nation, conceived in liberty, and dedicated to the proposition that all men are created equal. . . . That government of the people, by the people, for the people, shall not perish from the earth."[18]

Despite the tragedy of the Civil War, Lincoln never lost faith in democracy and the American people. The sincerity and personal commitment evident in Lincoln's words inspired future generations to believe in the American dream of democracy, freedom, and equal opportunity.

Lincoln believed that the Union was perpetual and that the argument that the states were sovereign and voluntarily associated with the Union was unconstitutional. In his First Inaugural Address, Lincoln made this basic concept clear when he said, "Perpetuity is implied, if not expressed, in the fundamental law of all national governments. It is safe to assert that no government proper, ever had a provision in its organic law for its own termination." He went on to say that the secessionists could not destroy the Union "except by some action not provided for in the instrument itself." Here Lincoln was referring to the Constitution.[19] While it was the slavery issue that provoked the potential breakup of the Union, the more fundamental constitutional issue was the sovereignty and supremacy of the federal government and the perpetuity of the Union. Lincoln realized that at some point, slavery must be eliminated and the war won in order for the Union to be preserved. It was slavery that had caused the house to divide, and slavery must be eliminated for the house to endure. The house would have to become all one or all the other.

From the start of his presidency, Lincoln had "a patient confidence in the ultimate justice of the people." With this statement, Lincoln was referring to a government by the people and was certain "that truth, and that justice, will surely prevail, by the judgment of this great tribunal, the American people."[20] With these and numerous other statements, Lincoln must be assured his place as the most eloquent spokesman for democracy. Indeed, his deeds spoke volumes as well; Lincoln's belief in the American people and democracy was remarkably demonstrated in the presidential election of 1864. In the middle of a Civil War, the chief executive was willing to run for reelection as the Constitution required. Lincoln believed he was ultimately responsible to the people, and if they disapproved of his actions, they could, through the ballot box, remove him from office. Ultimately, Lincoln had confidence in the wisdom of the American people. In many ways, the election of 1864 represented a remarkable test of the fundamental principles of American democracy and constitutional government.

Lincoln wanted to maintain the Union and persuade the American people to support the political system and the institution provided by the Constitution, and as long as he had the power, he could not allow secession to succeed. The bitterness caused by the American Civil War, with all its hatred and deprivation, while not lost on Lincoln, did not prevent him from seeking the reconciliation and unification of all Americans. It is difficult to imagine that any American would not be moved by Lincoln's words in his Second Inaugural Address when he said:

> With malice toward none; with charity for all; with firmness in the right, as God gives us to see the right, let us strive on to finish the work we are in; to bind up the nation's wounds; to care for him who shall have borne the battle, and for his widow, and his orphan—to do all which may achieve and cherish a just, and a lasting peace, among ourselves, and with all nations.[21]

More than a century later, Lincoln's words continue to clearly and eloquently express his vision for the future of America and the world. Generations of Americans have accepted Lincoln's vision and his commitment to retain American democratic principles.

Ultimately, the secession of the Southern slave states threatened the existence of constitutional democracy. Lincoln was correct when he predicted that a country could not endure permanently divided against itself. Despite the efforts of members of Congress and leading politicians to reach a compromise on the slavery issue, the house did divide, and the war came in April 1861.

Lincoln believed that secession was unconstitutional. As president, he had taken a solemn and sacred oath to uphold and defend the Constitution, and with that commitment, he was prepared to defend the democratic principles of a government that vested political power in the electorate.

When Lincoln took the oath of office in March 1861, the secession crisis was well under way, even though hostilities had not yet begun. Despite the new president's efforts to reassure the seceding states that the institution of slavery or their rights were not threatened, he was clearly prepared to bring the full force of the government to defend the Constitution and preserve the Union. Secession threatened the very existence of the Union, even if at first it did not threaten the existence of slavery. After all, the Union and constitutional government had always coexisted with slavery. Consequently, there was no legitimate reason, at least in Lincoln's mind, for the rebels to destroy the Union and with it the Constitution. The rebels could not be allowed to destroy a nation based on the will of the majority. Lincoln used force when it became necessary to reduce the threat to the country. He told his secretary John Nicolay on December 13, 1860, "The very existence of a general and national government lies in the legal power, right, and duty of maintaining its own integrity. This, if not expressed, is at least implied in the Constitution. The right of a state to secede is not an open or debatable question."[22]

Lincoln was not intolerant of dissent. He expected, and even appreciated, different positions and points of view. However, he was not prepared to tolerate or allow secession as a legitimate means of dissent in a democracy. Lincoln believed in, and was committed to, political party activism and saw politics and politicians as the best means to implement the will of the majority of the people.[23] In Lincoln's view, it was the responsibility of those seeking to represent the people to understand and be informed about the issues that confronted the people. He wanted to convince the people that his ideas and solutions to the problems they confronted were the best available. If he was successful in getting them to agree with his position, the people would vote for him, and he could present and argue for their political agenda. Lincoln managed to persuade the people to agree with him and therefore vote for him, rather than simply telling them what they wanted to hear. This concept may seem a bit simplistic in today's political arena; it was remarkably sophisticated in its application in the nineteenth century. Lincoln was a politician, and politics was his lifelong passion. He wanted to use the political system to make a difference for the greater good.

Lincoln was unable, despite his remarkable persuasive skills, to prevail upon the secessionists in the South to remain loyal to the Union. In 1860, the experiment in popular republican government that began in Philadelphia was now confronted with the prospect of complete failure. As much as anything else, the election of Abraham Lincoln in November triggered the potential breakup of the Union. The question before Lincoln and the country after his inauguration was whether a democracy could exist with a strong and militant minority that refused to submit to the will of the majority. Therein was the threat to democracy and popular government.

Lincoln rejected the Southerners' argument that they were fighting for self-government. The Southern stance was based on the refined positions taken by John C. Calhoun and, before him, Jefferson and Madison in the Kentucky and Virginia resolutions. The South maintained that the states had voluntarily entered the Union and temporarily surrendered part of their sovereign authority to the central government. Based on that premise, each state could withdraw from the Union of states when its local interest was threatened by continued participation. The secessionists referred to the revolutionary responsibility of the people to overthrow an oppressive government. Americans, including Southerners, relied on the philosophy of John Locke to legitimize the American Revolution and separate from the oppressive government of Great Britain. For Southerners, similar oppressions existed, and it was their moral obligation to conduct a revolution to obtain independence and form a new government.[24]

Lincoln argued that the purpose of secession was first to create a government that protected the institution of slavery. As he said in his First Inaugural Address:

> If, by the mere force of numbers, a majority should deprive a minority
> of any clearly written constitutional right, it might, in a moral point
> of view, justify revolution—certainly would, if such right were a vital
> one. But such is not our case. All the vital rights of minorities, and of
> individuals, are so plainly assured to them . . . in the Constitution,
> that controversies never arise concerning them.[25]

With this statement, Lincoln was simply saying that no constitutional right of any citizen or group of citizens had been encroached upon. Thus there was no legitimate justification for revolution, and secession was nothing more than a violent rebellion.

Lincoln concluded that secession was unconstitutional and therefore unlawful. He was convinced that if the country were allowed to break up, the world would lose "the last best, hope of earth." This hope was popular government, one that was responsible to the people. Lincoln expressed this view in his December 1862 message to Congress and the American people when he said, "Fellow-citizens, *we* cannot escape history. . . . The fiery trial through which we pass, will light us down, in honor or dishonor, to the latest generation. . . . In *giving* freedom to the *slave*, we *assure* freedom to the *free*. . . . We shall nobly save, or meanly lose, the last best, hope of earth."[26]

The fundamental question that still confronts a democracy is one of balance. It is appropriate and necessary in a democracy to protect the rights of a dissenting minority, but it is also necessary to prevent the dissenting minority from destroying the governing institutions established to maintain majority rule. The lofty and idealistic principles set forth in the Declaration of Independence can be sustained only by the practical application of the rule of law as defined in the Constitution.

Stated another way, Lincoln saw the Declaration of Independence as an expression of the inalienable rights of every person, while the Constitution provided the governing mechanisms and institutions for sustaining and protecting those fundamental freedoms. The Constitution legitimizes the institutions of government and protects the individual rights of people. At the heart of Lincoln's argument that secession was unconstitutional was his belief in the sovereignty of the national government. Moreover, the sovereign government was charged with the responsibility of making and upholding the rule of law.

Lincoln's constitutional arguments were unsuccessful in convincing Southerners that the doctrine of states' rights, as set forward by Jefferson and Madison and expanded by John C. Calhoun, did not legitimize secession. It was Appomattox that completely discredited Calhoun's argument once and for all. Nationalism triumphed, and with it a strong centralized government. Although the debate continued between the strong advocates for local government and those desiring more centralized governmental control, ultimately, it was the federal government that was sovereign. The defeat of the secessionist and the reconstruction that followed settled the major issue of sovereignty, and the Union survived.

The expansion and centralization of federal power during the Civil War was closely associated with the expansion of executive or presidential power. Lincoln believed that the power needed to meet the secession crisis was provided by the Constitution and was vested primarily in the president. Obviously, the rebellion was an emergency sufficient to justify the use of these extraordinary powers. However, the extent of the power needed, as defined in the Constitution, was determined by the magnitude of the emergency. Moreover, it was the president's responsibility to determine the magnitude of the emergency. The power to determine the parameters of presidential war powers and the power to determine whether the emergency justified their use was therefore vested in the president, in this case Lincoln. This extraordinary combination of powers vested in a single individual suggested the potential for the abuse of presidential power.

The expansion and consolidation of presidential power began with Lincoln's response to the Sumter crisis. After the failed attempt to resupply and reinforce Sumter, Lincoln took extraordinary and extraconstitutional action. He did not call Congress back into session, but he proclaimed the blockade of Southern ports, called for volunteers without authorization, directed the secretary of the Treasury to spend unauthorized government funds, and ultimately suspended the writ of habeas corpus in certain areas. Later on, as the war progressed, he introduced conscription, authorized military tribunals of civilians, condoned arbitrary arrest and imprisonment, suppressed newspapers, and emancipated the slaves. Lincoln justified these actions under his authority as commander in chief and as the exercise of his emergency war powers.

Lincoln believed that the power needed to meet the secession crisis was provided by the Constitution and was vested primarily in the president. He frequently cited the commander in chief clause of the Constitution, which required him to "take Care that the Laws be faithfully executed."[27] Furthermore, he took seriously the presidential oath of office, which included the promise to "preserve, protect and defend the Constitution of the United States," and even alluded that the oath was "registered in Heaven."[28] Obviously, in Lincoln's view, the rebellion was an emergency sufficient to justify the use of these extraordinary powers.

Undoubtedly, Lincoln understood from the very beginning of his presidency that he needed to resort to all means available to suppress the rebellion and uphold the Constitution. Throughout his presidency, Lincoln repeatedly communicated the seriousness of the crisis to the people's representatives and managed in a variety of ways and at the appropriate time to transform public opinion. His determination to create "a more perfect union" ultimately eliminated slavery and with it changed the fundamental structure of the federal republic.

It is worth noting that the Constitution Lincoln swore to protect and defend is not the Constitution of today's Americans. Lincoln's decisions and proclamations, and ultimately the outcome of the Civil War, set in motion a series of legislative actions and amendments to the Constitution that allowed dramatic new interpretations of that remarkable document. The Reconstruction Amendments—the Thirteenth, Fourteenth, and Fifteenth Amendments—required the federal government to protect the individual rights and freedoms of all Americans. The central government after the Civil War was charged with ensuring equal treatment under the law for all American citizens. The original drafters of the Constitution saw the central government as a potential threat to individual liberty and sought to protect Americans from the encroachment of centralized power. The post–Civil War Amendments reflected the changed expectations of the people and signaled a new relationship between the government and the governed in the United States.

In the final analysis, Lincoln believed the Constitution was essentially an extraordinary arrangement for the sharing of authority within a structure of popular government. In ordinary times, that meant that the legislative body, representing the diverse attitudes and interests of the people, would be the most influential of the three branches of government. However, with the Civil War and the secession crisis, this was no ordinary time. Lincoln realized that, as the chief executive and the commander in chief who was responsible for preserving both the Union and the Constitution. As he had pointed out to George Thompson and a group of antislavery visitors to the White House in 1864, preserving the Union was "the paramount idea of the Constitution." He went on to say, "It seems clear, then, that in the last extremity, if any local institution threatened the existence of the Union, the executive could not hesitate as to his duty."[29]

The power Lincoln assumed as the chief executive began a process that Arthur Schlesinger Jr. referred to as the road to an "imperial Presidency."[30] Modern communication and technology have forced recent presidents to become less imperial, but they remain nonetheless powerful. Moreover, if Schlesinger meant the arbitrary use of presidential power to manipulate the system, the imperial surge continues.

The constitutional crisis of 1860 and the war that followed demanded a great leader to persuade the American people to preserve the Union and constitutional democracy for all mankind. Lincoln was that visionary political leader. Throughout American history, the country has called forth great leaders in times of crisis. Americans will continue to seek political leaders, and they will emerge to implement the changes required to meet the challenges of the twenty-first century.

Notes

1. US Const. art. II, § 1, cl. 8.

2. Abraham Lincoln, "A House Divided," Speech at Springfield, Illinois, June 16, 1858, in *The Collected Works of Abraham Lincoln*, ed. Roy P. Basler et al. (New Brunswick, NJ: Rutgers University Press, 1953), 2:461.

3. Sean Wilentz, *The Rise of American Democracy: Jefferson to Lincoln* (New York: W. W. Norton, 2005), 736–38.

4. Lincoln, "House Divided."

5. *Dred Scott v. Sandford*, 60 US (19 How.) 393 (1856), 404–5, 451–52.

6. Allen C. Guelzo, *Lincoln's Emancipation Proclamation: The End of Slavery in America* (New York: Simon and Schuster, 2004), 200.

7. *Scott v. Emerson*, 15 Mo. 576 (1852).

8. Sarah Schultz, "Misconduct or Judicial Discretion: A Question of Judicial Ethics in the Connecticut Supreme Court," *Connecticut Law Review* 40 (2007): 549, 567n130; Lincoln, "House Divided." See James F. Simon, *Lincoln and Chief Justice Taney: Slavery, Secession, and the President's War Powers* (New York: Simon and Schuster, 2006), 98–132 for a detailed analysis of the *Dred Scott* case.

9. Lincoln, Speech at Springfield, Illinois, October 4, 1854, *Collected Works*, 2:254.

10. Francis Bicknell Carpenter, *Six Months at the White House with Abraham Lincoln: The Story of a Picture* (New York: Hurd-Huffington, 1866), 77.

11. Lincoln to Alexander H. Stephens, December 22, 1860, *Collected Works*, 4:160.

12. Lincoln, Address Delivered at the Dedication of the Cemetery at Gettysburg, November 19, 1863, *Collected Works*, 7:21.

13. See Alexis de Tocqueville, *Democracy in America*, ed. J. P. Mayer and Max Lerner, trans. George Lawrence (1835; repr., New York: Harper & Row, 1966).

14. See John Adams, *A Defence of the Constitutions of Government of the United States of America* (Philadelphia: William Cobbett, 1797); James Madison, "The Federalist, No. 10," in *The Federalist Papers*, ed. Willmoore Kendall and George W. Carey (New Rochelle, NY: Arlington House, 1966); John Stuart Mill, *On Liberty* (1859; repr., New Haven, CT: Yale University Press, 2003).

15. Lincoln, Address at Cooper Institute, New York City, February 27, 1860, *Collected Works*, 3:522–23; Harold Holzer, *Lincoln at Cooper Union: The Speech That Made Abraham Lincoln President* (New York: Simon and Schuster, 2008); Adams, *Defence of the Constitutions*.

16. Lincoln, First Inaugural Address, March 4, 1861, *Collected Works*, 4:262–71.

17. David Herbert Donald, *Lincoln* (New York: Touchstone, 1995), 599.

18. Lincoln, Address Delivered at the Dedication of the Cemetery at Gettysburg, November 19, 1863, *Collected Works*, 7:17–23.

19. Lincoln, First Inaugural Address, March 4, 1861, *Collected Works*, 4:264–65.

20. Ibid., 4:270.

21. Lincoln, Second Inaugural Address, March 4, 1865, ibid., 8:332, 333.

22. G. John Nicolay and John Hay, *Abraham Lincoln: Complete Works* (New York: Century Co., 1920), 3:248.

23. See "Circular from Whig Committee," March 4, 1843, ibid., 1:72, where Lincoln explains in some detail his position on party loyalty.

24. See Emory M. Thomas, *The Confederate Nation: 1861–1865*, ed. Henry Steele Commager and Richard B. Morris (New York: Harper and Row, 1979), 62.

25. Lincoln, First Inaugural Address, March 4, 1861, *Collected Works*, 4:267.

26. Lincoln, Annual Message to Congress, December 1, 1862, ibid., 5:537.

27. US Const. art. II, § 3. For example, Lincoln said in his First Inaugural Address, "I shall take care . . . that the laws of the Union be faithfully executed in all the states." March 4, 1861, *Collected Works*, 4:265.

28. US Const. art. II, § 1, cl. 8; Lincoln, First Inaugural Address, March 4, 1861, *Collected Works*, 4:262, 271.

29. Carpenter, *Six Months at the White House*, 77.

30. See Arthur M. Schlesinger Jr., *The Imperial Presidency* (New York: Houghton Mifflin Co., 1973).

Clement Vallandigham, a Democrat from Ohio whom Republicans often referred to as the leading Copperhead. Republicans associated these Peace Democrats with the poisonous copperhead snake. Courtesy of the Library of Congress, LC-DIG-cwpbh-01194.

ABRAHAM LINCOLN
AND CIVIL LIBERTIES
IN WARTIME

Frank J. Williams

Abraham Lincoln is remembered as one of America's greatest leaders. In poll after poll, Lincoln is ranked as the greatest of American presidents.[1] Chief among the characteristics that make a great leader is that of unshakable moral and political courage. Great leadership requires hope, confidence, commitment, and the ability to stay the course even when you stand alone. The circumstances that gave rise to the Civil War, which Lincoln inherited as president, presented opportunity after opportunity for him to demonstrate his leadership. Lincoln seized upon each of these opportunities and exhibited a brand of leadership distinguished by justice, integrity, unshakable moral and political courage, and a commitment to excellence.

From the time he took the oath as president, Lincoln was faced with difficult decisions that required him to exhibit the confidence that comes with great leadership. As chief executive, he sat atop a large, complex, and often conflict-ridden political organization that was charged with enforcing the law during a nationwide rebellion. As commander in chief, Lincoln sat atop a likewise large, complex, and often conflicted military organization charged with defeating an army composed entirely of fellow countrymen. He could not have functioned in either role without a great deal of confidence and the ability to project that confidence to his subordinates and his critics around the country.

Lincoln brought with him to the presidency not only confidence but also zealousness, a skill he had acquired during his time as a lawyer, which instilled in him the energy to put principle into practice. Principles are of little use without the necessary zeal to make a change. President Lincoln was zealous in many ways during his tenure, but his zeal was best exemplified in the actions he took to secure the Union during the early days of the Civil War.[2]

At the outset of the war, the single overarching principle that drove him was the Constitution's directive that as president and commander in chief, Lincoln had the duty "to take care that the laws be faithfully executed."[3] In the eighty days that elapsed between his April 1861 call for troops, which marked the beginning of the Civil War, and the convening of Congress in special session on July 4, 1861, Lincoln employed these clauses to implement a series of crucial acts by sheer assumption of presidential power, all in an effort to carry out his duty to preserve, protect, and defend the Constitution of the United States.

Lincoln foresaw the grave danger that the war would be lost if the Confederates seized the capital or caused its complete isolation. To ward off that prospect, Lincoln added twenty-three thousand men to the Regular Army and eighteen thousand to the navy,[4] called forty thousand volunteers for three years' service,[5] summoned the state militias into a ninety-day volunteer force,[6] paid $2 million from the Treasury's unappropriated funds for purposes unauthorized by Congress, closed the post office to "treasonable correspondence," and imposed a blockade on Southern ports.[7] Nevertheless, Lincoln was reluctant to suspend writ of habeas corpus, a procedural method by which one who is imprisoned can file the writ in an appropriate court to have his imprisonment reviewed.[8] Finally, at the urging of Secretary of State William H. Seward, Lincoln concluded that the suspension of habeas corpus could not wait.[9] Although Congress was in recess in April 1861, Lincoln was steadfast in his belief that his duty to protect the capital required immediate action. Thus, relying on the constitutional authorization that the framers had perceptively included years before, Lincoln issued a proclamation suspending the writ.[10]

Lincoln's unilateral suspension of habeas corpus between Washington and Philadelphia was instrumental in securing communication lines to the nation's capital.[11] It enabled military commanders to arrest and detain individuals indefinitely in areas where martial law had been imposed, many of whom had attempted to halt military convoys, and to divest the civil liberties of those who were disloyal and whose overt acts against the United States threatened its survival.[12]

Nevertheless, Lincoln's actions did not go unchallenged; criticism was rampant. His critics protested that his decisions were illegal acts of civil disobedience.[13] The ever-eloquent speaker responded to such criticism in a message to a special session of Congress on July 4, 1861. His words were filled with both power and substance:

The provision of the Constitution that "The privilege of habeas corpus, shall not be suspended unless when, in cases of rebellion or invasion, the public safety may require it," is equivalent to a provision—is a provision—that such privilege may be suspended when, in cases of rebellion, or invasion, the public safety *does* require it. It was decided that we have a case of rebellion, and that the public safety does require the qualified suspension of the privilege of the writ which was authorized to be made. Now it is insisted that Congress, and not the Executive, is vested with this power. But the Constitution itself, is silent as to which, or who, is to exercise the power; and as the provision was plainly made for a dangerous emergency, it cannot be believed that the framers of the instrument intended, that in every case, the danger should run its course, until Congress could be called together; the very assembling of which might be prevented, as was intended in this case, by the rebellion.[14]

Lincoln explained that his actions were not only justified but also required pursuant to his oath to preserve, protect, and defend the Constitution of the United States.[15] Less than a hundred days later, Congress ratified the president's actions.[16]

As a leader, Lincoln was also persistent. Persistence brings zealous action to fruition, regardless of criticism. A short burst of zealous action is often too little when faced with a problem of any great magnitude. Great lawyers are persistent, and so are great presidents.

Although Lincoln was acutely aware that some citizens would sharply criticize him for suspending the "Great Writ," the alternative was far worse. In Lincoln's estimation, nothing could be worse than allowing the nation to succumb to Confederate forces. In the face of sharp criticism for his "extra-constitutional measures," the ever-persistent Lincoln never denied his stretch in presidential power, but "these measures," he declared, "whether strictly legal or not, were ventured upon, under what appeared to be a popular demand, and a public necessity."[17] In the end, his critics notwithstanding, modern scholars ranked him as the nation's best leader, in part because of his broad definition of executive power.

Only a month after Lincoln's suspension of the writ of habeas corpus, Captain Samuel Yohe arrested John Merryman, a discontented citizen residing in Baltimore who had spoken out vigorously against President Lincoln and had actively recruited a company of Confederate soldiers. Merryman was arrested for various acts of treason, including his leadership of the secessionist group that conspired to destroy railroad bridges and ultimately did so after the Baltimore riots.[18] The government believed that Merryman's decision to form an armed group to overthrow the government was an act that went far beyond a simple expression of dissatisfaction.

Merryman's attorney sought a writ of habeas corpus,[19] directing his petition to US Supreme Court chief justice Roger Brooke Taney. Lawyers for Merryman suspected that Chief Justice Taney would entertain the petition in Washington,[20] but because Taney was then assigned to the circuit court sitting in Maryland, he took up the matter in Baltimore and granted the writ.[21] Taney acted as a circuit judge because the full Supreme Court was not sitting and higher court did not consider Merryman's petition. When Taney demanded that Merryman be brought before the court, the commander of the fort where Merryman was detained, George Cadwalader, respectfully refused, relying on President Lincoln's suspension of habeas corpus.[22] Outraged, Taney authored *Ex parte Merryman*, opining that Congress alone—and not the president—had the power to suspend the writ of habeas corpus.[23]

Although the case was published in the Federal Cases reporter and labeled a case from the April 1861 term of the Circuit Court for the District of Maryland, the original opinion, in Taney's longhand, was captioned, "Before the Chief Justice of the Supreme Court of the United States at Chambers."[24] As an "in chambers opinion," Chief Justice Taney's words carried no precedential value. Taney recognized this but forwarded his "in chambers opinion" to President Lincoln.[25] Ironically, it was Taney who, only a month before, had administered the president's oath,[26] which Lincoln now relied on to justify his actions.

If one thing is certain, it is that Chief Justice Taney's opinion did not deter the resolute Lincoln. Rather, Lincoln turned to Attorney General Edward Bates for confirmation that his decision to suspend habeas corpus was within his authority.[27] Bates responded as follows: "I am clearly of opinion that, in a time like the present, when the very existence of the nation is assailed, by a great and dangerous insurrection, the President has the lawful discretionary power to arrest and hold in custody persons known to have criminal intercourse with the insurgents, or persons against whom there is probable cause for suspicion of such criminal complicity."[28]

Having received Bates's confirmation, Lincoln disregarded the "in chambers opinion" of Chief Justice Taney and courageously broadened the scope of the suspension of the writ.[29] Courage is a leadership trait that is a difficult quality to define. At its most basic level, courage is the willingness to act or to refuse to act in the face of potential harm to oneself. Whether it involves advancing unpopular ideas or facing danger on the battlefield, courage is a key ingredient in greatness. This certainly was the case for Lincoln.

In the draft of Lincoln's report to Congress (the only extant copy of his speech from July 4, 1861), he passionately defended his position: "The whole of the laws which were required to be faithfully executed, were being resisted, and failing of execution, in nearly one-third of the States. Must they be allowed to finally fail of execution? . . . are all the laws, *but one*, to go unexecuted, and the government itself go to pieces, lest that one be violated?" Lincoln ardently explained that the outbreak of the Civil War made it necessary "to call out the war power of the Government; and so to resist force, employed for its destruction, by force, for its preservation." He professed that his actions, "whether strictly legal or not, were ventured upon under what appeared to be a popular demand and a public necessity, trusting then, as now, that Congress would readily ratify them."[30]

Although the Constitution is silent with respect to which branch of government is authorized to exercise the power to suspend habeas, Lincoln's words reflected his own belief that he had exercised a power that required at least some cooperation and approval from Congress.[31] Whatever confusion remained regarding the legality of Lincoln's unilateral suspension of habeas was quelled two years later when Congress, in addition to its previous ratification of August 6, 1861, enacted legislation empowering the president to suspend the writ nationwide while rebellion continued.[32]

By mid-1862, political conflicts roiled the nation, driving both sides to fight fiercely for a cause in which each strongly believed. Despair cast a dark cloud over the country, and casualties reached over two hundred thousand by the start of the next year.[33] Throughout the crisis, President Lincoln remained proactive, knowing that extraordinary measures were necessary to reunite the nation.

On September 24, 1862, responding to the grave political and military climate, Lincoln issued another proclamation, declaring martial law and authorizing the use of military tribunals to try civilians within the United States who were believed to be "guilty of disloyal practice" or who "afford[ed] aid and comfort to Rebels."[34] The following March, Lincoln appointed Major General Ambrose Burnside as commanding general of the Department of the Ohio.[35] Burnside took command at his headquarters in Cincinnati, where wholesale criticism of the war was rampant. Agitated by such anti-administration criticism, Burnside issued General Order No. 38, authorizing imposition of the death penalty for those who aided the Confederacy and who "declared sympathies for the enemy."[36]

Among those who particularly irked General Burnside was the Democratic former Ohio congressman Clement L. Vallandigham, the best known antiwar Copperhead of the Civil War and perhaps Lincoln's sharpest critic.[37] Active in politics throughout most of his life, Vallandigham was elected to the House of Representatives from Ohio in 1856, 1858, and 1860. General Burnside recalled him from several speeches that Vallandigham had given in Congress that gained considerable publicity. Vallandigham had charged Lincoln with the "wicked and hazardous experiment" of calling the people to arms without counsel and authority of Congress, with violating the Constitution by declaring a blockade of Southern ports, with "contemptuously" defying the Constitution by suspending the writ of habeas corpus, and with "cooly" coming before Congress and pleading that he was only "preserving and protecting" the Constitution, demanding and expecting the thanks of Congress and the country for his "usurpations of power."[38]

Learning that Vallandigham was scheduled to speak again at a Democratic mass meeting in Mount Vernon, Ohio, Burnside dispatched two captains in civilian clothes to listen to the former congressman's presentation. As anticipated, Vallandigham lambasted President Lincoln, referring to him as a political tyrant and calling for his overthrow. Vallandigham proclaimed, among other things, that "the present war was a wicked, cruel, and unnecessary war, one not waged for the preservation of the Union, but for the purpose of crushing out liberty and to erect a despotism; a war for the freedom of the blacks and the enslavement of the whites."[39]

With General Order No. 38 in place, Burnside ordered Vallandigham's arrest. On May 5, 1863, at 2:40 A.M., 150 Union soldiers arrived at the Copperhead's home in Dayton. The soldiers broke down Vallandigham's front door, forced their way inside, arrested him, and escorted him to Kemper Barracks, a military prison in Cincinnati.[40]

Although a US citizen would ordinarily be tried for criminal offenses in the civilian court system, Vallandigham was brought before a military tribunal a day after his arrest.[41] Vallandigham, an attorney by training, represented himself before the military officers and protested that the commission had no authority to try him.[42] His protestations fell on deaf ears, however, as the case before the tribunal proceeded. The tribunal found Vallandigham guilty of violating General Order No. 38 and sentenced him to imprisonment for the duration of the war. Vallandigham subsequently retained counsel, then applied to the US circuit court sitting at Cincinnati for a writ of habeas corpus—a procedural method by the imprisoned to have one's imprisonment reviewed—but the writ was denied.[43] He later sought a writ of certiorari from the US Supreme Court, which was likewise denied, the court ruling that it was without jurisdiction to review the military tribunal's proceedings.[44]

The arrest, military trial, conviction, and sentence of Vallandigham aroused excitement throughout the country. The "wiley agitator," as Lincoln later obliquely described the Ohioan,[45] found many supporters in New York, particularly in heavily Democratic Albany.

Sentiment in Albany held that Vallandigham's arrest was arbitrary and constituted an effort to exert military censorship of public discourse. One newspaper reported that the arrest was an experiment conducted by the Lincoln administration to test how much the public would tolerate. Many New Yorkers felt that Vallandigham's arrest posed a threat to them too. A Democratic newspaper speculated that "the blow that falls upon a citizen of Ohio to-day, may be directed at a Democrat of New York to-morrow. The blow, therefore, is a threat at every Democrat."[46] Days later, the paper drove home this idea: "The State of New York, and every citizen of the State, is equally threatened[.] We must make common cause with the citizens of other States, or we, too, are lost."[47]

Incensed by Vallandigham's arrest, the Democratic New Yorkers organized what the *Atlas & Argus* newspaper described as "one of the largest and most respectable meetings ever held at the Capitol" to protest against the case, which they believed was a "crime against the Constitution." New Yorkers arrived at the capitol in Albany in droves, and by 8 P.M., the broad walk leading to the capitol steps and the adjacent grounds were packed with citizens.[48]

Although unable to attend the public meeting, New York's Democratic governor Horatio Seymour forwarded a letter that was read aloud to the spirited crowd of three thousand that filled the capitol park.[49] Like many New Yorkers, Seymour was outraged at what he believed was a depredation of civil liberties. He wrote:

> The transaction involved a series of offences against our most sacred rights. It interfered with the freedom of speech; it violated our rights to be secure in our homes against unreasonable searches and seizures; it pronounced sentence without a trial, save one which was a mockery, which insulted as well as wrong. The perpetrators now

seek to impose punishment, not for an offence against the law but
for a disregard of an invalid order, put forth in an utter disregard of
principles of civil liberty.[50]

As the rally proceeded, fiery speeches criticized General Burnside for his
action against Vallandigham. Among those who spoke were Judge Amasa J.
Parker, Congressman Francis Kernan, and the Honorable John W. Murphy.
Orator after orator expressed outrage against the allegedly arbitrary action
of the administration. However, not everyone in attendance offered support
for the firebrands. Several soldiers who had just returned from the battlefield
displayed great dissatisfaction with the meeting's purpose, breaking chairs into
pieces and hurling them into the crowd. The *New York Times* reported that at
one point during the disruption, it appeared as though the soldiers might seize
control over the meeting. Eventually, the soldiers' efforts were thwarted and
the meeting returned to order.[51]

Ultimately, the attendees adopted a series of resolutions and ordered that
a copy of them be transmitted to the president "with the assurance of this
meeting of their hearty and earnest desire to support the Government in every
Constitutional and lawful measure to suppress the existing Rebellion." The
resolutions drove home the point that they considered Vallandigham's arrest and
imprisonment as illegal and unconstitutional. In the Albany Democrats' opinion:

> [The] assumption of power by a military tribunal, if successfully
> asserted, not only abrogates the right of the people to assemble and
> discuss the affairs of Government, the liberty of speech and of the
> press, the right of trial by jury, the law of evidence, and the privileges
> of *Habeas Corpus*, but it strikes a fatal blow at the supremacy of law,
> and the authority of the State and Federal Constitutions.[52]

On May 19, 1863, only days after this vocal public meeting, Albany's former
Democratic mayor, Erastus Corning, who had been elected as president of the
assemblage upon Henry S. Crandall's nomination, addressed the resolutions
to Republican president Lincoln. Corning also enclosed a brief note signed by
himself, as president of the assemblage, and by its vice presidents and secretaries.

In the weeks that followed the Albany meeting, similar gatherings were
held throughout the state of New York in protest of what organizers insisted
was the administration's infringement on the "most sacred rights of American

freemen." Mass meetings occurred in Utica, Troy, and Waterloo. While in Brooklyn, a subcommittee of the Democratic General Committee was appointed to "consider the subject of the recent arbitrary arrests by the Government, and draft resolutions expressive of the sense of the Union Democratic General Committee."[53]

These protests were challenged, however, by those loyal to the Union and the Republican administration. In Albany, hundreds assembled on May 20, 1863, "to give expression to their patriotic loyalty, and to vindicate the Capital of the State of New York from the imputation of indifference to the results of the war and to the integrity of the Nation."[54] The *Albany Evening Journal* described the assemblage of Albany Democrats as "a meeting to justify a bad man, and to denounce those who sought to punish him." The proadministration paper continued, "The meeting was, and will be, recognized as a meeting to approve what a man, who is at heart a traitor, has said and done, rather than what its responsible managers will wish it to be deemed, viz.: a meeting to maintain the supremacy of the civil law."[55]

It was not long before Lincoln himself replied to the Albany Democrats. As a lawyer, Lincoln's "intellectual integrity; his capacity for analysis and balanced decision; his practical, hardheaded approach to legal problems; his ability to strip away trivia and get to the heart of a matter; his sensitive consideration of others and his profound insight into the deep recesses of the human mind and heart, coupled with the gift of expressing himself in plain and pointed and unequivocal language," wrote biographer John Duff, "were precisely the essentials for success."[56] The same lawyerly traits allowed Lincoln to reason with the Albany Democrats.

In a closely reasoned document, constructed in lawyer-like fashion and sprawling over twenty pages of handwritten sheets, Lincoln justified the action of the administration in the arrest, trial, imprisonment, and his subsequent banishment of Vallandigham. He elaborated on his view that certain proceedings are constitutional "when in cases of rebellion or invasion, the public Safety requires them, which would not be constitutional when, in [the] absence of rebellion or invasion, the public Safety does not require them." Lincoln made sure copies of his letter went not only to Corning but also to pro-Republican newspapers such as the *New York Tribune*. As early as June 5, Lincoln had read the letter to his cabinet, prompting Secretary of the Navy Gideon Welles to write in his diary that it "has vigor and ability and with some corrections will be a strong paper."[57]

In Lincoln's opinion, the framers of the Constitution were wise to include such a provision allowing for the suspension of the writ of habeas corpus "when in cases of Rebellion or Invasion, the public Safety may require it," as such a suspension was necessary to prevent "sudden and extensive uprisings against the government." He explained to the Albany Democrats that Vallandigham's arrest was not, as they mistakenly believed, premised on his criticism of the administration.[58] Democrats in Albany had charged the Lincoln administration with arresting Vallandigham in an effort to silence him. The *Atlas & Argus* opined, "The arrest is a threat against every public man who refuses to advocate the extreme measures of the Abolition Cabinet."[59] Lincoln sought to assure those who harbored such mistaken beliefs that they were incorrect. He explained that Vallandigham had been arrested for his avowed hostility to the Union's war efforts, his laboring to prevent the raising of troops, and his encouragement of desertions from the army.[60]

Vallandigham's efforts, aimed at damaging the army and leaving the Union without an adequate military force to suppress the rebellion, were intolerable to the administration and antithetical to the Union's attempt to preserve the nation. Lincoln explained that experience had shown that armies cannot be maintained unless those who desert were punished by death. He believed that Vallandigham's efforts to encourage soldiers to desert the army were equally detrimental to the nation and should likewise be punished by death. With this came the most remembered passage of Lincoln's reply. The master lawyer-statesman wrote, "Must I shoot a simple-minded soldier boy who deserts, while I must not touch a hair of a wiley agitator who induces him to desert? . . . I think that in such a case, to silence the agitator, and save the boy, is not only constitutional, but, withal, a great mercy."[61]

Lincoln emphasized his belief that it was absolutely necessary to try insurrectionists, such as Vallandigham, before a military tribunal. In Lincoln's opinion, the civilian court system was woefully inadequate to handle such matters. He wrote to Corning that "a jury too frequently have at least one member, more ready to hang the panel than to hang the traitor." Lincoln recognized that the civilian court system was properly suited for trying individuals of crimes that were well defined in the law but was ill suited for trying those charged with insurrection. Driving home the point, Lincoln wrote, "He who dissuades one man from volunteering, or induces one soldier to desert, weakens the Union cause as much as he who kills a Union soldier in battle. Yet this dissuasion, or inducement, may be so conducted as to be no defined crime of which any civil court would take cognizance."[62]

Lincoln's perceptiveness in recognizing the need to try insurrectionists before a military tribunal, rather than in the civilian court system—as argued in his letter to Erastus Corning—would help the Union win the Civil War. As Lincoln recognized, without the power to punish those who deserted the army or encouraged others to desert, the Union would have been unable to maintain its force in numbers, certainly inhibiting its success. Indeed, the civil court system was wholly unable to prevent or punish desertion. Others similarly attributed the Union's success to Lincoln's suspension of the writ of habeas corpus and his willingness to try those detained before a military tribunal, but for an altogether different reason. Historian Phillip Shaw Paludan has surmised that "Lincoln kept the constitutional debate going throughout the war and thus propagandized to persuade the people that their constitutional system was adequate to survive and prosecute a war."[63] Lincoln, too, recognized the power of public sentiment, as he had remarked during his famous debates with Stephen A. Douglas that "public sentiment is everything."[64] The sixteenth president, through his letter to Corning, provided future wartime presidents with an invaluable tool: a brilliantly crafted, highly accessible, tightly reasoned legal argument justifying the trial of insurrectionists or other enemy combatants that would prove irresistible to his successors in later wars.

In the end, Lincoln's army won, leaving us with a United States that *is* and not states that *are*. Ultimately, "a trial lawyer named Abraham Lincoln gave us not only his courageous leadership . . . but also his life, during the most divisive period in our country's history."[65]

Notes

1. See, generally, Godfrey Sperling, "Rating Our Presidents," *Christian Science Monitor* (Boston, June 14, 2005), accessed May 4, 2014, http://www.csmonitor.com/2005/0614/p09s01-cogs.html; the American Flag Foundation, "Historical Bios: Abraham Lincoln," accessed May 4, 2014, http://www.americanflagfoundation.org/content/educationalresources_historicalbios.cfm; Lydian Saad, "Lincoln Resumes Position as Americas Top-Rated President," Gallup, February 19, 2007, accessed May 4, 2014, http://www.gallup.com/poll/26608/Lincoln-Resumes-Position-Americans-TopRated-President.aspx.

2. I have written more extensively on this subject elsewhere. Frank J. Williams, Nicole J. Dulude, and Kimberly A. Tracey, "Still a Frightening Unknown: Achieving a Constitutional Balance between Civil Liberties and National Security during the War on Terror," *Roger Williams University Law Review* 12, no. 3

(2007): 675; Frank J. Williams, *Lincoln as Hero* (Carbondale: Southern Illinois University Press, 2012).

3. US Const. art. II, § 3.

4. Henry J. Raymond, *The Life and Public Services of Abraham Lincoln* (Ann Arbor: University of Michigan Library, 2005): 380, accessed May 4, 2014, http://name.umdl.umich.edu/AAX3271.0001.001.

5. Abraham Lincoln, Proclamation Calling for 42,034 Volunteers, May 3, 1861, in *The Collected Works of Abraham Lincoln*, ed. Roy P. Basler et al. (New Brunswick, NJ: Rutgers University Press, 1953), 4:354–55.

6. Lincoln, Proclamation Calling Militia and Convening Congress, April 15, 1861, *Collected Works*, 4:332–33.

7. Lincoln, Proclamation of Blockade, April 19, 1861, *Collected Works*, 4:338–39; Lincoln, Proclamation of Blockade, April 27, 1861, ibid., 4:346–47.

8. Lincoln, Order to General Winfield Scott, April 27, 1861, ibid., 4:344.

9. William Rehnquist, *All the Laws but One: Civil Liberties in Wartime* (New York: Vintage, 2000), 23.

10. Lincoln, Order to General Winfield Scott, April 27, 1861, *Collected Works*, 4:344.

11. See William F. Duker, *A Constitutional History of Habeas Corpus* (Santa Barbara, CA: Greenwood Press, 1980), 146.

12. Michael Lind, *What Lincoln Believed: The Values and Convictions of America's Greatest President* (New York: First Anchor Books, 2004), 174; David Herbert Donald and Harold Holzer, *Lincoln in the Times* (New York: New York Times Co., 2005), 117; Richard A. Posner, *Not a Suicide Pact: The Constitution in a Time of National Emergency* (Oxford: Oxford University Press, 2006), 45.

13. Mark E. Neely Jr., *The Fate of Liberty: Abraham Lincoln and Civil Liberties* (Oxford: Oxford University Press, 1991), xvi; Posner, *Not a Suicide Pact*, 85–86; B. F. McClerren, Op-Ed, "Lincoln's Actions May Apply Today," *Charleston (IL) Times-Courier*, November 19, 2001.

14. Lincoln, Message to Congress in Special Session, July 4, 1861, *Collected Works*, 4:430.

15. Ibid. See also James M. McPherson, *This Mighty Scourge: Perspectives on the Civil War* (Oxford: Oxford University Press, 2007), 211.

16. Act of August 6, 1861, Ch. 63, § 3, 12 Stat. 326. See Brian McGinty, *Lincoln and the Court* (Cambridge, MA: Harvard University Press, 2008), 29.

17. Lincoln, Message to Congress in Special Session, July 4, 1861, *Collected Works*, 4:429.

18. Duker, *Constitutional History of Habeas Corpus*, 147.

19. *Ex parte Merryman*, 17 F. Cas., 144, 147 (C.C.D. Md.1861); Brian McGinty, *The Body of John Merryman: Abraham Lincoln and the Suspension of Habeas Corpus* (Cambridge, MA: Harvard University Press 2011), 73.

20. Arthur T. Downey, "The Conflict between the Chief Justice and the Chief Executive: *Ex parte Merryman*," *Journal of Supreme Court History* 31 (2006), 262–78.

21. *Ex parte Merryman*, 17 F. Cas., 145, 147.

22. Downey, "Conflict between the Chief Justice and the Chief Executive," 262–78.

23. *Ex parte Merryman*, 17 F. Cas., 147.

24. Carl B. Swisher, *The Oliver Wendell Holmes Devise: History of the Supreme Court of the United States* (Cambridge: Cambridge University Press, 1974), 848.

25. Daniel A. Farber, *Lincoln's Constitution* (Chicago: University of Chicago Press 2003), 17; see also Jeffrey Rosen, *The Supreme Court: The Personalities and Rivalries That Defined America* (New York: Times Books, 2007), 12.

26. McGinty, *Lincoln and the Court*, 4.

27. Lincoln to Edward Bates, May 30, 1861, *Collected Works*, 4:390; McGinty, *Body of John Merryman*, 104–7.

28. *Official Opinions of the Attorneys General of the United States, Advising the President and Heads of Departments in Relation to Their Official Duties*, ed. J. Hubley Ashton (Washington, DC: W. H. & O. H. Morrison, 1868), 10:81.

29. Lincoln to Henry W. Halleck, December 2, 1861, *Collected Works*, 5:35; Lincoln, Proclamation Suspending the Writ of Habeas Corpus, September 24, 1862, ibid., 5:436–37; Lincoln, Proclamation Suspending Writ of Habeas Corpus, September 15, 1863, ibid., 6:451–52; Farber, *Lincoln's Constitution*, 159.

30. Lincoln, Message to Congress in Special Session, July 4, 1861, *Collected Works*, 4:426, 429, 430.

31. Ibid., 431.

32. Habeas Corpus Act, ch. 80, 12 Stat. 755 (1863).

33. Civil War Battle Statistics Commanders and Casualties, http://www.AmericanCivilWar.com.

34. Lincoln, Proclamation Suspending the Writ of Habeas Corpus, September 24, 1862, *Collected Works*, 5:436–37.

35. See Michael Kent Curtis, "Lincoln, Vallandigham, and Anti-War Speech in the Civil War," *William & Mary Bill of Rights Journal* 7 (1998): 119.

36. General Order No. 38, in Benjamin Perley Poore, *The Life and Public Services of Ambrose E. Burnside, Soldier-Citizen-Statesman* (Providence: J. A. & R. A. Reid Publishers, 1882), 206.

37. Ibid., 208–9.

38. Cong. Globe, 37th Cong., 1st Sess. 57–59 (1861); Frank L. Klement, *The Limits of Dissent* (Bronx, NY: Fordham University Press, 1998).

39. *Ex parte Vallandigham*, 68 US 243, 244 (1864).

40. Curtis, "Lincoln, Vallandigham," 105, 107, 122; Poore, *Life and Public Services of Burnside*, 208; Rehnquist, *All the Laws but One*, 65–66; see also "Vallandigham Arrested," *Atlas & Argus*, May 6, 1863.

41. *Ex parte Vallandigham*, 68 US 244; see also Curtis, "Lincoln, Vallandigham," 105, 121.

42. *Atlas & Argus*, May 13, 1863.

43. *The Trial of Hon. Clement L. Vallandigham by a Military Commission and the Proceedings under His Application for a Writ of Habeas Corpus in the Circuit Court of the United States for the Southern District of Ohio* (Cincinnati: Rickey and Carroll, 1863), 33, 37–39.

44. *Ex parte Vallandigham*, 68 US 251.

45. Lincoln to Erastus Corning and Others, June 12, 1863, *Collected Works*, 6:266.

46. "Revival of Arbitrary Arrests," *Atlas & Argus*, May 12, 1863.

47. "The Vallandigham Outrage: Meeting at the Capitol in Behalf of Personal Freedom," *Atlas & Argus*, May 16, 1863.

48. "The Vallandigham Outrage: Immense Meeting at the Capitol," ibid., May 18, 1863; "The Arrest of Vallandigham," ibid., May 8, 1863, 2.

49. "General News," *New York Times*, May 19, 1863.

50. "The Vallandigham Outrage: Immense Meeting at the Capitol," *Atlas & Argus*, May 18, 1863.

51. "Vallandigham Indignation Meeting at Albany, Letter from Gov. Seymour—An Attempt Made to Break Up the Meeting," *New York Times*, May 17, 1863.

52. "The Vallandigham Outrage: Immense Meeting at the Capitol," *Atlas & Argus*, May 18, 1863.

53. "The Vallandigham Outrage: The Voice of the People," *Atlas & Argus*, May 26, 1863.

54. "The Union Must and Shall Be Preserved," *Albany Evening Journal*, May 19, 1863; see also "The Great War Meeting," *Albany Evening Journal*, May 21, 1863.

55. "The Vallandigham Meeting," *Albany Evening Journal*, May 18, 1863.

56. John J. Duff, *A. Lincoln Prairie Lawyer* (New York: Bramhall House, 1960), 301.

57. Lincoln to Erastus Corning and Others, June 12, 1863, *Collected Works*, 6:267, 269n2.

58. Ibid., 264, 266.

59. "Revival of Arbitrary Arrests," *Atlas & Argus*, May 12, 1863.

60. Lincoln to Erastus Corning and Others, June 12, 1863, *Collected Works*, 6:266.

61. Ibid., 266–67.

62. Ibid., 264.

63. Phillip Shaw Paludan, "'The Better Angels of Our Nature': Lincoln, Propaganda, and Public Opinion in the North during the Civil War," in *On the Road to Total War: The American Civil War and the German Wars of Unification, 1861–1871*, ed. Stig Forster and Jorg Nagler (Cambridge: German Historical Institute, 1997), 357.

64. Lincoln, First Debate with Stephen A. Douglas at Ottawa, Illinois, August 21, 1858, *Collected Works*, 3:27.

65. Charles Wirken, "It's a Wonderful Profession—Let's Defend It!," *Arizona Attorney* 41 (January 2005): 6.

From Francis Carpenter's painting of the first reading of the Emancipation Proclamation before Lincoln's cabinet. Carpenter resided in the White House for six months and had access to the president during that time. Courtesy of the Library of Congress, LC-DIG-pga-03452.

"I CLAIM NOT TO HAVE CONTROLLED EVENTS": LINCOLN, LEADERSHIP, AND THE EMANCIPATION STRUGGLE

Edna Greene Medford

Despite his acknowledgment that the Emancipation Proclamation was "the central act" of his administration and "the great event of the nineteenth century,"[1] Abraham Lincoln likely would be surprised by all the attention he has received over the last 150 years as the "Great Emancipator" image has been promulgated, contested, and embraced anew. In a letter he wrote to Kentucky newspaper editor Albert Hodges in the spring of 1864, he suggested that his actions were less certain or deliberate than we imagine today. "I claim not to have controlled events," he told Hodges, "but confess plainly that events have controlled me."[2] If we are to extend this self-assessment to include his role in ending slavery, we could conclude with some degree of reasonableness that he had not begun his presidency with the aim to emancipate the enslaved population. In fact, when he stood before the American people in his First Inaugural Address, he declared emphatically that he had neither the inclination nor the authority to end the institution where it already existed.[3] Yet twenty months into the war, he issued a proclamation that freed enslaved people in the states that were still in rebellion. In the final year of the conflict, he helped secure passage of the Thirteenth Amendment, thus legally guaranteeing the freedom that he had declared was the right of all humankind.

Lincoln's conversion to abolitionism came neither swiftly nor directly, but he was not a passive actor in the emancipation drama.[4] Frederick Douglass declared at the dedication of the Freedmen's Memorial to the martyred president that, compared with ardent abolitionists, Lincoln was "tardy, cold, dull, and indifferent." Measured by the times and by public sentiment, however, "he was swift, zealous, radical, and determined."[5] Lincoln's monumental task had been to reconcile public will with national interest in a time of unprecedented crisis. As he attempted to do so, he drew on his knowledge and understanding of his countrymen, skillfully managing competing agendas while pursuing a solution that did not compromise the rule of law.

Lincoln was hardly an ideal candidate for national executive, especially during a time of crisis. The son of an uneducated, hardscrabble farmer who, like many on the frontier, spent his days struggling with nature to provide for his family, Lincoln had little in the way of personal background to recommend him. Neither was he one of the most nationally prominent politicians of his day. Before winning the presidency, his political career had consisted of four terms in the Illinois legislature and one in the US House of Representatives, all elections that depended on a local constituency rather than statewide support. His unremarkable military background consisted of a brief stint of less than three months in the 1832 Black Hawk War, in which his only combat was in "bloody struggles with the musquetoes."[6] If not for the national debate over slavery, he might have passed his days satisfied with providing legal representation to common folk and the railroads or entertaining the local people with his folksy joke-telling, as he traveled Illinois' Eighth Judicial Circuit.

However, Lincoln lived in tumultuous times. His coming of age coincided with the growing debate over slavery's place in a nation committed, at least in principle, to freedom and equality. He was a passionate supporter of the Declaration of Independence, a document that promised the basic rights of humanity—"Life, Liberty, and the pursuit of Happiness"—to all. Yet from its founding, the nation had grappled with the denial of these rights to the vast majority of African Americans. Compelled to labor for someone else's benefit, subject to being sold like cattle, and refused the basic rights of self-determination, enslaved men and women were both an embarrassment and a reminder of America's hypocrisy. A series of compromises, beginning with the Constitution, had kept the struggle over slavery from rending the nation. During the crucial decade of the 1850s, the sectional conflict intensified and propelled the country ever closer to irreconcilability. Before the decade ended, the Whig Party, in which Lincoln held membership, had been destroyed, and the Democratic Party had been splintered along sectional lines. A new party committed to antislavery—the Republican Party—had emerged from this struggle and had absorbed former Whigs, certain disaffected Democrats, and "free soil" proponents. Many of these new Republicans, including Lincoln, chose to remain outside the abolitionist camp while pledging to limit slavery to where it already existed. In this war of containment, the territories became the battleground that would determine America's future. "We want [the territories] for the homes of free white people," Lincoln had declared. "This they cannot be . . . if slavery shall be planted within them."[7]

Lincoln's response to the problem of slavery was shaped by two influences: his certainty that the founding fathers had anticipated the eventual extinction of slavery and his recognition that enslaved people were legally held property. Unable to rid themselves of the institution at the nation's founding because of the Southern delegation's insistence on keeping it, the framers of the Constitution had attempted to limit its impact as much as possible and even excluded the words "slave" and "slavery" from the founding document. "The plain unmistakable spirit of that age, towards slavery," Lincoln argued, "was hostility to the PRINCIPLE, and toleration, ONLY BY NECESSITY."[8]

However uncomfortable they were with the idea of slavery, the Founding Fathers acknowledged, and Lincoln concurred, that enslaved people were property, implicitly protected by constitutional guarantees. Whatever may have been its moral implications, American law sanctioned the institution. The slaveholder had a *legal* right to his human property. Hence emancipation would require the consent of the local communities, and slaveholders would have to be compensated for their loss.

Unlike the abolitionists, many of whom favored immediate and unconditional divestment from slavery, Lincoln believed that emancipation should be carried out gradually in order to "spare both races from the evils of sudden derangement."[9] Slaveholders would have time to shift to free labor and become accustomed to a new economic system, while the enslaved would be eased into freedom and prepared for the responsibilities that came with it. To Lincoln's thinking, this was a reasonable plan.

Lincoln's views on slavery matured during the 1850s as proslavery forces sought to extend the institution's reach. In 1854, Senator Stephen A. Douglas, a fellow Illinoisan, introduced a bill to organize the Kansas-Nebraska territory. The impetus for such action was the proposed transcontinental railroad, which Douglas hoped would be built with Chicago as its terminus. The bill, which became law with Southern support, created a political firestorm because Douglas had proposed that the local people should decide the issue of slavery. Opponents argued that the slavery question had already been settled in the Kansas-Nebraska region thirty-four years earlier through the provisions of the

Missouri Compromise. Abolitionists and other opponents of slavery responded to Douglas's bill with alarm. The ensuing struggle destroyed the Whig Party, prompting Lincoln to share his views on the extension of slavery. He declared that he hated the institution because of its "monstrous injustice" and because it "deprive[d] our republican example of its just influence in the world."[10] When, a few years later, the US Supreme Court ruled in *Dred Scott v. Sandford* that African Americans were not citizens and that Congress had no authority to outlaw slavery in the territories, Lincoln again objected, arguing that the authors of the Declaration of Independence had intended that African Americans be included in the phrase "all men" in the sense that they were entitled to unalienable rights. He declined to accept any notion, however, that black men were equal to white men in every respect.[11]

In a series of statewide debates in 1858 with Senator Douglas, Lincoln polished his skills as an orator and as a proponent of freedom. The two candidates for the US senatorial seat jointly crisscrossed the state, visiting seven cities in total. Each provided his perspective on slavery and its expansion. In response to Douglas's race-baiting in a region with strong antiblack sentiment, Lincoln uttered the infamous words that still give his detractors cause for criticism and make his admirers cringe. To Douglas's charge that Lincoln was in favor of "producing a perfect equality" between African Americans and white people, Lincoln declared:

> I am not, nor ever have been, in favor of bringing about in any way the social and political equality of the white and black races . . . I am not nor ever have been in favor of making voters or jurors of negroes, nor of qualifying them to hold office, nor to intermarry with white people; . . . there is a physical difference between the white and black which I believe will forever forbid the two races living together on terms of social and political equality.[12]

Although Lincoln lost the election, the debates introduced him to the nation. Thus when he traveled to New York to speak at Cooper Union two years later, he was recognized as an authority on the subject of slavery's extension and the intentions of the Founding Fathers.[13]

The Cooper Union address helped elevate Lincoln's stature from that of a regional politician to a national spokesperson. It also confirmed him as a moderate in an increasingly volatile debate. Hence the man who could not win a statewide election just two years before was now viewed as a serious contender for the Republican nomination for the presidency. When the party met in convention in Chicago a few months later to select its nominee, Lincoln's supporters employed their considerable political influence to help him defeat the more radical but better- known candidates, William Seward and Salmon Chase.

The Republican Party's championing of the nonextension of slavery into the territories guaranteed Southern opposition to the party and its candidate. A divided Democratic Party met in two separate conventions, one representing Northern interests and the other committed to upholding the rights of the Southern people. Each offered a candidate for the presidency. Although he did not carry a single state that would secede from the Union in the winter of 1860–61, Lincoln won the election. The following month, unwilling to remain in a nation led by even a moderate Republican, South Carolina seceded. Over the next several months, ten states joined it and eventually formed a government whose constitution explicitly protected slavery in the member states and sanctioned it in any territory acquired by the new nation.[14]

Believing that it was inappropriate for the president-elect to respond publicly to the unfolding developments, Lincoln made his sentiments known in private correspondence.[15] In a letter to his friend Lyman Trumbull, fellow Republican and US senator from Illinois, Lincoln urged, "Let there be no compromise on the question of *extending* slavery. If there be, all our labor is lost, and, ere long, must be done again. The dangerous ground—that into which some of our friends have a hankering to run—is Pop[ular] Sov[ereignty]. Have none of it. Stand firm. The tug has to come, & better now, than any time hereafter."[16] In another private communication, he responded to the call for his support of a constitutional amendment that would prohibit the federal government from abolishing slavery. Supported by Peace Democrats and others who sought to divert disunion, the proposed amendment guaranteed that the South's "peculiar institution" would be protected in perpetuity. Citing his lack of desire for such an amendment, Lincoln nevertheless was willing to bow to the will of the people and acknowledge their right to consider any solution.[17] Although Congress passed the amendment, war erupted before the requisite number of states could ratify the law. Had it gone into effect, it would have become, ironically, the Thirteenth Amendment. In a third letter, this time to secretary of state designate William Seward, Lincoln reiterated that he was "inflexible" and would not compromise with any plan that would allow slavery's extension. Other issues involving slavery were negotiable as long as "what is done be comely, and not altogether outrageous."[18]

When Lincoln took office on March 4, 1861, seven Southern states had already withdrawn from the Union. In the weeks and months to come, various groups competed for his attention and for the opportunity to influence his response. He had to contend with the Peace Democrats, who opposed the war and consistently tried to undermine his policies. They favored settling with the Confederacy, even if it meant preserving slavery. One of them, Ohio congressman Clement Vallandigham, had urged Union soldiers to desert their units and had proposed a bill to imprison the president. Conservatives within Lincoln's own party, many of them longtime friends, criticized him whenever they felt his policies regarding slavery attacked the institution or, conversely, did too little to protect it. At the same time, he had to contend with the Radical Republicans, many of them abolitionists, who believed he moved too slowly toward emancipation. Newspaper editors excoriated him at every turn; generals in the field ignored his orders; and certain members of his own cabinet held him in contempt.

Virtually powerless but determined, African Americans presented a different problem. While free men and women of color in the North pressed the Lincoln administration to combine the fight for the Union with emancipation, the enslaved took flight at the first sign that white men were divided. Fugitives quickly overwhelmed the capacity of the federal government to respond to their presence, leading Union commanders to decide individually what to do with them. Significantly, the contrabands, as they became known, arrived with news that those still enslaved in the Confederacy provided coerced assistance in the war effort, thus pressuring the Lincoln administration to acknowledge their value to the enemy. These competing groups challenged the president and put his leadership skills to the test throughout the war.

During his first weeks in office, Lincoln focused on managing the secession crisis. In an effort to allay Southern fears, he set a course of appeasement and conciliation, beginning with his inaugural address, in which he attempted to convince the secessionists and those who were similarly inclined that their rights as American citizens would be protected. Federal legislation such as the Fugitive Slave Act, which obligated Northerners to assist in the apprehension of runaways, would be upheld. In Lincoln's estimation, the seceded states had not actually dissolved their association with the Union because they could not legally do so.

The Confederate assault on Fort Sumter disrupted Lincoln's plan of appeasement and removed the possibility of a peaceful resolution to the crisis. The Federal installation in Charleston Harbor was the first test of the president's resolve to maintain national authority. In his response to Southern aggression, Lincoln convened Congress and called for the levying of seventy-five thousand men drawn from the various state militias. Still, he sought to reassure, promising in his proclamation authorizing military action, "The utmost care will be observed . . . to avoid any devastation, any destruction of, or interference with, property."[19] Rather than easing tensions, however, Lincoln's decision to respond militarily drove four additional states into the Confederate camp, thereby expanding the conflict.

Before either side shouldered arms, enslaved people had taken advantage of the disruptions to escape their bondage. Flight increased as the Union army advanced and as the Confederate government authorized impressment of enslaved men for military labor. Within weeks of Fort Sumter's bombardment, fugitives seeking asylum had presented themselves at Federal installations, thus testing the administration's resolve to maintain a policy of noninterference and creating a dilemma for military commanders, who responded to such action according to the circumstances and their own personal sentiment. General Benjamin F. Butler's acceptance of the fugitives as contraband encouraged a policy shift among certain commanders in the field that remained unofficial long after the first men sought sanctuary with the Union forces at Fortress Monroe.

Fully aware that African Americans who remained behind Confederate lines were compelled to aid the Southern cause, Congress attempted to remove the advantage. In August 1861, it passed an act that allowed for the confiscation of any property, including slave labor, used to wage war against the Union.[20] Lincoln signed the measure, but he simultaneously pursued a course that he hoped would render any future congressional *or* executive action unnecessary.

Fearing that the border states would soon join the Confederacy, Lincoln adopted a plan of action that required him to balance their interests and national survival. His strategy in the first few months of the war was to keep those states loyal. So while his responses to the events unfolding had a great deal to do with what he viewed as constitutional constraints, he also was influenced by the anticipated and actual reactions of the border states. Hence when General John C. Frémont, commander of Union forces in Missouri, issued a proclamation declaring enslaved laborers of rebels in the state free, Lincoln asked him to modify it to conform to the First Confiscation Act.[21] As expected, the president received a great deal of criticism from the abolitionists for this action. In a letter to his friend Orville H. Browning, Republican senator from Illinois, Lincoln communicated his reasons for not seizing the opportunity presented by the situation. "General Frémont's proclamation, as to confiscation of property, and the liberation of slaves, is *purely political*, and not within the range of *military law or necessity*," he wrote. Equally important, he seemed to suggest, was the attitude of Kentucky: "The Kentucky Legislature would not budge till that proclamation was modified. I think to lose Kentucky is nearly the same as to lose the whole game. Kentucky gone, we can not hold Missouri, nor, as I think, Maryland. These all against us, and the job on our hands is too large for us."[22]

Lincoln knew he might be successful in preventing defection of the remaining slave states if he could convince them that it would be in their best interest to eliminate slavery. State-imposed emancipation solved existing constitutional constraints, and it placed the process in the hands of those who would be most affected by it. Believing Delaware to be a good place to start, in November 1861, Lincoln drafted two bills of gradual, compensated emancipation, which he proposed to the state's congressional representatives. Delaware appeared to be ideal for such an undertaking, as it had fewer than two thousand enslaved people resident within its borders. Lincoln's first proposal called for the freeing of a few hundred adults each year until 1867, when all remaining men and women and all children would be freed. The second proposal called for the elimination of slavery by 1893, with all persons over thirty-five receiving immediate freedom and others becoming free after they reached that age. Hence the young and fit would remain available to the slave owner for a while longer. Lincoln left open the possibility that children born to enslaved mothers after passage of the act would be apprenticed to the mother's owner for a specified period of time.[23]

Despite his efforts, the president's plan for Delaware never reached the state's legislature. The slaveholding power would brook no tampering with its institution, even to save the Union. Yet Lincoln held to his plan of gradual, compensated emancipation within the border states. In his message to Congress on March 6, 1862, he proposed the adoption of a joint resolution calling for the government to provide aid to any state that adopted a gradual plan. Reiterating the necessity for such a policy, he argued that the Confederate states must be dissuaded from the idea that the border states would ever join them. By abolishing slavery, even gradually, the tie would be removed that bound the loyal slaveholding states to those in rebellion.[24]

One month later, Congress responded favorably to the president's proposal by approving funding for emancipation, but the border states remained unconvinced. Undeterred, Lincoln employed personal persuasion. He invited the states' congressional representatives to the White House, where he appealed to their sense of duty, patriotism, and self-interest. He assured them that they possessed the power to bring the war to a speedy conclusion. If they failed to take the initiative, they risked the real possibility that slavery would "be extinguished by mere friction and abrasion—by the mere incidents of the war." If that happened, they would forfeit the opportunity to be compensated for their loss. Ever the gradualist, he assured them that they need not emancipate immediately; he merely wanted them immediately to agree to emancipate over a period of time. Any resistance from local residents who feared an unrestrained black presence could be assured by a plan of colonization. He suggested that African Americans would embrace colonization "when numbers shall be large enough to be company and encouragement for one another."[25]

While Lincoln was pursuing state-imposed emancipation, Congress exercised its authority over the District of Columbia. In 1850, it had abolished the heinous slave trade in the city, where human commodities were bought and sold in the shadow of the Capitol. In the District of Columbia, with just over three thousand enslaved people, slavery had been modified by urban constraints and necessities. The population of enslaved people consisted primarily of domestic servants, who, although they shared some of the same horrors and indignities of slavery with their Deep South counterparts, had grown to be independent in ways unimaginable to plantation laborers. District slaveholders objected to abolition, but they had no mechanism by which to give official voice to their dissent. This troubled Lincoln, who believed that emancipation without local consent violated constitutional guarantees to ownership of property. He delayed signing the bill into law for two days, perhaps because of this concern. Orville Browning, however, suggested a rather unsettling motive for the delay. Browning purportedly visited Lincoln during this time of apparent indecision and claimed that the president had confided to him that he was delaying official action at the request of former governor Charles Wickliffe. The Kentucky congressman, it seems, needed additional time to remove two enslaved people from the city who he thought would not benefit from freedom because of their advanced age.[26]

With emancipation implemented by congressional action in the District of Columbia, Lincoln experienced increasing pressure from abolitionist groups and from those convinced that the only way to save the Union was to deprive the Confederacy of its enslaved labor force. In August 1862, *New York Tribune* editor Horace Greeley criticized Lincoln for his ineffectual enforcement of the First and Second Confiscation Acts, the latter being a more sweeping law that Lincoln had objected to and hinted that he would not sign unless modified.

Greeley charged him with being "unduly influenced by the counsels, the representations, the menaces, of certain fossil politicians hailing from the Border Slave States."[27] Lincoln's response, intended for a wider audience, outlined the rationale for his evolving policies on slavery. He assured Greeley:

> My paramount object in this struggle *is* to save the Union, and is *not* either to save or destroy slavery. If I could save the Union without freeing *any* slave I would do it, and if I could save it by freeing *all* the slaves I would do it; and if I could save it by freeing some and leaving others alone I would also do that. What I do about slavery, and the colored race, I do because I believe it helps to save the Union; and what I forbear, I forbear because I do *not* believe it would help to save the Union.[28]

Lincoln concluded that this was his view of "official duty," but he continued to believe personally that all men should be free. A couple of weeks later, he reiterated his position in a meeting with a group of Chicago churchmen who had presented him with a memorial calling for emancipation. "What good would a proclamation of emancipation from me do, especially as we are now situated?" he asked. "I do not want to issue a document that the whole world will see must necessarily be inoperative, like the Pope's bull against the comet!" Lincoln left the door open to future executive action, suggesting that "as commander-in-chief of the army and navy, in time of war," he believed that he had the right to act in any way that might defeat the enemy. "I view this matter as a practical war measure, to be decided on according to the advantages or disadvantages it may offer to the suppression of the rebellion," he told the delegation. Lincoln assured them that he had not "decided against a proclamation of liberty to the slaves, but [would] hold the matter under advisement." Whatever he did, he told his visitors, would be guided by "God's will."[29]

Lincoln's cagey response to those pressing for emancipation in the summer of 1862 personified his leadership style. At the very time that he was suggesting that he had not made up his mind about issuing an emancipatory decree, he was actually writing the preliminary proclamation. The less harried environment of the Soldiers' Home, where he spent his nights between late spring and early fall during the second, third, and fourth years of his presidency, had afforded him the ideal conditions in which to sharpen his ideas regarding how to deal with slavery. Lincoln based his decision on the legal precedents of wartime emancipation—governed by the international law of war—and constitutional authority. He later argued the constitutionality of his actions, declaring that the founding document "invests its Commander-in-chief, with the law of war, in time of war." Although enslaved people were legally property, he asked:

> Is there—has there ever been—any question that by the law of war, property, both of enemies and friends, may be taken when needed? And is it not needed whenever taking it, helps us, or hurts the enemy? Armies, the world over, destroy enemies' property when they can not use it; and even destroy their own to keep it from the enemy. Civilized belligerents do all in their power to help themselves, or hurt the enemy, except a few things regarded as barbarous or cruel.[30]

On July 22, Lincoln broached the subject of military emancipation to his cabinet members. Weighing their concerns, he decided to withhold the decree until the Union could claim a victory on the battlefield. That opportunity came on September 17, when Federal forces prevailed at the Battle of Antietam, albeit ever so slightly. Five days later, Lincoln issued the Preliminary Emancipation Proclamation, an ultimatum to the Confederate states that their slaves would be freed if they did not return to the Union by January 1 of the following year. Although taking control of the emancipation process, he had not abandoned the idea of the border states implementing plans of action. He again promised them assistance in their efforts to develop programs of gradual, compensated emancipation with the potential for colonization. Such state action to end slavery remained necessary, since the border states did not meet the criteria for military emancipation and hence would not be included in the proclamation.

If the preliminary proclamation reflected changes in Northern sentiment regarding slavery, it also aimed at preparing white men and women to accept an extraordinary transformation in the nation's commitment to freedom. War had convinced ambivalent Northerners that the demise of slavery was the only solution to the problem of disunion, but uneasiness remained. Lincoln understood that Northerners preferred gradual, compensated emancipation, with provisions for colonization. The preliminary decree was intended to signal that they need not share America with the freed people.

Even before he issued the preliminary proclamation, the president had begun to garner the support of white Americans by telling them what many wanted to hear: America could be a white man's nation if black people voluntary removed themselves from it. As calls for abolition increased, he invited a committee of five African American men to the White House, where he proposed a solution to the supposed irreconcilable differences between the races. In a one-way conversation that saw the president offering his opinions but showing no desire to solicit the thoughts of his guests, he suggested that the presence of black people in America had caused the war. The eradication of slavery, he continued, would not end the discrimination and ill use that had characterized the lives of the vast majority of African Americans. "Even when you cease to be slaves," he argued, "you are yet far removed from being placed on an equality with the white race . . . on this broad continent, not a single man of your race is made the equal of a single man of ours. Go where you are treated the best, and the ban is still upon you."[31] The meeting and Lincoln's remarks received significant attention in the press. It doubtless assured Northerners that they need not fear being overrun by hordes of freed people.

The next hundred days bridging the preliminary proclamation and the final decree were, at best, challenging for the president. Perhaps better than anyone else, he understood that in issuing the proclamation, he risked greater dissension among the Northern people. His fears were realized when the Republican Party suffered reversals in the fall elections, losing thirty-four seats in Congress to the Democrats and being forced to relinquish control of certain state legislatures. Yet the party managed to hold on to a twenty-five-seat majority in the House of Representatives and claimed seventeen of nineteen governorships. The discord caused by the preliminary proclamation momentarily dampened the enthusiasm and the optimism of abolitionists, who feared that Lincoln might be persuaded to reverse position.

Their apprehensions seemed justified when, in December, just weeks before the final proclamation was to take effect, Lincoln used the occasion of his annual message to Congress to outline a proposed constitutional amendment that would provide for compensation for any state that attempted to end slavery by 1900. In his estimation, such action would shorten the war and restore the Union more quickly. Although he indicated that the plan was "recommended as a means, not in exclusion of, but additional to, all others," its proposal so close to the January 1, 1863, deadline for the proclamation to take effect caused some to question his commitment to the decree.[32] Frederick Douglass remained optimistic that Lincoln would follow through with the promise to emancipate, but Douglass confessed that the president's failure to refer directly to the proclamation in his message, combined with his tendency to be overly concerned with border state sentiment, gave lovers of freedom cause for concern.[33]

Private and public pressures notwithstanding, Lincoln kept his promise. The final Emancipation Proclamation freed approximately three million people while exempting areas that were already under Union control. Inexplicably, colonization had been removed from the emancipation plan, and Lincoln no longer advocated compensation for owners. He pledged the military to secure and ensure the freed people's liberty and encouraged them to behave in a peaceful manner,[34] a directive that doubtless was intended to stifle criticism that he was encouraging servile insurrection by freeing the enslaved.

Lincoln's proclamation also authorized the use of black men for military service. From the very beginning of the war, African Americans, seeing the potential that the conflict held for their own elevation, had sought to enter the fight. Lincoln had ignored such pressure out of deference to the border states and because he feared the reaction of white Union soldiers. He also had initially doubted the capacity of black men to serve effectively and courageously. When pressured to accept them into military service, he had remarked that if the Union made soldiers of black men, "in a few weeks the arms would be in the hands of the rebels."[35] However, the war's attrition necessitated the enlistment of African Americans. Nearly two hundred thousand black men eventually served in the army and navy, which constituted roughly one-tenth of all Union military personnel. They saw action in 449 engagements, 39 of which were major, including Port Hudson and Milliken's Bend, Louisiana; Fort Wagner, South Carolina; and Petersburg, Virginia. Their bravery and devotion to the cause of freedom and the Union proved Lincoln and the skeptics wrong and earned the president's private and public acknowledgement of their assistance in winning the war.

The valor of black soldiers helped seal Lincoln's commitment to the Emancipation Proclamation, but such sentiment was not universally shared. While many at home and abroad praised Lincoln for his bold effort to save the Union by freeing enslaved people, others took every opportunity to criticize him. Lincoln responded to such challenges with sound arguments that were hard to counter. When he was invited by a group of Republicans (or unconditional Union men) to speak in Springfield, Illinois, in August 1863, Lincoln seized the chance to present his defense of emancipation. Although the demands of

his office required him to decline the invitation, he wrote a letter that he requested be read to the assembled audience. Lincoln skillfully addressed those
who criticized his policies: "You dislike the emancipation proclamation; and,
perhaps, would have it retracted." However, he said:

> [T]he proclamation, as law, either is valid, or is not valid. If it is not
> valid it needs no retraction. If it is valid, it can not be retracted, any
> more than the dead can be brought to life . . . [S]ome of the com-
> manders . . . who have given us our most important successes, believe
> the emancipation policy, and the use of colored troops constitute the
> heaviest blow yet dealt to the Rebellion.[36]

Lincoln reminded his critics why he had issued the proclamation in the first
place: "You say you will not fight to free negroes. I issued the proclamation on
purpose to aid you in saving the Union. Whenever you shall have conquered
all resistance to the Union, if I shall urge you to continue fighting, it will be an
apt time, then, for you to declare you will not fight to free negroes." Lincoln
suggested that through the proclamation, the nation had made a promise.
"Negroes, like other people, act upon motives," he wrote. "If they stake their
lives for us, they must be prompted by the strongest motive—even the promise
of freedom. And the promise being made, must be kept."[37]

The promise was kept, despite attempts to persuade him otherwise. When,
in the summer of 1864, he was faced with the possibility of having to negotiate
peace with the Confederacy, Lincoln considered what would happen to those
black men and women trapped behind Confederate lines. Enlisting the aid
of Frederick Douglass, he requested that a plan be devised to help secure the
freedom of those who did not know about the proclamation or who had yet to
act upon it.[38] Douglass accepted the challenge, but more favorable Union outcomes on the battlefield made his plan unnecessary. The fact that Lincoln had
sought a contingency for African Americans beyond his reach had impressed
Douglass and had convinced him that the president was guided as much by
moral conviction on the issue of slavery as by military necessity.

As Union victory loomed, the supporters of universal emancipation escalated their campaign for a law that would forever ban slavery from the United
States. In late 1863 and early 1864, several proposals for a constitutional amendment were offered, including ones from Congressman James Ashley of Ohio,

Congressman James Wilson of Iowa, and Senator Charles Sumner of Massachusetts. In response, Missouri senator John Henderson offered a joint resolution that incorporated the sentiment of Ashley's proposal as well as of the others that had been introduced. Despite a noble effort on the part of amendment supporters, the bill did not receive the required number of votes to pass the House of Representatives, but on April 8, 1864, a stronger Republican presence in the Senate secured the votes needed in that chamber.

During the debates that ensued, the president maintained an official silence. It was not for lack of interest that he did so. He had always questioned whether the Emancipation Proclamation, a measure implemented out of military necessity, could withstand legal challenge once that necessity had been removed. The proposed constitutional amendment contradicted his continuing belief, despite the Emancipation Proclamation, that abolition should be mandated and imposed by individual states. He was not yet prepared to retreat from that position. Adding to this was the very real doubt he faced over his prospects for reelection. Opponents of his tendency toward caution as well as those who demanded peace, even at the expense of black freedom, stood ready to assail him at every turn. Support for a constitutional amendment would appease one element of the opposition but would stoke the passions of others against him. As he always did in such instances, he waited.

The president's position on the constitutional amendment became evident when the Republican Party met in convention in June 1864. By spring, two factions of the party had formed. One, calling itself the Radical Democracy Party, met in Cleveland in May and nominated Frémont. The second, renamed temporarily the National Union Party, met in Baltimore and adopted a platform that supported a constitutional amendment abolishing slavery. Lincoln exerted significant influence in this decision, instructing the keynote speaker to make the amendment the center of his speech.[39] Later, in response to his renomination by the party, Lincoln publicly and officially declared his support for a thirteenth amendment. Citing the ultimatum of September 22, 1862, he suggested that the Confederate states' failure to comply justified the proposed amendment as "a fitting, and necessary conclusion to the final success of the Union cause." He urged his fellow countrymen, "In the joint names of Liberty and Union," to "labor to give it legal form, and practical effect."[40]

After he won reelection, using all the resources at his disposal as chief executive, Lincoln vigorously pushed for passage of the proposed amendment.

On January 31, 1865, the House approved it by a vote of 119 to 56, and Lincoln sent it forward for ratification. Formally prohibiting slavery throughout the nation, the amendment stipulated that "neither slavery nor involuntary servitude, except as a punishment for crime whereof the party shall have been duly convicted, shall exist within the United States, or any place subject to their jurisdiction."[41]

When the amendment was before the Senate, Senator Charles Sumner had attempted to introduce a measure that, if ratified, not only would have ended slavery but also would have proclaimed the equality of all persons before the law. There is no indication that Lincoln publicly supported so sweeping a measure. On April 11, 1865, in his last public address, he offered his own vision of what the future might hold. At a gathering assembled to celebrate Grant's victory over Lee's army, he declared that he preferred to see the elective franchise conferred on those African American men whom he declared to be "the very intelligent" and "those who serve our cause as soldiers."[42] In doing so, he reminded Americans—at once boldly *and* cautiously—that a debt was owed to people of color.

Lincoln's perspective on black freedom, many years in the making, had been altered by four years of war. Given the unfolding events that shaped the national crisis, it is hardly surprising. Lincoln was an astute politician and a pragmatic strategist; he possessed the ability to evaluate new realities with a practical eye, weigh shifting options, and change course when necessary. What is surprising, perhaps, is the facility with which he brought a significant segment of the North along with him. That success doubtless arose from the extraordinary skills he brought to the presidency and his commitment to finding a solution to the crisis within the parameters established by law. He may not have controlled events, but he was adept at making effective use of every opportunity those events offered.

Notes

1. Francis B. Carpenter, *Six Months at the White House with Abraham Lincoln* (New York: Hurd and Houghton, 1866), 90.

2. Abraham Lincoln to Albert G. Hodges, April 4, 1864, in *The Collected Works of Abraham Lincoln*, ed. Roy P. Basler et al. (New Brunswick, NJ: Rutgers University Press, 1953), 7:282.

3. Lincoln, First Inaugural Address, March 4, 1861, ibid., 4:263.

4. For recent works on Lincoln's role in bringing about black freedom, see Allen Guelzo, *Lincoln's Emancipation Proclamation: The End of Slavery in America* (New York: Simon and Schuster, 2004); Eric Foner, *The Fiery Trial: Abraham Lincoln and American Slavery* (New York: W. W. Norton and Company, 2010); Lerone Bennett, *Forced into Glory: Abraham Lincoln's White Dream* (Chicago: Johnson Publishing, 2000); Burris Carnahan, *Act of Justice: Lincoln's Emancipation Proclamation and the Law of War* (Lexington: University of Kentucky Press, 2007); James Oakes, *Freedom National: The Destruction of Slavery in the United States, 1861–1865* (New York: W. W. Norton, 2013); Louis Masur, *Lincoln's Hundred Days: The Emancipation Proclamation and the War for the Union* (Cambridge, MA: Belknap Press, 2012); and Harold Holzer, Edna Greene Medford, and Frank Williams, *The Emancipation Proclamation: Three Views* (Baton Rouge: Louisiana State University Press, 2006).

5. Frederick Douglass, "Oration in Memory of Abraham Lincoln, Delivered at the Unveiling of the Freedmen's Monument in Memory of Abraham Lincoln, in Lincoln Park, Washington, D.C., April 14, 1876," in *Frederick Douglass: Selected Speeches and Writings*, ed. Philip S. Foner and abridged and adapted by Yuval Taylor (Chicago: Lawrence Hill Books, 1999), 621.

6. Lincoln, Speech to the House of Representatives, July 27, 1848, *Collected Works*, 1:510.

7. Lincoln, Speech at Peoria, Illinois, October 16, 1854, ibid., 2:268.

8. Ibid., 2:275.

9. Lincoln, Annual Message to Congress, December 1, 1862, ibid., 5:531.

10. Lincoln, Speech at Peoria, Illinois, ibid., 2:255.

11. Lincoln, Speech on the Dred Scott Decision, June 26, 1857, ibid., 2:405.

12. Lincoln, Fourth Debate with Stephen A. Douglas at Charleston, Illinois, September 18, 1858, ibid., 3:145–46.

13. Harold Holzer, *Lincoln at Cooper Union: The Speech That Made Abraham Lincoln President* (New York: Simon and Schuster, 2004).

14. See Constitution of the Confederate States of America, art. IV, § 2, paras. 1 and 3, and § 3, para. 3, http://Avalon.law.yale.edu/19_century/csa_csa.asp.

15. For an account of Lincoln's attitude and actions during the months between the 1860 election and his inauguration, see Harold Holzer, *Lincoln, President-Elect: Abraham Lincoln and the Great Secession Winter, 1860–1861* (New York: Simon and Schuster, 2008).

16. Lincoln to Lyman Trumbull, December 10, 1860, *Collected Works*, 4:149–50.

17. Lincoln to Duff Green, December 28, 1860, ibid., 4:162.

18. Lincoln to William H. Seward, February 1, 1861, ibid., 4:183.

19. Lincoln, Proclamation Calling Militia and Convening Congress, April 15, 1861, ibid., 4:332.

20. "An Act to Confiscate Property Used for Insurrectionary Purposes," August 6, 1861, Freedmen & Southern Society Project, http://www.freedmen.umd.edu.

21. Lincoln to John C. Frémont, September 2, 1861, *Collected Works*, 4:506.

22. Lincoln to Orville H. Browning, September 22, 1861, ibid., 4:532.

23. Lincoln, Draft of Bill for Compensated Emancipation in Delaware, ibid., 5:29–30.

24. Lincoln, Message to Congress, March 6, 1862, ibid., 5:144–45. See also Oakes, *Freedom National*, and James Oakes, *The Scorpion's Sting: Antislavery and the Coming of the Civil War* (New York: W. W. Norton, 2014), in which he argues that the Republican Party believed that surrounding the slaveholding states with free states would eventually cause the institution to be destroyed. It was a strategy that was devised before the secession crisis began.

25. Lincoln, Appeal to Border State Representatives to Favor Compensated Emancipation, July 12, 1862, *Collected Works*, 5:318.

26. See Edna Greene Medford, "'Some Satisfactory Way': Lincoln and Black Freedom in the District of Columbia," *Washington History* 21 (2009): 5–6.

27. Horace Greeley to Abraham Lincoln, "The Prayer of Twenty Millions," August 19, 1862, *New York Tribune*, August 20, 1862.

28. Lincoln, Reply to Horace Greeley's "Prayer of Twenty Millions," August 22, 1862, *Collected Works*, 5:388–89.

29. Lincoln, Reply to Emancipation Memorial Presented by Chicago Christians of All Denominations, September 13, 1862, ibid., 5:420–25.

30. Lincoln to Hon. James C. Conkling, August 26, 1863, ibid., 6:407. See also Burris Carnahan, *Act of Justice: Lincoln's Emancipation Proclamation and the Law of War* (Lexington: University of Kentucky Press, 2007).

31. Lincoln, Address on Colonization to a Deputation of Negroes, August 14, 1862, *Collected Works*, 5:371–72.

32. Lincoln, Annual Message to Congress, December 1, 1862, ibid., 5:530.

33. *The Life and Writings of Frederick Douglass*, ed. Philip Foner (New York: International Publishers, 1975), 3:309.

34. Lincoln, Emancipation Proclamation, January 1, 1863, *Collected Works*, 6:28.

35. Lincoln, Reply to the Emancipation Memorial Presented by Chicago Christians . . . , ibid., 5:423.

36. Lincoln to James C. Conkling, August 26, 1863, ibid., 6:408.

37. Ibid., 409.

38. *Frederick Douglass: Autobiographies*, ed. Henry Louis Gates Jr. (New York: Library of America, 1994), 796.

39. For a discussion of Lincoln's role in the successful passage of the constitutional amendment in 1865, see Michael Vorenberg, *Final Freedom: The Civil War, the Abolition of Slavery, and the Thirteenth Amendment* (New York: Cambridge University Press, 2001).

40. Lincoln, Reply to Committee Notifying Lincoln of His Renomination, June 9, 1864, *Collected Works*, 7:380.

41. Thirteenth Amendment to the US Constitution, *Our Documents*, http://www.ourdocuments.gov.

42. Lincoln, Last Public Address, April 11, 1865, *Collected Works*, 8:403.

THE QUALITY OF MERCY: ABRAHAM LINCOLN AND THE PRESIDENTIAL POWER TO PARDON

Ron Soodalter

*Pardon: The action of an executive official
of the government that mitigates or sets
aside the punishment for a crime.*

Article II, Section 2, of the Constitution states clearly that the president "shall have the Power to grant Reprieves and Pardons for Offenses against the United States." There are no qualifiers, no conditions; the president can pardon whomever he chooses. No president in the history of this nation has been so praised, or so criticized, for his use of the pardoning power as Abraham Lincoln.

Generations of Americans have envisioned Lincoln as something of an "aw-shucks" backwoodsman, who somehow found himself at the nation's helm during its greatest crisis. We often tend to forget that Lincoln did not become his party's nominee to the highest office in the land by accident; he knew and played the political game with finesse. As Lincoln biographer William Lee Miller noted, he was not a "folksy and jocular countryman swapping yarns at the village store or making his way to the White House by uncertain and awkward steps or presiding like a father, a tear in his eye, over the tragedy of the Civil War." To the contrary, he was "intent, self-controlled, strong in intellect, tenacious of purpose."[1] And as an experienced and successful trial attorney, he was certainly familiar with the law.

This being said, there is no question that Lincoln was blessed—or perhaps cursed—with a highly compassionate nature. It is possible that the vicissitudes of his upbringing accounted for his inordinately warm heart. As Miller wrote, "Those who knew him in Illinois before he became president said he was an unusually generous human being. He was reported to have more sympathy with the suffering of his fellow creatures than was really advantageous in a ruler—not only for lost cats, mired-down hogs, birds fallen out of the nest,

Harper's Weekly *print of the execution of Nathaniel Gordon. Abraham Lincoln's compassionate nature did not extend to a convicted slave trader. Courtesy of the Library of Congress, LC-DIG-ds-00692.*

but also for his fellow human beings."[2] As president, Lincoln was called upon time and again to draw from this seemingly bottomless well of compassion.

Early in his administration, Lincoln earned a reputation for the liberal use of the power to pardon. He was to some a man of kindness and mercy, to others a sentimental meddler who was continually undermining military discipline and the sanctity of the courts. Three men who felt that Lincoln had to be protected from his own kinder instincts were members of his cabinet— Secretary of the Navy Gideon Welles, Treasury Secretary Salmon P. Chase, and Attorney General Edward Bates.

The president, Welles confided to his diary, "is always disposed to mitigate punishment, and to grant favors. Sometimes this is a weakness."[3] Chase felt that Lincoln's tendency to pardon soldiers would ultimately weaken the war effort. "Such kindness to the criminal," he wrote, "is cruelty to the army, for it encourages the bad to leave the brave and patriotic unsupported."[4] Bates defined Lincoln as an ideal man with but one failing:

> I have sometimes told him . . . that he was unfit to be entrusted with the pardoning power. Why, if a man comes to him with a touching story his judgment is almost certain to be affected by it. Should the applicant be a woman—a wife, a mother or a sister,—in nine cases out of ten her tears, if nothing else, are sure to prevail.[5]

The pardon clerk for the Justice Department wrote, "My chief, Attorney Bates, soon discovered that my most important duty was to keep all but the most deserving cases from coming before the kind Mr. Lincoln at all, since there was nothing harder for him to do than to put aside a prisoner's application and he could not resist it when it was urged by a pleading wife and a weeping child."[6] And Lincoln's own correspondence secretary, William O. Stoddard, said that Lincoln was "downright sure to pardon any case" in which he saw "a fair excuse for pardoning. . . . Some people think he carries his mercy too far."[7]

It is hard to imagine the constant assault upon Lincoln's sensibilities by the petitions of desperate people. Take, for example, the letter of young Sally Petty, of which this is a brief excerpt:

> Mr. President Lincoln
>
> Dear Sir I take my pen in hand with a broken heart to try to write you a few lines. . . . I cannot write for weeping. I am a poor little helpless girl of 13 years. . . . O Mr. Lincoln they have sentenced my

papa . . . to be shot. O . . . won't you pardon him. . . . how can I
live and no papa to protect me. . . . O Mr. Lincoln . . . If you let
my papa be killed it will kill me and mother too.[8]

There were three areas in which Lincoln's pardoning power pertained. The
first of these related to cases in the civil courts; these included murder, treason,
assault, mutiny, embezzlement, rape, violations of the Fugitive Slave Act, and the
slave trade. According to the records of the State and Justice Departments, Lincoln reviewed 456 civil cases; 375 of them—over 82 percent—received pardons.[9]

The second category in which Lincoln had pardoning power was in military cases. It was here that Lincoln received the most criticism for what was
perceived—not without some justification—as his interference in the flow
of military justice and discipline. Lincoln did, in fact, have a tendency to
pardon boys who had fallen asleep on guard duty or who had deserted. His
inclination toward mercy was certainly not lost on his officers. General William Tecumseh Sherman made his frustration known in an 1864 letter to the
judge advocate general, writing that he planned to "execute a good many spies
and guerillas—without bothering the President. Too many spies and villains
escape us . . . and we all know that it is very hard for the President to hang
spies, even after conviction, when a troop of his friends follow the sentence
with earnest . . . appeals."[10]

General Joseph Hooker once sent an envelope to the president containing
the cases of fifty-five convicted and doomed deserters; Lincoln merely wrote,
"Pardoned," on the envelope and returned it to Hooker.[11] Colonel Theodore
Lyman, serving under General George Meade in the Army of the Potomac,
was frustrated by what he referred to as Lincoln's "false merciful policy,"
opining, "If we attempt to shoot a deserter, you pardon him and our army is
without discipline."[12]

Looked at objectively, Lincoln probably did interfere too freely in affairs of
military discipline. More than a few believed that greater restraint would prove
the kinder path in the long run. General Sherman once commented, "Forty or
fifty executions now would in the next twelve months save a thousand lives."[13]

Lincoln's approach to clemency for those in the ranks was neither whimsical
nor haphazard. He was pragmatic—or, as one historian put it, "discriminat-
ing."[14] He believed that the most serious offenders should be punished, and
they often were. Certain crimes aroused his righteous anger; neither wanton
murderers nor rapists could expect to receive his consideration. The military
executed 267 men during the war, and each order required Lincoln's signature.

But he would not countenance taking life if no good would be served. He made it clear to General Meade that he was "unwilling for any boy under eighteen to be shot."[15] As a rule, he disallowed shooting men for desertion. In justifying his arrest of Clement L. Vallandigham, Ohio Democratic congressman and virulent antiwar Copperhead, Lincoln wrote, "Must I shoot a simple minded soldier boy who deserts, while I must not touch a hair of a wily agitator who induces him to desert? I think that in such a case to silence the agitator and save the boy, is not only constitutional but withal a great mercy."[16]

Lincoln was not unaware of the impact the wholesale execution of deserters would have on those on the home front, many of whom had sent husbands, fathers, brothers, and sons into battle. In 1862, at a time when desertion was rife, he was asked why he repeatedly refused to enforce the prescribed penalty. "Because you cannot order men shot by the dozens and twenties," he replied. "People won't stand it, and they ought not stand it."[17]

The third class of cases calling for Lincoln's presidential review—and possibly his clemency—had to do with those in rebellion against the government. This being the Civil War, nearly half the country fell into this category. Lincoln's attitude toward the South reflected the greatest expression of his mercy. He wanted nothing more than a return of the seceded states to their former place in the Union and was ready at any time to grant a general amnesty with a remission of all penalties, except the loss of property in slaves, if the measure hastened the return of peace and the end of the Confederacy.

Not all of Lincoln's pardons were expressions of kindness and compassion. Being an astute politician, he was not above granting clemency for the sake of expedience. During the presidential campaign of 1864, Lincoln pardoned a condemned contractor at the urging of three prominent New York statesmen. He did so in order to help secure New York State's votes in the upcoming election. In another instance, Lincoln bowed to the request of prominent—and influential—Massachusetts senator Charles Sumner and pardoned a group of Boston contractors who had been convicted of defrauding the government in filling naval contracts.[18]

Lincoln's old friend and former law partner, William Herndon, wrote that the president "would strain a point to be kind, but he never strained it to breaking. He would be just as kind and generous as his judgment would let him be—no more."[19] Lincoln brought to each case his fine sense of justice, and he generally knew when to let the law take its course. He offered no pardon to bounty jumpers or recruiters for the Confederacy. He refused to show favoritism to officers over enlisted men and turned a deaf ear to the pleas of repeat deserters and of soldiers whose offenses smacked of meanness or brutality. Lincoln always looked to the consequences of his actions.

When Illinois congressman Henry Bromwell, a friend of Lincoln's, visited the White House in 1865, the president complained of the constant pressure to pardon or reprieve men. He spoke of the unending line of petitioners:

> "It seems to me," he said, "they will wear the very life out of me; but then all these other matters are nothing to these cases of life and death—and there are so many of them, and they all fall on me. I reckon there never was a man raised in the country, on a farm, where they are always butchering cattle and hogs and think nothing of it, that ever grew up with such an aversion to bloodshed as I have and yet I've had more questions of life and death to settle in four years than all the men who ever sat in this chair put together. But, I've managed to get along and do my duty, as I believe, and still save most of them. . . . But there must have been some of them I couldn't save—there are some cases where the law must be executed."[20]

The Lincoln we see here is a man who is empathetic and kind, but he is also the leader of a powerful, war-torn nation, keenly aware that his decisions—great and small—inevitably have to reflect that nation's greater good. Of the hundreds of cases, both civilian and military, that called on Lincoln's much-touted sense of compassion, a handful stand out, not as incidences in which Lincoln extended his mercy, but as examples of cases where—in deference to the law and to the nation's well-being—he withheld it.

TO HANG A SLAVER

Early in the war, Lincoln found himself considering clemency for Nathaniel Gordon, a young New England sea captain who had been sentenced to die. A noted reverend from Portland, Maine, wrote an impassioned letter to the president, avowing that the condemned had been a member of his Sunday school when a boy and came from solid New England stock. Petitions containing thousands of names came to Lincoln's desk seeking clemency. The law under which the man had been condemned, they said, had been a dead letter for decades and did not justify taking a man's life. He had harmed no Americans, they argued, and committed no act of treason. Have pity, they pleaded, on his poor widowed mother and on his young wife and small son. Rhoda White, the wife of a New York judge—a strong Lincoln supporter—came to the White House, bringing with her Gordon's wife and mother. It was a particularly difficult time for the Lincolns; two of their sons had contracted typhoid, and although young Tad eventually recovered, eleven-year-old Willy lay dying. He was Lincoln's pet, and President and Mrs. Lincoln were beside themselves with grief.

Mrs. White, aware of the situation in the White House, wrote Lincoln exactly the type of entreaty that had worked so often in the past: "I would not intrude upon the sanctity of your sick room and upon your hours of grief but for the sake of Mercy, and for the sake of an afflicted Mother and wife who are bowed down with sorrow and look to God and to you to lift the heavy burden they are suffering under."[21]

This time, however, the usual entreaties failed; the merciful Lincoln, the supposed "soft touch" for a weeping wife and grieving mother, refused to see them. And so they were given an audience with Mary Lincoln. The condemned man's wife gave the First Lady a poem of her own composition. It begins:

> Within your power it lies to save
> My husband from an early grave;
> And rescue from a life of shame,
> The wife and child who bear his name.[22]

Mary, coming fresh from her dying son's bed, was deeply moved. She attempted to discuss a commutation with her husband; he flatly refused.

What was it about this case that the pleas for clemency failed to call forth Lincoln's widely touted mercy? The answer lies in the nature of Nathaniel Gordon's crime. His ancestors, who had arrived on these shores in 1621, had always made their living from the sea. His chosen method was both disreputable and illegal: he was a professional slave trader. He would sail to Africa's coastal slave markets, fill his hold with hundreds of suffering captives, and sell them on the blocks of Rio and Havana. Although this was a stunningly profitable enterprise, there was no uglier path to wealth. As the commander of Britain's Royal Africa Company had written centuries before, "Your captains and mates . . . must neither have dainty fingers or dainty noses; it's a filthy voyage and few men are fit for [it] but them that are bred up to it."[23] Nathaniel Gordon was such a man. He had completed at least three voyages and was caught at sea on his fourth, with nearly nine hundred Africans—half of them children—in the hold of his small ship.

The law, which had been passed more than forty years earlier, was clear: if you trafficked in slaves, you would hang. Unfortunately, the government, the courts, and the military did not take the law very seriously; in over four decades, not a single slaver had been executed, and few had been punished at all. Juries were either bribed or unwilling to hang an American for simply conveying slaves from Africa to a foreign country, when it was perfectly legal to sell and transport slaves from, say, Virginia to Louisiana.

It had taken two trials to convict Gordon; the first ended in a hung jury, almost certainly because of bribery. The prosecutor was Edward Delafield Smith, a recent Republican appointee to the office of US attorney. He was intent on driving the burgeoning slave trade from New York and determined to see a slave trader punished to the full extent of the statute. William Davis Shipman, an honest jurist who was trying his first slaving case, was outraged at the nature of Gordon's offense and saw no reason why the slaver should not receive the death penalty. Now it was up to President Lincoln to decide whether the law forbidding human trafficking was, in fact, a dead letter.

Most people of the mid-nineteenth century, just as with people today, were oblivious to the terrible nature of the slave trade—and terrible it was. The horrors of a typical slaving voyage strained credulity. Deaths were inevitable; it was just a question of numbers. The deaths were so frequent that the crewmen of slavers often told of schools of sharks following their ships all the way from Africa to their final destination. Much has been written about the horrors of the Middle Passage—the voyage from Africa to America, Brazil, or the islands of the Caribbean—which took from several weeks to three months. In the 1850s, US Navy lieutenant T. A. Craven recorded his firsthand impressions of the conditions aboard a slaver, where the captives were already debilitated, often ill, and half-starved after making the trek from the African interior to the coast and the waiting slave ship:

> The negroes are packed below in as dense a mass as it is possible for human beings to be crowded; the space allotted them being . . . about four feet high between decks, there, of course, can be but little ventilation. . . . These unfortunate creatures are obliged to attend to the calls of nature in this place—tubs being provided for the purpose— and here they pass their days, their nights, amidst the most horribly offensive odors of which the mind can conceive, and this under the scorching heat of the tropical sun, without room enough for sleep;

with scarcely space to die in; with daily allowance of food and water barely sufficient to keep them alive. . . . [A]nd when [the voyage] has much exceeded the shorter time disease has appeared in its most appalling forms, the provisions and water are nearly exhausted, and their sufferings are incredible.[24]

The death rate among the captives varied, depending on the length of the voyage, the severity of conditions onboard, and the callousness of captain and crew. During the early 1800s, it averaged 17.5 percent among American slavers; out of every 1,000 Africans shipped as slaves, approximately 175 perished. They died of disease, thirst, starvation, suffocation, exhaustion, suicide, and sometimes simply despair.[25]

Stories abound of slaver captains who chose to jettison their cargo rather than face fines, imprisonment, or forfeiture of their vessels. One such slaver, an Englishman named Homans, had already completed ten successful voyages, delivering about five thousand Africans to the shores of Brazil and Cuba. On the return of his eleventh voyage, he found his brig, the *Brillante*, surrounded by four cruisers. He immediately had his cargo of six hundred manacled captives herded to the rail and bound to the anchor chain. When the cruisers' boats made for the *Brillante*, Homans had the anchor thrown over the side; it plummeted to the ocean floor, carrying with it every man, woman, and child. When the warships' crews boarded the *Brillante*, they found clear evidence that several hundred human beings had occupied the hold only moments before, but they could do nothing. They were forced to release the brig, as Homans "jeered in their faces and defied them as they stood on his deck."[26]

What would allow for such a callous disregard for life? In a word, greed. A successful slaving voyage was profitable beyond all reason. It has been estimated that during the mid-1800s, a slave purchased in Africa for approximately $40 worth of trade goods would bring a price ranging from $400 to $1,200. Therefore, the selling price of a cargo of, say, eight hundred slaves ranged between $320,000 and $960,000. Even after factoring in the cost of outfitting the ship, paying off all the people involved in the voyage, and the inevitable loss of "inventory," a successful slaving expedition realized a profit many times in excess of the initial investment. Consider that $100 in the 1850s would be worth around $4,000 today, and the allure of such a venture becomes apparent. Given such returns, one successful trip could easily make the fortunes of investors and captain.[27]

Lincoln had always been clear on his feelings toward the *institution* of slavery, as he stated in 1858: "I have always hated slavery, I think as much as any Abolitionist." But he made no secret of his position on the legality of slavery where it already existed: "I have said it a hundred times, and I have now no inclination to take it back, that I believe there is no right, and ought to be no inclination in the people of the free States to enter into the slave states, and interfere with the question of slavery at all. I have said that always."[28] If slavery was to end, it must be through the force of law, and Lincoln—whose background as a lawyer had instilled in him an abiding respect for the Constitution—was fully prepared to put aside his personal feelings, strong though they might be, in deference to it.

Lincoln had no such ambivalence regarding the slave trade; he abhorred it. Slavery was bad enough, but to make one's fortune through the buying and selling of human beings was beyond evil. And what was more, the law forbade it. In an early campaign speech, he had painted the slave trader as an arch villain: "The poor Negro has some natural right to himself. . . . [T]hose who deny it, and make mere merchandise of him, deserve kickings, contempt and death."[29]

Now was his chance to put the force of law behind his words, and he was firmly resolved to do so. On one of the numerous occasions when he was asked to consider mercy for Gordon, he responded:

> I think I would personally prefer to let this man live in confinement and let him meditate on his deeds, yet in the name of justice and the majesty of law, there ought to be one case, at least one specific instance, of a professional slave-trader, a Northern white man, given the exact penalty of death because of the incalculable number of deaths he and his kind inflicted upon black men amid the horror of the sea-voyage from Africa.[30]

Just weeks before his own death, Lincoln told Congressman Bromwell, "There was that man who was sentenced for piracy and slave-trading on the high seas. . . . [Y]ou don't know how they followed and pressed to get him pardoned, or his sentence commuted, but there was no use of talking. It had to be done; I couldn't help him."[31]

Aware that the condemned man had been misled by his lawyers and supporters into believing he would live, Lincoln gave him a two-week reprieve to make his peace with God. On February 21, 1862, Nathaniel Gordon was hanged in the courtyard of New York City's prison.

PHYSICIAN, HEAL THYSELF

The following year, an unusual capital case arose that called on Lincoln's mercy. The condemned man, Dr. David M. Wright, was a highly revered citizen of Norfolk, Virginia. When he moved there from North Carolina a decade earlier, the local newspaper cited his "personal character" as "untarnished," describing him as a "gentleman in all aspects." By 1863, there was no question that Dr. Wright's standing in the community was stellar.[32]

Norfolk, a vital naval center in the state that contained the Rebel capital, had been in Federal hands since March 1862, and the populace bridled at the occupation. On July 11, 1863, as Dr. Wright watched from a storefront, a company of Union soldiers marched up the sidewalk on which he was standing. They were the men of Company B, First Regiment—and they were black.

When President Lincoln issued his Emancipation Proclamation on January 1, 1863, he had included a controversial provision stating that African Americans would "be received into the armed forces of the United States." Racism was endemic in America at the time, and while many in the North had difficulty accepting the fact of black men in Union blue, Southerners were apoplectic. The Confederate Congress passed a resolution dictating that African American officers, when captured, were to be "put to death or otherwise punished" as the Rebel commanders saw fit.[33] Black enlisted prisoners were to be "returned" to slavery—even if they had enlisted as free men. Rather than distinguishing between officers and enlisted men, some Rebel commanders simply chose to kill any and all black troops they captured wearing Federal uniforms. With the Confederate government itself mandating a no-quarter treatment of African American prisoners, it followed that—to the citizens of Norfolk and the slave-bound South in general—the only thing more hateful than the sight of a Yankee soldier was that of a *black* Yankee soldier.

As Dr. David Wright watched indignantly, a "colored" company was marching up the Main Street sidewalk—*his* sidewalk. Commanding the unit was a twenty-one-year-old Vermonter, Lieutenant A. L. Sanborn. A number of citizens shouted epithets at the soldiers as they passed. Dr. Wright, however, apparently outdid himself, flinging insults at the young officer that he later admitted were "offensive." Furious, Lieutenant Sanborn sent for the provost marshal. According to the July 25, 1863, edition of the *Caledonian* of St. Johnsbury, Vermont, "The lieutenant halted his company, and walking toward the doctor, said, 'I am a United States officer, consider yourself under arrest.'"[34] Producing a Colt revolver from behind his back, Wright fired three shots into Sanborn, who managed to bring Wright to the ground before expiring. Only the timely intervention of the colonel of a nearby regiment kept Sanborn's outraged troops from bayoneting Wright on the spot. As the doctor was being led away under arrest, he suddenly remembered his calling and said, "Let me do something for this man," indicating the young lieutenant, who lay bleeding to death as a result of Wright's bullets. His offer was ignored.[35]

Northern and Southern iterations of the story sprang up practically overnight. The words of Confederate secretary of war James Seddon typified the Southern viewpoint. Seddon made no claim of self-defense on Wright's part, but rather of "natural indignation" at seeing the "shameful spectacle" of "colored" troops in the streets of his hometown. Seddon justified Wright's actions as a "prompt vindication of his honor"—as no doubt did countless thousands of Southerners.[36]

To the Northerners, however, and most specifically to Judge Advocate General Joseph Holt, it was an "unprovoked assassination," and that is precisely how Holt later described it to President Lincoln in his summary of the case. Because Norfolk was under the command of the Union army, Wright was tried before a military commission consisting of three officers. According to the charge, to which Dr. Wright entered a "not guilty" plea, he "did willfully, feloniously, and with malice aforethought kill and murder A. L. Sanborn . . . by shooting him to death with a pistol."[37]

Wright's two-man legal team was well chosen. Both were highly skilled lawyers and staunch Union men, one a US senator and the other a former US attorney and a congressman-elect. Their defense was singular, to say the least. First they challenged the military court's jurisdiction, and failing that, they claimed the defendant was not guilty on the recently recognized grounds of temporary insanity. Just four years earlier, congressman, scoundrel, and now Union general Daniel Sickles had accosted and cold-bloodedly slain his wife's lover, Washington district attorney Philip Barton Key. Sickles's attorneys invoked the "temporary insanity" defense for the first time in legal history and got him acquitted.[38] Dr. Wright's lawyers reasoned that if it had worked once, it could work again.

When the court refused to allow them to introduce evidence supporting the insanity claim, Wright's lawyers withdrew from the trial and applied directly to President Lincoln for a pardon. Wright, suddenly left without counsel, now had to represent himself and soon proved the old adage that "a man who is his own lawyer has a fool for a client." Friends had advised him to remain mute, but given the opportunity to address the court, Wright insisted on explaining himself—which, fatally for his case, he did. He lodged his self-justification in a long-winded speech on Southern honor—and blatant, unfettered racism. "Who does not know," he asked, presumably rhetorically, "that these creatures, the Negroes, when restraint is removed, become unmanageable savages?" Wright went on, growing increasingly passionate and emphatic as he spoke: "[I]s it to be supposed that a citizen of Norfolk, himself an owner of slaves, not knowing what some of my slaves was in that company, would submit to be arrested by Negroes, and marched off to the guard house? No, sir, I would not submit to that."[39]

So much for a temporary insanity defense. By his own admission, he had simply refused "to be arrested by Negroes." Soon the trial transcript would pass up the ladder of command to the president. Wright's remarks would prove anything but helpful to him when it came time for Lincoln to consider a pardon. Realizing how badly he had damaged his own case, Wright asked the court to exclude his remarks from the record—to no avail.

Had he been tried by a jury of his fellow citizens, Southerners who shared Wright's views of honor and race, he might well have gotten off. However, the military court declared him guilty and sentenced him to die on the gallows. Dr. David Wright's life now lay in the hands of President Lincoln.

The petitions flooded in, as Wright's supporters extolled the condemned man's fine qualities and sterling reputation. Just one month after the Battle of Gettysburg, with its tens of thousands of casualties, had earned the distinction of being the bloodiest battle in American history, Lincoln gave the case of this one Southern doctor his full attention. He ordered the execution halted until he had a chance to examine the papers, which, as a former trial attorney of some repute, he was more than qualified to do. He subsequently reviewed the transcript and, after satisfying himself that there had been no improprieties in the conduct of the trial, summoned Wright's two lawyers to present their purported "mass of testimony" in proof of their client's insanity. Wright himself had all but placed the noose around his own neck by acknowledging that he had shot Lieutenant Sanborn—a total stranger to him until that moment—in defense of his Southern sense of outraged racial purity. As Lincoln saw it, the only possible justification for a pardon now lay in establishing that Wright had not been in his right mind at the time of the murder.

Secretary of State William Seward recommended to Lincoln the name of a leading mental health specialist, Dr. John P. Gray, editor of the *American Journal of Insanity*, whom the president engaged and sent to Fort Monroe to examine Dr. Wright. Lincoln ordered a hearing and assigned a judge advocate to the case. Presiding over what was in fact a second, civilian, trial, Dr. Gray called twenty-six witnesses: thirteen for the defense and thirteen for the prosecution. Finally, satisfied that the case for temporary insanity had not been satisfactorily established, Dr. Gray wrote his report to the president.

On October 7, Lincoln recorded his actions and the grounds for his subsequent decision:

> Being satisfied that no proper question remained except as to the insanity of the accused, I caused a very full examination to be made on that question, upon a great amount of evidence, including all offered by counsel of accused, by an expert of high reputation in that professional department, who thereupon reports to me, as his opinion, that the accused Dr. David M. Wright, was not insane prior to or on the 11th day of July, 1863, the date of the homicide of Lieutenant Sanborn; that he has not been insane since, and is not insane now.[40]

As he had done with Nathaniel Gordon, Lincoln allowed Wright a one-week reprieve to make "his preparation." One of Wright's lawyers sought to make good use of the time and requested that Lincoln receive the doctor's wife. Again Lincoln refused to entertain the pleas of a distraught woman, responding, "It would be useless for Mrs. Dr. Wright to come here. . . . [T]he case is settled."[41]

After a foiled escape attempt, an unsuccessful bribe offer, and a rejected plea for an exchange of prisoners, Dr. Wright was hanged at Fort Monroe on October 23, 1863. As he stood on the gallows, he assured the gathered throng, "The act which I committed was done without the slightest malice."[42] President Lincoln, who had devoted more than a reasonable amount of time and attention to the case, found otherwise.

IN THE DEFENSE OF MY COUNTRY

One of the most dramatic cases in which Lincoln withheld his mercy was that of the Confederate officer John Yates Beall. Beall was the embodiment of the Victorian concept of chivalry—young, handsome, and selflessly dedicated to the Southern cause. Born to an old and distinguished Virginia family, he studied law at the University of Virginia, returning home to run the family plantation, Walnut Grove, at his father's death. When the war began, Beall enlisted in the legendary Stonewall Brigade of the Second Virginia Regiment. He fought bravely, suffering a serious lung wound during a charge at the Battle of Falling Waters.

After recovering from his wound, Beall put together a ranger company with the authorization of Confederate president Jefferson Davis. He staged raids against Union shipping along the Lower Potomac, where he became known as the "Mosby of the Chesapeake."

In late 1864, Beall received Davis's approval to attack the Union prison on Johnson's Island in Lake Erie and liberate the three thousand Confederate prisoners of war—all officers—incarcerated there. He and his nineteen-man force commandeered two vessels and steamed toward Johnson's Island, but somehow their plan had been discovered, and they were forced to flee to Canada with a Yankee gunboat in hot pursuit. Less than three months later, Beall made his way to upstate New York, where he was arrested in an attempt to stop a Union train carrying seven Confederate generals on their way to Fort Lafayette Military Prison. He was tried by a military court on charges of being a spy and a "guerrillero," or guerrilla, and was sentenced to hang.[43]

Media coverage of Beall and his trial was fairly extensive, and the case became something of a cause célèbre. Lincoln's office was flooded with appeals for clemency, including letters from ninety-two members of Congress. Lincoln personally received as supplicants in his office the librarian of Congress, the president of the Baltimore and Ohio Railroad, former postmaster general Montgomery Blair, and the governor of Massachusetts. General and future president James A. Garfield asked Lincoln to grant the young man a reprieve. At one point, Lincoln received a visit from Roger Pryor, the recently released Confederate general who had shared a cell with Beall and who now spoke eloquently of the young man's fine qualities. The reasoning was consistent: John Yates Beall was merely following his superiors' orders as a loyal and dedicated officer.

Orville Browning, a prominent attorney and an old friend of Lincoln's, was retained by several Beall supporters in the hope that he might sway the president. Confederate president Jefferson Davis took time away from a war that was going badly to write to the court affirming that Beall had been acting under his orders. The court, however, would not admit the letter into evidence. Beall's sister visited the White House to plead with the president for mercy. And through a friend, Beall sent the trial record to President Lincoln along with a dignified letter stating, "Some of the evidence is true, some false. I am not a spy nor a guerrilla. The execution of the sentence will be murder."[44]

The end of the war was only weeks away, and many made the argument that nothing would be gained by the death of this young man. However, the commander of the Eastern District, General John Dix, had sworn to hang any

Rebel operatives he apprehended, and he pressured Lincoln not to interfere in the interest of the "security of the community."

There was more to Dix's "national security" position than simply the desire to execute captured Rebels. By late 1864, it was obvious to all but the most benighted that the South was losing the war. Approved and financed by President Davis and his cabinet, the Rebels hatched a number of desperate secret plots, many of them originating with the Confederate Secret Service branch operating out of a base in Ontario. Their main objective was the dissemination of death and terror throughout the North.

One of the most chilling plots involved the attempted burning of New York City. Conceived to disrupt the November 1864 elections, aid in a hoped-for Copperhead uprising, and bring home to the North a taste of the destruction the Union forces had been visiting on the South, the plan was configured to destroy Manhattan, as well as other major Union cities. On November 25, rooms in about thirteen New York hotels, as well as various public buildings, including theaters and P. T. Barnum's Broadway museum of curiosities, were set ablaze using the highly volatile chemical agent known as Greek fire. However, a combination of an unreliable incendiary and the plotters' inexperience ensured that the damage was relatively slight. Only one Rebel operative was caught, he was subsequently tried, condemned, and hanged at Fort Lafayette.[45]

Other plots involved the distribution (by a doctor, no less) of blankets infected with yellow fever, the poisoning of a major city's water supply, and the demolition of the White House. A Rebel cavalry detachment rode out of Canada into a small Vermont community, robbed its banks, killed a local, and attempted to burn the town to the ground. It was exactly these types of behind-the-lines activities, aimed at an interminable war of attrition rather than a swift resolution to the conflict, that the Union administration and the nation at large had come to fear.

Lincoln must have personally sympathized with Beall, a sincere, appealing, and devout young man who had acted on behalf of his country. A visit to the White House by Beall's tearful sister certainly caught Lincoln where he was most vulnerable. Although Beall was a sympathetic and attractive character, however, he had been caught behind enemy lines dressed in civilian clothes after a failed attempt to derail a train—a desperate act that might well have resulted in several deaths and that today would be considered an act of domestic terrorism. As a lawyer, Lincoln was keenly aware not only of the severity of Beall's actions but also of their legal ramifications. After much deliberation, Lincoln determined to allow the sentence to stand.

John Yates Beall was hanged on Governor's Island in New York Harbor on February 24, 1865. On the morning of his execution, he asked to have his picture taken for his family, fiancée, and friends; the resulting photograph shows a serene-appearing young man, strong of feature, with a well-trimmed goatee. Nothing in his manner suggests the fate awaiting him outside his cell. As he approached the gallows, flanked by Union soldiers, he remarked, "The sun shines brightly; I now see it for the last time." When asked if he had anything to say, Beall responded in a clear voice, "I protest against the execution of this sentence. It is absolute murder—brutal murder. I die in the defense and service of my country."[46]

The editor of the *Richmond Examiner*, outraged at Beall's execution, wrote, "True to their cowardly instincts, the Yankees carried out their mad purpose of hanging Captain Beall. . . . The Yankees, it will be recollected, trumped up the charge against him of being a 'spy and guerilla,' but the truth is, he was merely a prisoner of war."[47]

The president was deeply affected by the execution. A full month after the event—and shortly before his assassination—he confided to Henry Bromwell:

> That was a case where there must be an example. They tried me every way. They wouldn't give up; but I had to stand firm on that, and I even had to turn away his poor sister when she came and begged for his life, and [I] let him be executed, and he was executed, and I can't get the distress out of my mind yet.[48]

LINCOLN AND THE INDIANS

Very few people are aware that Abraham Lincoln was responsible for the largest mass execution—and the greatest act of executive clemency—in our nation's history. The case, which had nothing to do with the Civil War, placed perhaps the greatest demand of all on Lincoln's sense of mercy and of justice.

The history of our government's relations with the Indians is disgraceful. It is fair to say that Congress never made a treaty that it was not more than willing to break at the slightest provocation. Throughout the eighteenth and nineteenth centuries, tribe after tribe was left with no recourse other than rebellion or starvation. The Dakota Sioux were no exception. In 1851—ten years before the Civil War and Lincoln's assumption of the presidency—the United States signed two treaties with the Sioux that resulted in the tribe giving up huge portions of Minnesota. In exchange, they were promised compensation in the form of cash and trade goods and directed to live on a reservation along the upper Minnesota River. The thoroughly corrupt Bureau of Indian Affairs was responsible for overseeing the terms of the treaties; this was akin to entrusting the sheep to a pack of wolves. Not surprisingly, many of the trade goods were substandard and overvalued by several hundred percent. The promised payments often were not forthcoming—either never sent or stolen by Washington functionaries, crooked traders, and Indian agents.

This situation continued for years. Finally, in 1858—the year Minnesota entered the Union—a party of Sioux led by Chief Little Crow visited Washington to see about proper enforcement of the treaties. It did not go the way they had hoped; instead of acknowledging the Sioux grievances, the US government took back half their reservation and opened it up to white settlement. The land was cleared, and the hunting and fishing that had sustained the Sioux virtually ended. The situation worsened with each passing year, with the Sioux suffering increasing hunger and hardship. They had tried in vain to appeal to the traders; the traders' representative—a clod of a fellow named Andrew Jackson Myrick—responded with the comment "So far as I am concerned, if they are hungry, let them eat grass or their own dung."[49]

In August 1862, the powder keg exploded. Under the leadership of Little Crow, several bands held a war council and set about attacking the new settlements, killing white settlers and burning the buildings. According to some accounts, Myrick was one of the first casualties, and when his body was discovered, his mouth was stuffed with grass.[50] In response to the uprising, a combined force of militia and volunteer infantry set out to subdue the hostiles; the result was a resounding defeat for the army. Emboldened by victory, roving bands of Sioux destroyed entire townships, plundering and killing as they went.

A number of desperate appeals for help had gone to Lincoln, but at this juncture, he was immersed in such day-to-day matters as the stunning disaster at Second Bull Run, Lee's invasion of Maryland, McClellan's heartbreaking failure to end the war at Antietam, and the release of the Preliminary Emancipation Proclamation. Finally, more than a month after the Sioux outbreak, President Lincoln responded by assigning the pompous General John Pope, fresh from his defeat at Bull Run, the task of ending the uprising. Pope declared it his "purpose to utterly exterminate the Sioux," saying, "They are to be treated as maniacs and wild beasts."[51] The army finally subdued the Indians. Those who surrendered were promised safety. The butcher's bill at the end of the hostilities totaled about seventy-seven soldiers killed, seventy-five to one hundred Sioux, and somewhere between three hundred and eight hundred settlers; no one took an accurate count.

Hundreds of Sioux were arrested—some of whom had had nothing to do with the uprising—and summarily tried by a five-man military commission. The trials were perfunctory affairs, some lasting less than five minutes. More than forty cases were judged in one day alone. Due process played no part; the defendants—many of whom spoke no English—did not have a clue what was happening, and if any admitted to so much as firing a gun, he was condemned. Of the 393 tried for "murder and other outrages," 323 were convicted, with 303 sentenced to hang—including those who had surrendered with a promise of safety.

As always, the final approval for the executions rested with the president. General Pope, seeking a quick and dramatic finish to the affair, pressured Lincoln to sign the orders for all 303 executions. Nor was he alone; outraged newspaper editors and congressmen advocated a speedy hanging as well. The governor of Minnesota—who had made a fortune cheating the Sioux—threatened that if the president did not hang all the condemned, the citizens of his state would.[52]

Instead, Lincoln personally examined every case on its own merits. After thorough analysis, he found that only a portion of the condemned number could be proven to have participated in the uprising. Lincoln immediately approved the execution order for these 38 Sioux and commuted the sentences of the remaining 265. In a finish that is pure Lincoln, the president handwrote the list of long, difficult, phonetically spelled Sioux names and advised the telegrapher on the vital necessity of sending them correctly, lest the wrong men be hanged.[53]

On December 26, 1862—the day after Christmas—thirty-eight Dakota Sioux were led to the gallows. They sang their death songs as they walked, and when they had mounted the scaffold and the hoods were drawn down over their faces, they continued to sing and sway and clasp each other's manacled hands. At a drum signal, the trap was sprung.

Given the mood of the country regarding what were seen as unprovoked savage attacks, what impelled Lincoln to spare the lives of so many Sioux? As we have seen, Lincoln was indeed a man of mercy; but he was no soft touch. Kind though he was, he was still very much a product of his time. His grandfather had been slaughtered by Indians in Kentucky—"by stealth," Lincoln recalled, "when he was laboring to open a farm in the forest."[54] Lincoln's father was only six at the time, and Lincoln always saw this as the reason his father grew up a rootless laborer and he was raised in poverty. As an American of the Victorian era, Lincoln was a firm believer in the superiority of the white race and in our right to a westward expansion limited only by the edge of the sea. Those who did not clear the way would be forcibly removed. If they responded violently, they would be met with violence. Lincoln defended Andrew Jackson's policy of Indian removal, and in an 1863 address to a visiting delegation of Indians—about fifteen chiefs of the Arapaho, Cheyenne, Kiowa, Comanche, and Apache nations—Lincoln advised them that the only hope for their survival lay in abandoning the old ways and taking up farming. Then Lincoln, commander in chief in a conflict that would ultimately claim the lives of some three quarters of a million Americans, had the temerity to lecture the chiefs on violence: "Although we are now engaged in a great war between one another, *we* are not, as a race, so much disposed to fight and kill one another as our red brethren."[55]

The wonder is not that Lincoln allowed more than three dozen men to hang; it is that he took the time away from a war that was going badly, and that threatened the very existence of our nation, to examine, one at a time, the cases of more than three hundred men and to spare the lives of all but thirty-eight. While Lincoln felt that there must be a reckoning and that the wholesale killing of settlers could be neither condoned nor ignored, he would not allow the law to be used for indiscriminate revenge, despite the tremendous pressure on him to do so. When it was suggested to him that he would have garnered political support by allowing the original order to stand, he responded, "I could not afford to hang men for votes."[56] Selectively allowing the executions of the thirty-eight Sioux was to Lincoln an act not of vengeance, but of justice.

The burden of leadership, the duty to administer justice within the context of the law, and the awesome responsibility that derived from presidential power weighed heavily on Lincoln daily. He was arguably the most kindhearted man ever to occupy the White House. However, as is clear in the cases of Gordon, Beall, Dr. Wright, and the thirty-eight Sioux, as well as the hundreds of others he allowed to perish in the course of the nation's greatest conflict, Lincoln had the remarkable ability to balance his merciful inclinations with his profound sense of justice. In the end, Lincoln refused to save these men because, at bottom, he felt the sentences to be right. Theirs was not the case of a sixteen-year-old boy falling asleep on picket duty or of a frightened soldier running from the terrors of battle. In the final analysis, there was nothing in their offenses to call forth that remarkable compassion for which Abraham Lincoln was so well and so rightly known.

Notes

1. William Lee Miller, *Lincoln's Virtues* (New York: Alfred A. Knopf, 2002), 16.
2. William Lee Miller, *President Lincoln: The Duty of a Statesman* (New York: Alfred A. Knopf, 2008), 5.

3. Gideon Welles, *Diary of Gideon Welles, Secretary of the Navy under Lincoln and Johnson* (Boston: Houghton Mifflin Company, 1911), 2:207.

4. Miller, *President Lincoln*, 5.

5. William Lee Miller, "Lincoln's Mercy," *Miller Center Report*, Scholar's Corner, University of Virginia (Summer 2001): 30.

6. Ibid.

7. Harold Holzer, ed., *Dear Mr. Lincoln* (New York: Addison-Wesley Publishing Co., 1993), 71–72.

8. Ibid., 84.

9. J. T. Dorris, "President Lincoln's Clemency," *Journal of the Illinois State Historical Society* 20 (January 1928): 551. Although nearly a century old, Dorris's study is rich with fact and anecdote, both of which stand up well to modern scholarship.

10. Ibid., 550.

11. Miller, "Lincoln's Mercy," 32.

12. Miller, *President Lincoln*, 341.

13. Dorris, "President Lincoln's Clemency," 551.

14. Miller, "Lincoln's Mercy," 10.

15. Ibid., 12.

16. Abraham Lincoln to Erastus Corning, in Douglas L. Wilson, *Lincoln's Sword: The Presidency and the Power of Words* (New York: Vintage Books, 2006), 173–74.

17. Miller, *President Lincoln*, 343.

18. Dorris, "President Lincoln's Clemency," 556.

19. William H. Herndon, *Herndon's Life of Lincoln* (Rockville, MD: Wildside Press, 2008), 430.

20. Interview in the *Denver Tribune*, May 18, 1879, reprinted in the *New York Times*, May 27, 1879, in Don E. Fehrenbacher and Virginia Fehrenbacher, eds., *Recollected Words of Abraham Lincoln* (Stanford, CA: Stanford University Press, 1996), 40–41.

21. US Library of Congress, the Abraham Lincoln Papers at the Library of Congress, Rhoda White plea for clemency, February 17, 1862.

22. Robert Murray, "The Career of Gordon the Slaver (1866)," transcribed by Walter Brewer, 1950 (unpublished), 64–65.

23. Hugh Thomas, *The Slave Trade: The Story of the Atlantic Slave Trade: 1440–1870* (New York: Simon and Schuster, 1997), 291.

24. Warren S. Howard, *American Slavers and the Federal Law, 1837–1862* (Berkeley: University of California Press, 1963), 1.

25. William Dillon Piersen, *From Africa to America: African American History from the Colonial Era to the Early Republic, 1526–1790* (New York: Simon and Schuster, 1996), 30.

26. John R. Spears, *The American Slave-Trade* (New York: Charles Scribner's Sons, 1900), 145–46.

27. Calvin Lane, "The African Squadron: The U.S. Navy and the Slave Trade, 1820–1862," *Log of Mystic Seaport* 50, no. 4 (Spring 1999): 7.

28. Abraham Lincoln, Speech at Chicago, July 10, 1858, in *The Collected Works of Abraham Lincoln*, ed. Roy P. Basler et al. (New Brunswick, NJ: Rutgers University Press, 1953), 2:492.

29. Lincoln, Speech at Peoria, Illinois, October 16, 1854, ibid., 2:265.

30. "Lincoln Let Him Hang," *Civil War Times* (March 1998): 37.

31. Ibid., 41.

32. Miller, *President Lincoln*, 273ff.

33. Ibid., 276

34. "Murder of a Vermonter," *Caledonian* (St. Johnsbury, VT), July 24, 1863.

35. Miller, *President Lincoln*, 277.

36. Ibid., 278.

37. Ibid., 279.

38. Thomas Keneally, *American Scoundrel: The Life of the Notorious Civil War General Dan Sickles* (New York: Doubleday, 2002), 197.

39. Miller, *President Lincoln*, 281–83.

40. Ibid., 287.

41. Lincoln to John G. Foster, October 15, 1863, *Collected Works*, 6:514; Lincoln to John G. Foster, October 17, 1863, ibid., 6:522.

42. Miller, *President Lincoln*, 288.

43. John W. Headley, *Confederate Operations in Canada and New York* (Honolulu: University Press of the Pacific, 2003), 231ff, 301ff.

44. Ibid., 360.

45. Ibid., 321ff.

46. Ibid., 364, 366.

47. "The Execution of John Yates Beall, CSN," *Richmond Examiner*, March 1, 1865.

48. Fehrenbacher and Fehrenbacher, *Recollected Words*, 40–41.

49. Miller, *President Lincoln*, 323, 458n.

50. Ibid., 458n.

51. Ibid., 323.

52. David A. Nichols, *Lincoln and the Indians: Civil War Policy and Politics* (St. Paul: Minnesota Historical Society Press, 2012), 111.

53. Miller, *President Lincoln*, 324–25.

54. Ibid., 319.

55. Ibid., 321.

56. Nichols, *Lincoln and the Indians*, 118.

LINCOLN AND
THE LAW OF WAR

Burrus M. Carnahan

A popular misconception is that a formal declaration of war was never issued in the Civil War. In fact, on May 6, 1861, the Provisional Confederate Congress in Montgomery, Alabama, passed an act "recognizing the existence of war between the United States and the Confederate States; and concerning letters of marque, prizes and prize goods." A declaration of war can either initiate a state of war or, like this one, assert that a war already exists, usually because of actions of the enemy, in this case President Lincoln's blockade of Southern ports and proclamation calling seventy-five thousand militia into Federal service following the Confederate attack on Fort Sumter in South Carolina.[1]

By this action, the Confederate Congress underlined a fundamental disagreement between the two sides over the nature of their conflict. Declarations of war are issued only in international armed conflicts. The Confederates believed they were a sovereign nation fighting an international war against another sovereign nation and were therefore entitled to all the rights and privileges of a belligerent state under the law of war. President Lincoln, on the other hand, never accorded any legitimacy to the Confederate States of America and always regarded the enemy as an organized group of individual insurgents. Asking Congress for a declaration of war would have implicitly recognized the Confederacy as an independent nation; the United States would have given up some of the core values it was fighting for—that the Union was indissoluble and secession unconstitutional.

Just as it refused out of principle to call for a declaration of war, so too was the Lincoln administration initially reluctant to apply the international law of war to the enemy. Within a few months after the firing on Fort Sumter,

Francis Lieber, a Prussian immigrant and professor of political science at Columbia University. Courtesy of the Library of Congress, LC-BH82-4591.

however, it became clear to the administration that it was impractical to maintain a steadfast, unyielding refusal to apply the law of war to the Confederate armed forces. The erosion started with President Lincoln's declaration of a blockade on Confederate ports. Blockade was an institution of international law, and invoking the term had the effect of recognizing the Confederacy as a "belligerent"—that is, a rebel government that had some limited rights in nineteenth-century international law, in particular, rights to trade with neutral nationals and for its warships to use neutral ports for provisions and supplies.

The Lincoln administration had initially considered trying to avoid the consequences of declaring a blockade by simply proclaiming that all ports under Confederate control were closed to international commerce under US customs laws. On March 25, 1861, Secretary of State William Seward floated this idea to European diplomats during a dinner party at the British legation in Washington. It was immediately rejected by the ministers of Great Britain, France, and Russia as an illegitimate attempt to impose a de facto blockade without following the rules and procedures required under international law. Lord Lyons, the British minister, suggested that if the United States followed this course of action, the result might be recognition of the Confederacy by Great Britain and war between his government and the United States.[2] The Lincoln administration had to follow the law of war if its acts were to be accepted as lawful by the major neutral powers.

A further retreat followed on July 13, 1861, when Major General George McClellan, operating in the pro-Union northwestern counties of Virginia, accepted the surrender of Confederate lieutenant colonel John Pegram and five hundred of his soldiers after promising that they would be treated as prisoners of war in accordance with the law of war. McClellan at once telegraphed the War Department asking "immediate instructions by telegraph as to the disposition to be made of officers and men taken prisoners of war."[3] The following day, the commanding general of the army telegraphed McClellan that Pegram's men should be treated as prisoners of war, establishing a precedent that would be followed for the remainder of the war.[4]

As a practical matter, the Lincoln administration had little choice but to apply the international law of war to Confederate soldiers. Theoretically, one alternative would have been to charge Pegram and his men with the civil crime of treason against the United States. In the summer of 1861, however, there was no US District Court with jurisdiction over McClellan's area of operations. (The northwestern counties of Virginia were later organized as the new state of West Virginia, but it was not admitted to the Union until 1863.) Even if such a court had existed, trying more than five hundred treason cases would have overtaxed any nineteenth-century court.

Another possibility would have been to hold these men as "prisoners of state," without any clearly defined rights or status, as the army did with persons suspected of disloyal activities in areas of the North where the privilege of the writ of habeas corpus had been suspended.[5] This option was politically unattractive, however. The Confederate government undoubtedly would have retaliated by denying prisoner-of-war treatment to captured Union soldiers, leading to a backlash against the Lincoln administration by the voting friends and relatives of captured soldiers.

Threat of retaliation became a reality in late 1861, when the US District Court in Philadelphia convicted Confederate naval lieutenant William Smith of piracy and sentenced him to hang.[6] President Lincoln, in response to reports that the Confederate government was considering licensing privately owned warships, called privateers, to prey on Union merchant shipping, included in his April 19, 1861, blockade proclamation a threat that "if any person under the pretended authority of the said [Confederate] States . . . shall molest a vessel of the United States, or the persons or cargo on board of her, such persons will be held amenable to the laws of the United States for the prevention and punishment of piracy."[7] The prosecution of Lieutenant Smith, who had served on the privateer *Jeff Davis*, was an implementation of this policy. In response, Confederate president Jefferson Davis had Colonel Michael Corcoran of the 69th New York State Militia, captured at the First Battle of Bull Run, separated from other prisoners of war as a hostage for Lieutenant Smith. Thirteen other Union officers were similarly treated as hostages for other Confederate privateer crewmen being held for trial in New York. By flag of truce, the US War Department was notified that the fate of the hostages would parallel that of the captured Confederates.[8] After fruitless attempts to negotiate a more limited solution, the Lincoln administration finally capitulated at the end of January 1862, reversing the policy of treating privateer crewmen as pirates rather than prisoners of war.[9]

Shortly thereafter, in early February 1862, Secretary of War Stanton authorized the commander of Fortress Monroe, a Union enclave in Virginia at the tip of the peninsula between the York and James Rivers, to begin negotiations with his Confederate counterpart at Norfolk, Virginia, for a formal agreement to govern exchanges of prisoners of war during the conflict.[10] Such agreements, known as "exchange cartels," were common in European wars of the eighteenth and nineteenth centuries, but Lincoln was initially concerned that agreeing to prisoner exchanges would amount to recognition of the Confederacy. As he explained to Episcopal bishop Thomas Clark in 1861, "I don't like to think of our men suffering in the southern prisons; . . . but you don't want me to recognize the Southern Confederacy, do you? Well, I can't propose an exchange of prisoners without recognizing the existence of the Confederate government."[11] Attorney General Edward Bates expressed similar worries at a cabinet meeting as late as December 10, 1861.[12]

There was, however, considerable political pressure from the Northern public to conclude an exchange cartel, and the government finally adopted the position of Dr. Francis Lieber, a professor at Columbia University who had argued, on the basis of state practice, that the United States could agree to exchange prisoners with Rebel authorities as a humanitarian measure, without according the Rebels political recognition.[13] After negotiations were authorized in February, they led to the signing on July 22, 1862, of the Dix-Hill Cartel for exchange of prisoners. It worked well for ten months, but in the summer of 1863, general exchanges were suspended by President Lincoln after the Confederate government refused to recognize African American soldiers as legitimate prisoners of war.[14]

By mid-1862, it was therefore the policy of the United States to apply the international law of war to its conflict with the Confederate States of America. This gave rise to another problem—educating the officers and men of the Union army on what the law of war did and did not require of them. At the start of 1861, the US Army consisted of sixteen thousand officers and men. By the end of the Civil War, the Union army had almost a million men under arms. The vast majority of the officers in this expanded army were appointed from civilian life and had no knowledge of the law of war.[15] This problem was addressed in the winter of 1862–63, when the War Department appointed Dr. Francis Lieber, along with four generals, to draft "a code of regulations for the government of armies in the field, as authorized by the laws and usages of war."[16] The eventual result was a concise restatement of the law of land warfare in 157 articles, published by the War Department, after approval by President Lincoln, as "Instructions for the Government of Armies of the United States in the Field," and issued as General Orders No. 100, April 24, 1863.[17] It is usually referred to as the Lieber Code after its principal drafter.

One of the Union officials who needed education in the law of war was the president himself. In 1867, Congressman Thaddeus Stevens quoted Lincoln as having declared, early in the war, that he did not "know anything about the law of nations." He continued, "I'm a good enough lawyer in a western law court, but we don't practice the law of nations up there." He later supposedly said to Attorney General Bates, "I'm not much of a prize lawyer," at a time when prize law was an important part of the law of naval warfare.[18] While some have doubted the authenticity of these quotations, they are consistent and, more to the point, they are true—Lincoln did not have occasion to deal with the international law of war before he became commander in chief of the army and navy. With his keen analytical mind and lifelong practice of self-education, the president soon grasped the general principles, if not all the technical details, of the nineteenth-century law of war. For a man who read Euclid's geometry for recreation, learning international law posed few intellectual challenges.

Legal historian Stephen Neff has called the Lieber Code "something of a legal masterpiece—a sort of pocket version of Blackstone's famous *Commentaries on the Laws of England*, though confined to the particular subject of the laws of land warfare." More than simply a list of rules, it was, "in addition, a miniature commentary on those rules, explaining, if only in the briefest terms, the basic principles underlying the specific commands and prohibitions."[19] By mid-1863, President Lincoln was able to produce miniature legal masterpieces of his own. A prime example is the public letter addressed to Illinois politician James C. Conkling in August 1863. Conkling had asked Lincoln to return to Springfield, Illinois, to address a mass rally of Union supporters, including at least some who supported the war but not the Emancipation Proclamation. Citing his official duties, the president declined but instead sent a letter to be read to the crowd. One paragraph defended the Emancipation Proclamation as justified under the law of war:

> You dislike the emancipation proclamation; and, perhaps would have it retracted. You say it is unconstitutional—I think differently. I think the constitution invests its commander-in-chief, with the law of war, in time of war. The most that can be said, if so much, is, that slaves are property. Is there—has there ever been—any question that by the law of war, property, both of enemies and friends, may be taken when needed? And is it not needed whenever taking it, helps us, or hurts the enemy? Armies, the world over, destroy enemy's property when they can not use it; and even destroy their own to keep it from the enemy. Civilized belligerents do all in their power to help themselves, or hurt the enemy, except a few things regarded as barbarous or cruel. Among the exceptions are the massacres of vanquished foes, and non-combatants, male and female.[20]

This paragraph summarizes, in plain language, important law-of-war concepts still applicable today. In particular, it explains the legal principle of military necessity without using the term. Lieber had defined military necessity as including "those measures which are indispensable for securing the ends of the war, and which are lawful according to the modern law and usages of war."[21] In practice, governments at war have not taken literally the term *necessity*. If there is a rational connection between a specific war measure and the defeat of the enemy's armed forces, the measure would be justified by military necessity.[22] Lincoln's statement that armies may "do all in their power to help themselves, or hurt the enemy," including taking of property, clearly restates the essence of the principle in layman's language. The Conkling letter also clearly explains the limits of military necessity. It does not justify acts "regarded as barbarous or cruel" under the law of war, such as "massacres of vanquished foes, and non-combatants." Like the Lieber Code itself, this paragraph is a miniature legal masterpiece.

Another example of Lincoln's mastery of the law of war, and his ability to write a pithy explanation of complex rules, was penned in 1865. In response to a complaint from a woman in Arkansas, President Lincoln wrote the following to the commanding general of the Department of Arkansas:

Washington, Jan. 20th, [1865]

Major General Reynolds,

It would appear by the accompanying papers that Mrs. Mary E. Morton is the owner, independently of her husband, of a certain building, premises and furniture, which she, with her children, has been occupying and using peaceably during the war, until recently, when the Provost-Marshal has, in the name of the U.S. Government, seized the whole of said property, and ejected her from it. It also appears by her statement to me, that her husband went off in the rebellion at the beginning, wherein he still remains.

It would seem that this seizure has not been made for any military object, as for a place of storage, a hospital, or the like, because this would not have required the seizure of the furniture, and especially not the return of furniture previously taken away.

The seizure must have been on some claim of confiscation, a matter of which the courts, and not the Provost-Marshals, or other military officers, are to judge—In this very case, would probably be the questions: "Is either the husband or wife a traitor?" "Does the property belong to the husband or to the wife?" "Is the property of the wife confiscable for the treason of the husband?" and other similar questions, all which it is ridiculous for a Provost-Marshal to assume to decide.

The true rule for the military, is to seize such property as is needed for Military uses and reasons, and let the rest alone. Cotton and other staple articles of commerce are seizable for Military reasons; Dwelling-houses and furniture are seldom so—. If Mrs. Morton is playing traitor, to the extent of practical injury, seize her, but leave her house to the courts.—Please revise and adjust this case upon these principles.

Yours &c

A. Lincoln[23]

While the letters to James Conkling and General Reynolds reflect principles of law still applicable today, in other respects the mid-nineteenth-century law of war was much harsher than the international humanitarian law in force today. This is most clearly reflected in the tactics regular armies were permitted to use in response to enemy irregulars. According to the Lieber Code:

Men, or squads of men, who commit hostilities, whether by fighting, or inroads for destruction or plunder, or by raids of any kind, without commission, without being part and portion of the organized hostile army, and without sharing continuously in the war, but who do so with intermitting returns to their homes and avocations, or with the occasional assumption of the semblance of peaceful pursuits, divesting themselves of the character or appearance of soldiers—such men, or squads of men, are not public enemies, and, therefore, if captured, are not entitled to the privileges of prisoners of war, but shall be treated summarily as highway robbers or pirates.[24]

The implication is that guerrillas meeting this definition could be executed without trial when captured.

The problem with this approach is that summary punishment could be applied only to guerrillas taken into custody, and guerrillas operating amid a sympathetic civilian population are notoriously difficult for regular armed forces to find and capture. To dissuade civilians from supporting guerrillas, the nineteenth-century law of war allowed military commanders to hold hostile civilian populations collectively responsible for guerrilla activities in their midst. Collective responsibility most commonly took the form of punitive monetary assessments, destruction of civilian property near the site of a guerrilla attack, exiling civilians or taking hostages.[25] In Missouri, for example, the Union command set up a formal system for assessing collective fines against "disloyal" persons. A collective fine of $5,000 would be assessed on civilians in the vicinity for every Federal soldier or pro-Union civilian killed by guerrillas, and fines between $1,000 and $5,000 for each one wounded.[26]

When guerrillas in Tennessee attacked Union steamboats, General Sherman took harsher measures, burning a town in the vicinity of the attacks and planning further retaliation if the attacks continued. He reported to General Grant:

> Guerrillas have twice attacked boats near Randolph, on both of which were many lady and children passengers. The attacks were wanton and cruel. I caused Randolph to be destroyed, and have given public notice that a repetition will justify any measures of retaliation, such as loading the boats with their captive guerrillas as targets (I always have a lot on hand), and expelling families from the comforts of Memphis, whose husbands and brothers go to make up those guerrillas. I will watch Randolph closely, and if anything occurs there again I will send a brigade by land back of Randolph and clean out the country.[27]

In extreme cases, civilian hostages or prisoners of war might be executed in retaliation for guerrilla attacks. In July 1864, for example, the Union commander in Kentucky ordered that four captured guerrillas be shot for every Union soldier or pro-Union citizen killed by guerrillas. Earlier, in 1862, ten hostages had actually been executed at Palmyra, Missouri, after a pro-Union civilian who had acted as a guide for the US Army was seized by guerrillas and not returned within ten days, as demanded by the Union commander. On the Confederate side, North Carolina governor Zebulon Vance ordered his Home Guard to confine the families of pro-Union guerrillas as hostages, and in West Virginia, Confederate guerrilla John Imboden threatened to execute two Union officers for every Confederate executed.[28]

Francis Lieber recognized the legitimacy of retaliation but cautioned that it must "never be resorted to as a measure of mere revenge, but only as a means of protective retribution, and moreover, cautiously and unavoidably; that is to say, retaliation shall only be resorted to after careful inquiry into the real occurrence, and the character of the misdeeds that may demand retribution."[29] This one of six places in which the Lieber Code declared acts of revenge or cruelty to be unlawful.[30]

These rules resonated with Lincoln. From an early age, he had been repelled by cruelty, even against animals, an unusual attitude on the frontier.[31] Acts of revenge also represented the triumph of an emotion—hatred—over reason, and Lincoln believed that reason should be used to control passion, not surrender to it.[32] An early example of his aversion to cruelty and revenge occurred in 1832, while he was serving as a militiaman during the Black Hawk War. Lincoln's unit had passed through an abandoned Indian village, where the men had seen what they believed to be scalps of white women and children. Later, when an elderly Indian entered their camp, most of the men wanted to kill him, but Lincoln defended the old man and prevented the other militiamen from harming him.[33]

As president, when required to determine to legitimacy of collective punishments or other questionable acts of his generals, Lincoln followed Lieber's approach. In some cases, he sensed that the military had taken retaliatory action before conducting a "careful inquiry into the real occurrence." In 1863, for example, persons unknown destroyed a Federal lighthouse on the Eastern Shore of Virginia. Suspecting the local population of sabotage, the regional military commander imposed a collective fine of $20,000 on members of the local population thought to be disloyal. When local authorities appealed to Lincoln, he suspended the fine. The assessments were "very strong measures," he noted, "and as I have to bear the responsibility of them, I wish them suspended till I can at least be better satisfied of their propriety than I now am."[34] In this case, the president's instincts were correct. The lighthouse had in fact been destroyed by a raiding party from the Confederate navy, not the local inhabitants.[35] In other cases, the decisive issue for President Lincoln was whether the military's action served a rational military purpose or was merely an expression of cruelty and revenge. Lincoln's approach can be illustrated by considering his treatment of two incidents, one in 1862 and the other in 1864.

As a result of various acts of corruption and inefficiency by government Indian agents and local white traders, the Sioux in Minnesota went to war against the United States in August 1862. Although the rebellion was quickly suppressed, the impact on the white population was significant. A contemporary account estimates that 644 white civilians were killed.[36] Thirty thousand others were forced to flee their homes; one Lincoln biographer has concluded that this brief conflict was "the bloodiest massacre of American civilians on U.S. soil prior to September 11, 2001."[37]

A military commission convened by the local commander proceeded to try all the Sioux men, and one woman, who had participated in the uprising. Of the more than 400 defendants, 303 were convicted and sentenced to hang (the female defendant was found not guilty). The commission seems to have regarded the Sioux fighting men as illegitimate combatants, not entitled to prisoner-of-war status. While some were charged with rape and the murder of specific civilians, many were convicted merely for participating in battles against US troops and Minnesota militia. A contemporary participant in the trials stated that all that was required for conviction was testimony or an admission by the accused "that he had fired in the battles, or brought ammunition, or acted as commissary in supplying provisions to the combatants." Forty cases were sometimes disposed of in one day.[38]

In the summer of 1862, Congress passed a law providing that in courts-martial and military commission trials, "no sentence of death . . . shall be carried into execution until the same shall have been approved by the President."[39] In accordance with this act of Congress, on November 7, 1862, Major General John Pope, commanding the Department of Minnesota, telegraphed the president the names of three hundred of the Indians sentenced to death, asking that he approve the sentences.[40] (It is not clear why Pope did not include all the defendants sentenced to death by the military commission. He also did not inform the president that the military commission members had recommended clemency for one of the accused, who had acted as a government witness in the prosecution of others.)

Lincoln replied two days later, asking Pope to send him the trial records for review. "If the record does not fully indicate the more guilty and influential of the culprits," he said, "please have a careful statement made on these points and forwarded to me."[41] Pope immediately responded by telegraph, "The only distinction between the culprits is as to which of them murdered most people or violated most young girls[;] all of them are guilty of these things in more or less degree,"[42] a description unsupported by the records of trial sent to Washington. Only two men, for example, had been convicted of rape. Moreover, Pope could not have known in detail what all three hundred condemned men had done because, according to the person who took the records of trial to Pope's headquarters, they were not delivered there until November 15.

The Minnesota public was outraged that the president would even consider clemency for the three hundred Indians. Riots and lynching of the condemned were widely expected if any of them were spared the noose. On November 28, about the time the trial records arrived in Washington, Minnesota Governor Ramsey telegraphed Lincoln, "Nothing but the Speedy execution of the tried and convicted Sioux Indians will save us here from Scenes of outrage. If you prefer it turn them over to me & I will order their Execution."[43]

The telegrams from General Pope and Governor Ramsey probably had an unanticipated effect on the president that was the opposite of what they had intended. Pope's hasty assertion that all three hundred prisoners were equally guilty and the governor's prediction that "Scenes of outrage" would occur unless all were quickly executed suggest that both men were seeking revenge, not justice. When the trial records arrived in Washington around November 28, Lincoln delegated review of the records to two civil servants with legal backgrounds, directing them to determine which of the condemned had committed rape or "participated in massacres as distinguished from participation in battles." On December 5, they reported to the president that two of the accused had committed both rape and murder of civilians, and thirty-eight others had deliberately killed civilians. Lincoln granted clemency to one of the latter, as recommended by the military commission, and approved the execution of thirty-nine Sioux.[44] Executive clemency was later extended to another of the condemned when evidence was presented that exonerated him of murder. The remaining thirty-eight were hanged at Mankato, Minnesota, on December 26, 1862.[45]

The records of trial never received a full-scale legal review. On November 27, Judge Advocate General Joseph Holt, Lincoln's advisor on military law, began prosecuting the court-martial of a Union general, a task that occupied him full-time until early 1862. Even as a review for executive clemency, the procedure Lincoln adopted was hasty and rough. Three hundred military commission records were scrutinized in the space of only eight or nine days, and it appears that at least one prisoner who had merely participated in a battle had his death sentence approved.

However, by refusing to approve 262 death sentences, President Lincoln was, in effect, treating the Sioux as legitimate combatants and prisoners of war. This was in accordance with the Lieber Code, which stated that a "prisoner of war is subject to no punishment for being a public enemy"—that is, an enemy soldier. But the code also said that a "prisoner of war remains answerable for his crimes committed against the captor's army or people, committed before he was captured, and for which he has not been punished by his own authorities," in this case rape and killing civilians.[46] Later in the nineteenth century, the judge advocate general of the army followed Lincoln's precedent and ruled that the law of war, as defined in the Lieber Code, applied in conflicts between the United States and Native Americans.[47]

In contrast to the clemency granted to most of the Sioux fighting men in 1862, President Lincoln deferred to the military commander on the scene in an 1864 case involving retaliatory executions. Missouri was plagued by guerrilla warfare throughout the Civil War.[48] In the fall of 1864, a Confederate guerrilla band led by Timothy Reeves captured and executed Union major James Wilson of the 3rd Missouri State Cavalry, along with five of his men. Reportedly, Wilson met his fate with a stoicism that led Reeves to tell him, "Major, you are a brave man—but you never showed my men quarter, neither will I give you quarter."[49] In retaliation, Major General William Rosecrans, commanding the Department of the Missouri, ordered the execution on November 11, 1864, of Confederate major Enoch Wolf, a prisoner of war of equal rank.[50] Wolf had no personal involvement with Wilson's death, and at the last moment, several prominent Missourians intervened with President Lincoln to request clemency on his behalf.[51] By telegraph, Lincoln ordered Rosecrans to suspend the execution and report the facts of the case to the White House.[52]

Rosecrans replied the following day, arguing that Confederate general Sterling Price and men under his command had actively encouraged and supported guerrillas in Missouri.[53] Retaliation against prisoners from Price's command was, as he saw it, necessary for the safety of Union men taken prisoner by these guerrillas. Rosecrans told Lincoln:

> In compliance with your telegraphic orders of the 10th instant I transmit . . . a printed statement of the case of Major Wolf, C. S. A. and of the other rebels who were executed by my orders, for the purpose of teaching the enemy that if the laws of war and humanity are not sufficient to secure our prisoners from murder, I will add to their force the motive of personal interest. . . .
>
> As to the policy of doing as I have done I leave you to judge after reading the records in this case. All other motive having failed to secure my soldiers who have surrendered themselves prisoners of war from cold blooded assassination or official murder by Price's Command, I

felt bound to appeal to the sense of personal security by declaring to these men that I should hold them individually responsible for the treatment of my Troops while prisoners in their hands.[54]

Arguably, General Rosecrans had a valid military reason for ordering Major Wolf's execution. In this case, Lincoln deferred to Rosecrans's military judgment while cautioning him not to act out of revenge:

A Major Wolf, as it seems, was under sentence, in your Department, to be executed in retaliation for the murder of a Major Wilson; and I, without any particular knowledge of the facts, was induced, by appeals for mercy, to order the suspension of his execution until further order. Understanding that you so desire, this letter places the case again within your control, with the remark only that I wish you to do nothing merely for revenge, but that what you may do, shall be solely done with reference to the security of the future.[55]

The president's admonition seems to have had its intended effect. In the end, General Rosecrans or his successor in command of the Department of the Missouri, Grenville Dodge, reconsidered the matter and decided not to execute Wolf, who was later exchanged as a prisoner of war.[56]

The Conkling letter and Lincoln's communications with Generals Reynolds, Pope, and Rosecrans illustrate how well the president had mastered the principles of the law of war as summarized by the Lieber Code. As a wartime leader, however, Lincoln's handling of these issues deviated radically from the practices of modern presidents, who issue hundreds of executive orders giving general policy guidance to the departments and agencies of the federal government. President Lincoln, on the other hand, dealt with the law of war on an ad hoc basis, acting only on appeals and decisions in specific cases.

In the terminology of modern management theory, Lincoln's leadership followed the practice of "management by exception." Under this approach, managers interfere with their subordinates' decisions only in exceptional cases, when a serious problem arises.[57] This practice can encourage initiative on the part of subordinates and avoid the morale problems caused by micromanagement by superiors. Management by exception is illustrated by many of Lincoln's law-of-war decisions discussed above, including the initial 1861 decision to treat Confederate soldiers as prisoners of war, the commutation of Sioux Indian death sentences in 1862, the case of Major Wolf in 1864, and the 1865 letter on Mrs. Morton's property in Arkansas. This style of leadership was consistent with Lincoln's approach to military matters in general. In his study of civilian leadership in wartime, the political scientist Eliot Cohen concluded that rather than issue direct orders to his subordinates, President Lincoln tended "to question, prod and suggest."[58] The problem was that President Lincoln tended to rely almost solely on management by exception, and aside from the prisoner-of-war issue, his administration did not follow decisions in specific cases with more general guidance to subordinates in the field. In one of the few instances where the president did try to establish a general policy on treatment of civilian property, the results were inconclusive at best.

Destruction of private property, including houses, was a standard response to guerrilla activity, but in 1864, this practice seemed to be spiraling out of control. On May 21 of that year, Major General David Hunter assumed command of the Department of West Virginia, with orders to advance up the Shenandoah Valley and clear it of Confederate forces. Two days later, persons unknown fired on a column of Union supply wagons at Newtown, Virginia. In retaliation, Hunter sent a force of cavalry that burned three houses belonging Confederate sympathizers. On May 24, he issued a warning that all houses of "Secessionists resident in the Valley" within five miles of the scene of any guerrilla attacks would be burned. He had another house burned that was believed to be a meeting place for guerrillas and near which five Union soldiers had been killed. Yet another was burned because the owner was thought to have killed Union stragglers. By June 11, Hunter's forces had captured Lexington, Virginia, where the house of former Virginia governor John Letcher was burned for Letcher's encouragement of guerrilla attacks on Hunter's forces. The Virginia Military Institute was also burned after debate among Hunter's staff over whether it was primarily an education institution or a military installation. The general inclined towards the latter view and had it burned.[59]

Confederate general Jubal Early drove Hunter's forces from the Shenandoah Valley and then initiated a raid through Maryland to the outskirts of Washington. During the raid, a detachment of Confederate cavalry burned the home of Maryland governor Augustus Bradford in retaliation for the burning of Letcher's home. The home of Postmaster General Montgomery Blair in Silver Springs, Maryland, was also burned in what appeared to be another act of retaliation. In retaliation for the burning of Governor Bradford's house, General Hunter began a new round of house burnings in West Virginia and

Maryland on July 16.[60] On July 25, in retaliation for Hunter's latest burnings, General Early ordered General John McCausland to take a force to Chambersburg, Pennsylvania, where he was to demand a payment of $100,000 in gold or $500,000 in greenbacks, supposedly for Hunter's victims, or the town would be burned. The town could not raise the money, so on July 30, it was set on fire and about three hundred families lost their homes.[61] As Francis Lieber had warned, "Inconsiderate retaliation removes the belligerents farther and farther from the mitigating rules of regular war, and by rapid steps leads them nearer to the . . . wars of savages."[62]

On August 14, 1864, President Lincoln sent a telegram to Ulysses Grant, proposing that the general negotiate an end to retaliatory burning of houses by both sides. "The Secretary of War and I concur that you had better confer with Gen. Lee and stipulate for a mutual discontinuance of house-burning and other destruction of private property. The time and manner of conference, and particulars of stipulation we leave, on our part, to your convenience and judgment."[63] Grant replied that he opposed such negotiations because he did not think the Confederates would respect any resulting agreement. "Experience has taught us that agreements made with rebels are binding upon us but are not observed by them longer than suits their convenience," he said.[64] The president and Stanton dropped the matter. So ended the only effort by Lincoln to negotiate a general agreement with the enemy on the treatment of civilian property.

Considering all his responsibilities during the Civil War, it is probably expecting too much of Abraham Lincoln to have gone beyond management by exception and issued as many executive orders as a modern president. The administrative resources available to draft executive orders were very limited in the mid-nineteenth century. Whereas the modern White House operates with a staff of hundreds, Lincoln had only three young secretaries to help run the entire government. What is clear from the historical record is that the president, although initially reluctant to apply the law of war to Confederate armed forces, eventually developed considerable expertise in this branch of international law and effectively applied this knowledge where his duties required.

Notes

1. James Matthews, ed., *The Statutes at Large of the Provisional Government of the Confederate States of America, from the Institution of the Government, February 8, 1861, to Its Termination, February 18, 1862, Inclusive* . . . (Richmond, VA:

R. M. Smith, 1864), 100–4, accessed June 30, 2013, http://docsouth.unc.edu/imls/ 19conf/19conf.html#p100. A "letter of marque" was government license to operate a privately owned warship and use it to capture enemy merchant vessels on the high seas. Ships operating under a letter of marque were called "privateers." After capture, the enemy vessel and its cargo would be brought before a "prize court" of the nation that had issued the letter of marque for adjudication as to whether the capture was lawful. If the capture was upheld as a lawful prize, the ship and its cargo would typically be auctioned and the proceeds divided among the government, the crew, and the owner of the privateer. Most of the act of May 6, 1861, set out the rules that Confederate privateers were required to follow. Naval warfare could be a profitable business in the mid-nineteenth century. See, generally, Donald A. Petrie, *The Prize Game: Lawful Looting on the High Seas in the Days of Fighting Sail* (Annapolis, MD: US Naval Institute Press, 1999); William Morrison Robertson Jr., *The Confederate Privateers* (Columbia: University of South Carolina Press, 1994).

2. See, e.g., Walter Stahr, *Seward: Lincoln's Indispensable Man* (New York: Simon and Schuster, 2012), 263–64; Howard Jones, *Blue & Gray Diplomacy: A History of Union and Confederate Foreign Relations* (Chapel Hill: University of North Carolina Press, 2010), 25–27; Dean B. Mahin, *One War at a Time: The International Dimensions of the American Civil War* (Dulles, VA: Brassey's, 1999), 45–46.

3. McClellan to Townsend, July 13, 1861, in *War of the Rebellion: Official Records of the Union and Confederate Armies* (US Government Printing Office, 1880–1901), ser. 2, vol. 3, 9 (hereafter *Official Records*). For a fuller account of the circumstances surrounding this incident, see Burrus M. Carnahan, *Act of Justice: Lincoln's Emancipation Proclamation and the Law of War* (Lexington: University Press of Kentucky, 2007), 58–65.

4. Scott to McClellan, July 14, 1861, *Official Records*, ser. 2, vol. 3, 10–11.

5. Mark E. Neely Jr., *The Fate of Liberty: Abraham Lincoln and Civil Liberties* (Oxford: Oxford University Press, 1991), 77, 120.

6. *United States v. William Smith*, October 22, 1861 (US Dist. Court for the Eastern Dist. of Pa.), *Official Records* ser. 2, vol. 3, 58. For general background on privateers, see Petrie, *Prize Game*, and Robertson, *Confederate Privateers*.

7. Abraham Lincoln, Proclamation of a Blockade, April 19, 1861, in *The Collected Works of Abraham Lincoln*, ed. Roy P. Basler et al. (New Brunswick, NJ: Rutgers University Press, 1953), 4:338–39.

8. Cogswell to Thomas, November 11, 1861, *Official Records*, ser. 2, vol. 3, 130–31.

9. Seward to U.S. Marshals, January 31, 1862, *Official Records*, ser. 2, vol. 3, 229; Wool to Huger, February 10, 1862, ibid., 250. See also John Fabian Witt, *Lincoln's*

Code: The Laws of War in American History (New York: Free Press, 2012), 157–64; Carnahan, *Act of Justice*, 65–70.

10. Stanton to Wool, February 11, 1862, *Official Records*, ser. 2, vol. 3, 254.

11. Don E. Fehrenbacher and Virginia Fehrenbacher, eds., *Recollected Words of Abraham Lincoln* (Stanford, CA: Stanford University Press, 1996), 106.

12. David Donald, ed., *Inside Lincoln's Cabinet: The Civil War Diaries of Salmon P. Chase* (New York: Longmans, Green and Company, 1954), 48–49.

13. Frank Freidel, *Francis Lieber: Nineteenth-Century Liberal* (1947; repr., Gloucester, MA: Peter Smith, 1968), 320.

14. The cartel was named after the negotiators, Major General John A. Dix for the US Army and Major General D. H. Hill for the Confederate army. Dix-Hill Cartel, *Official Records*, ser. 2, vol. 4, 266. Article 1 expressly provided that privateer crewmen were to be treated as officers and men of the respective navies. On Lincoln's suspension of exchanges without permission from the War Department, see Hitchcock to Stanton, November 30, 1863, *Official Records*, ser. 2, vol. 6, 607, 608–9.

15. David J. Eicher, *The Longest Night: A Military History of the Civil War* (New York: Simon and Schuster, 2001), 58, 785; Bryon Farwell, *The Encyclopedia of Nineteenth Century Land Warfare* (New York: W. W. Norton & Company, 2001), s.vv. "Union Army," "United States Army."

16. Para. 5, Special Orders No. 399, War Department, Adjutant General's Office, Washington DC, December 17, 1862, *Official Records*, ser. 3, vol. 2, 951.

17. "Instructions for the Government of Armies of the United States in the Field," General Orders No. 100, War Department, Adjutant General's Office, Washington, DC, April 24, 1863, *Official Records*, ser. 3, vol. 3, 148–64 (hereafter Lieber Code). On the general background and influence of the Lieber Code, see Witt, *Lincoln's Code*, 193–95, 231–49; Stephen C. Neff, *Justice in Blue and Gray: A Legal History of the Civil War* (Cambridge, MA: Harvard University Press, 2010), 56–101; Burrus M. Carnahan, "The Civil War Origins of the Modern Rules of War: Francis Lieber and Lincoln's General Order No. 100," *Northern Kentucky Law Review* 39 (2012): 661.

18. Fehrenbacher and Fehrenbacher, *Recollected Words*, 109, 423. The Fehrenbachers give both statements a rating of "D," which meant that they believed that there was "more than average doubt" as to their authenticity.

19. Neff, *Justice in Blue and Gray*, 57.

20. Lincoln to James C. Conkling, August 26, 1863, *Collected Works*, 6:406, 408.

21. Lieber Code, Art. 14.

22. For example, Article 15 of the Lieber Code explains, regarding the principle of military necessity:

[It] admits of all direct destruction of life or limb of armed enemies, and of other persons whose destruction is incidentally unavoidable in the armed contests of the war; it allows of the capturing of every armed enemy, and every enemy of importance to the hostile government, or of peculiar danger to the captor; it allows of all destruction of property, and obstruction of the ways and channels of traffic, travel, or communication, and of all withholding of sustenance or means of life from the enemy; of the appropriation of whatever an enemy's country affords necessary for the subsistence and safety of the army, and of such deception as does not involve the breaking of good faith.

23. Lincoln to Joseph J. Reynolds, January 20, 1865, *Collected Works* 8:228–29. A provost marshal was an "officer appointed in every army in the field to command those serving as military police and to secure prisoners." Farwell, *Encyclopedia of Nineteenth Century Land Warfare*, s.v. "provost marshal."

24. Lieber Code, Art. 82.

25. See, generally, Clay Mountcastle, *Punitive War: Confederate Guerrillas and Union Reprisals* (Lawrence: University Press of Kansas, 2009); Daniel E. Sutherland, *A Savage Conflict: The Decisive Role of Guerrillas in the American Civil War* (Chapel Hill: University of North Carolina Press, 2009). Collective punishment of civilians in occupied territory is now prohibited by Art. 33, Convention Relative to the Protection of Civilian Persons in Time of War, August 12, 1949, 6 UST 3516, T.I.A.S. 3365, 75 UNTS 287 (Fourth Geneva Convention).

26. General Order No. 3, Headquarters District of Missouri, Saint Louis, June 23, 1862, *Official Records*, ser. 1, vol. 13, 446–47.

27. Sherman to Grant, October 4, 1862, *Official Records*, ser. 1, vol. 17, pt. 2, 259, 261–62.

28. Sutherland, *Savage Conflict*, 162, 222, 249; Mark E. Neely Jr., *The Civil War and the Limits of Destruction* (Cambridge, MA: Harvard University Press, 2007), 42–44.

29. Lieber Code, Art. 28. Article 27 of the Lieber Code recognizes the legitimacy of retaliation in principle: "The law of war can no more wholly dispense with retaliation than can the law of nations, of which it is a branch. Yet civilized nations acknowledge retaliation as the sternest feature of war. A reckless enemy often leaves to his opponent no other means of securing himself against the repetition of barbarous outrage."

30. For the others, see Lieber Code, Art. 11 (the law of war "disclaims . . . all acts of private revenge, or connivance at such acts"); Art. 16 ("Military necessity does

not admit of cruelty—that is, the infliction of suffering for the sake of suffering or for revenge, nor of maiming or wounding except in fight, nor of torture to extort confessions"); Art. 56 ("A prisoner of war is subject to no punishment for being a public enemy, nor is any revenge wreaked upon him by the intentional infliction of any suffering, or disgrace, by cruel imprisonment, want of food, by mutilation, death, or any other barbarity"); Art. 60 ("It is against the usage of modern war to resolve, in hatred and revenge, to give no quarter"); Art. 68 ("Unnecessary or revengeful destruction of life is not lawful").

31. See, e.g., David Herbert Donald, *Lincoln* (New York: Touchstone, 1995), 27.

32. See, e.g., Allen C. Guelzo, Abraham Lincoln: Redeemer President (Grand Rapids, MI: Wm. B. Eerdmans Publishing Co., 1999), 361–62; Donald, *Lincoln*, 82–83.

33. Interview with Royal Clary, October 1866, in *Herndon's Informants: Letters, Interviews, and Statements about Abraham Lincoln*, ed. Douglas L. Wilson and Rodney O. Davis (Urbana: University of Illinois Press, 1998), 370, 372; William G. Greene to Herndon, May 30, 1865, and November 1, 1866, ibid., 17–18.

34. Lincoln to Edwin M. Stanton, September 1, 1863, *Collected Works*, 6:427. See also Lincoln to Joseph Segar, September 5, 1863, ibid., 6:434.

35. Eric Mills, *Chesapeake Bay in the Civil War* (Centreville, MD: Tidewater Publishers, 1996), 214.

36. Isaac D. Heard, *History of the Sioux War and Massacres of 1862 and 1863* (1863; repr., Nabu Press, n.d.), 243. For modern accounts of the war, trials, and executions, see Scott W. Berg, *38 Nooses: Lincoln, Little Crow and the Beginning of the Frontier's End* (New York: Pantheon Books, 2012); Duane Schultz, *Over the Earth I Come: The Great Sioux Uprising of 1862* (New York: St. Martin's Press, 1992); Kenneth Carley, *The Dakota War of 1862*, 2nd ed. (St. Paul: Minnesota Historical Society Press, 1976).

37. Michael Burlingame, *Abraham Lincoln: A Life* (Baltimore: Johns Hopkins University Press, 2008), 2:480.

38. Heard, *History of the Sioux War*, 255, 269. Heard, a Minnesota lawyer, was the official recorder of the military commission trials and had also served in the militia suppressing the uprising.

39. Act of July 17, 1862, ch. 201, § 5, 12 Stat. 597 (1862).

40. Pope to Lincoln, November 7, 1862, Abraham Lincoln Papers, Library of Congress.

41. Lincoln to John Pope, November 10, 1862, *Collected Works*, 5:493.

42. Pope to Lincoln, November 11, 1862, Lincoln Papers; Riggs to Lincoln, November 17, 1862, ibid.

43. Ramsey to Lincoln, November 28, 1862, ibid.

44. "Message of the President in Answer to a Resolution of the Senate of the 5th Instant in Relation to the Indian Barbarities in Minnesota," December 11, 1862, S. Exec. Doc. No. 7, 37th Cong., 3rd sess.

45. See, e.g., Schultz, *Over the Earth I Come*, 255–64; Carley, *Dakota War of 1862*, 68–75.

46. Lieber Code, Arts. 56, 59.

47. See William Winthrop, *A Digest of the Opinions of the Judge Advocates General of the Army*, (Washington, DC: US Government Printing Office, 1895), 451–53.

48. See, generally, Thomas Goodrich, *Black Flag: Guerrilla Warfare on the Western Border, 1861–1865* (Bloomington: Indiana University Press, 1995); Michael Fellman, *Inside War: The Guerrilla Conflict in Missouri during the American Civil War* (Oxford: Oxford University Press, 1989).

49. Fellman, *Inside War*, 182.

50. Wolf to Rosecrans, November 8, 1864, *Official Records*, ser. 2, vol. 7, 1111. Five enlisted prisoners of war had been executed on October 29, 1864, in retaliation for the deaths of Major Wilson's men. Lincoln to William S. Rosecrans, November 10, 1864, *Collected Works*, 8:102n1. Article 59 of the Lieber Code also said, "All prisoners of war are liable to the infliction of retaliatory measures," but retaliation against prisoners of war is now prohibited by Art. 13, Convention Relative to the Treatment of Prisoners of War, August 12, 1949, 6 U.S.T. 3316, T.I.A.S. No. 3364, 75 UNTS 135 (Third Geneva Convention).

51. Able and Terry to Lincoln, November 10, 1864, and Yeatman to Lincoln, November 10, 1864, Lincoln Papers.

52. Lincoln to William S. Rosecrans, November 10, 1864, *Collected Works*, 8:102.

53. In 1862, Price admitted to the Union commander in Missouri, at that time Henry Halleck, that that he had "specially appointed and instructed" guerrillas "to destroy railroads, culverts and bridges" behind Union lines. He argued that because he had authorized these attacks, the men should not be punished but should be treated as prisoners of war. Halleck rejected the argument. Price to Halleck, January 12, 1862, and Halleck to Price, January 22, 1862, *Official Records*, ser. 2, vol. 1, 255–56, 258–59.

54. Rosecrans to Lincoln, November 11, 1864, ibid., ser. 2, vol. 7, 1118–19.

55. Lincoln to William S. Rosecrans, November 19, 1864, *Collected Works*, 8:116.

56. *Official Records*, ser. 2, vol. 7, 1118n. Rosecrans was relieved of command of the Department of the Missouri on December 9, 1864, and replaced by Grenville Dodge. See Frank J. Welcher, *The Union Army, 1861–1865*, 2:93 (Bloomington: Indiana University Press, 1993).

57. *Cambridge Business Dictionary*, s.v. "management by exception," accessed September 13, 2013, http://dictionary.cambridge.org/us/dictionary/business-english/management-by-exception; Phyllis G. Holland, *YourDictionary*, s.v. "management by exception—business definition," accessed September 13, 2013, http://www.yourdictionary.com/management-by-exception.

58. Eliot A. Cohen, *Supreme Command: Soldiers, Statesmen, and Leadership in Wartime* (New York: Free Press, 2005), 41.

59. See, e.g., Report of Major General Hunter, Headquarters Department of West Virginia, Harper's Ferry, August 8, 1864, *Official Records*, ser. 1, vol. 37, pt. 1, 96; Scott C. Patchan, *The Battle of Piedmont and Hunter's Raid on Staunton* (Charleston, SC: History Press, 2011), 28–29; Edward A. Miller, *Lincoln's Abolitionist General: The Biography of David Hunter* (Columbia: University of South Carolina Press, 1997), 170–72, 192–95.

60. See, e.g., Marc Leepson, *Desperate Engagement: How a Little-Known Civil War Battle Saved Washington, D.C., and Changed American History* (New York: Thomas Dunne Books, 2007), 136; Fritz Hasselberger, *Confederate Retaliation: McCausland's 1864 Raid* (Shippensburg, PA: Burd Street Press, 2000), 55–59; Miller, *Lincoln's Abolitionist General*, 220–25. In at least one case, President Lincoln ordered that a house not be burned after an appeal from the owner's wife. Lincoln to Franklin G. Martindale, c. July 17, 1864, *Collected Works*, 7:445.

61. See, e.g., Hasselberger, *Confederate Retaliation*, 63, 92–96; Miller, *Lincoln's Abolitionist General*, 229–30.

62. Lieber Code, Art. 28.

63. Lincoln to Ulysses S. Grant, August 14, 1864, *Collected Works*, 7:493.

64. Grant to Lincoln, August 17, 1864, ibid., 7:493n. According to Major General Ethan Allen Hitchcock, the Union officer in charge of prisoner exchanges, the Confederates had already violated the Dix-Hill Cartel on prisoner exchanges by refusing to recognize African American soldiers as prisoners of war, and they had again violated the cartel by declaring the Confederate troops paroled by General Grant to have been exchanged, and therefore released from parole, without following the procedure laid down in the cartel. Hitchcock to Stanton, November 30, 1863, *Official Records*, ser. 2, vol. 6, 607–14.

Wisconsin representative John F. Potter, who was given the nickname of "Bowie Knife Potter" and was known for his passionate personality. Potter formed the Congressional Committee on the Loyalty of Clerks and Other Persons Employed by the Government, commonly known as the "Potter Committee." Courtesy of the Library of Congress, LC-DIG-ppmsca-26834.

LINCOLN AND THE POTTER CONGRESSIONAL COMMITTEE CONCERNING THE LOYALTY OF GOVERNMENT EMPLOYEES

Natalie Sweet

On January 28, 1862, a select committee headed by Wisconsin representative John Potter released its report on the loyalty of clerks and others employed by the government to the Thirty-Seventh Congress. The report questioned the Union loyalty of more than five hundred individuals, whose names and places of employment appeared throughout the report. Local and national newspapers quickly picked up the accusations and broadcast the listed names. Notably, secret testimony condemned many, and none of the accused were allowed to present evidence on their behalf. Potter repeatedly asserted throughout the committee's investigations that the civil liberties of the accused were not infringed on because those named were simply under congressional investigation, not judicial trial.

Significantly for the president, four of the accused individuals worked within the White House. Despite the public clamor for immediate action against his household staff, Lincoln refused to immediately remove any of those who were named in his own household. Instead, he approached the issue as an attorney would. He looked for witnesses and documents that would corroborate the charges. While he searched, he knew that some in the public viewed the Potter Committee's investigation as having real implications for Sixth Amendment rights. He also knew that others viewed whether he would allow the possibility of "traitors" working within the Executive Mansion as a test of the president's leadership. Relying on the skills he possessed as a lawyer to confirm that the accused within his home were being tried without proper evidence in the court of public opinion, Lincoln resisted the Potter Committee's challenge and stood

strong in the face of the select committee's attempt to exert congressional jurisdiction over the executive office.

FORMATION OF A COMMITTEE IN A TIME OF FEAR

Throughout the course of Potter's investigation, Lincoln's desire to steadily
pursue evidence against the accused in his household was challenged by the
culture of fear that had developed in Washington, DC. The unease that Union-
ists felt about their Southern neighbors in the first year of the war cannot
be underestimated or easily dismissed. The District of Columbia had been a
Southern, slave-trading city prior to 1850, and slavery still existed within the
capital in 1860. Numerous presidents who had called the Executive Mansion
home were originally from South of the Mason-Dixon Line. Southern vitriol
had seethed within the halls of the Capitol building over the past decade. Even
the weather conspired with the city's Southern aristocratic pretensions, as the
New York Herald noted that the capital was "the abode of a very slow and respectable people, who cool themselves during the hot weather by the delightful
remembrance that they are of gentle blood."[1]

The *National Republican*, however, perhaps best captured the paranoia
over Washington's Southern bent in the winter of 1861–62 when one writer
exclaimed, "Washington is to-day nearly as rotten as Richmond, all things
considered. You meet traitors on every corner of the street, every hour in the
day. They are hatched nightly. We ought to have had martial law here for the
last eight months. It would have saved hundreds, perhaps thousands, of valuable lives, and millions of money." The author identified himself only by "Pro
Patria" and signed off on this declaration with "Let traitors, and those who
defend them, have all they deserve; then, and not till then, the country is safe.
God save the Republic!"[2]

The mood within the city was tense, to say the least. Many had uneasily
watched as conflict brewed on their doorstep in the years leading up to the
Civil War. In the interim between Abraham Lincoln's election and his inauguration, soldiers patrolled the streets, and men carried guns for safety on their
way to gather news at the local hotels and kept their weapons close by their
beds even in respectable neighborhoods.[3] In May 1856, antislavery proponent
and Massachusetts senator Charles Sumner was nearly beaten to death with a
cane in the Senate chamber by South Carolina representative Preston Brooks.
A few years later, another near duel between politicians spoke to the increasing
violence that had entered the US political halls: Wisconsin representative John

Potter and Virginia representative Roger Pryor nearly came to fatal blows in April 1860 after a shouting match erupted over the topic of slavery between Northern and Southern representatives. When Pryor issued his challenge, Potter accepted. He proposed that the two representatives come together "in a closed room with bowie knives of equal size and weight and length of blade," earning him the nickname of "Bowie Knife" Potter and a reputation for immediate action in the face of a challenge. District police arrested both representatives before the duel could occur.[4]

By the time the 37th Congress gathered in July 1861, with fears of disloyalty high in Washington, John Potter became the perfect individual to challenge the existence of potential traitors within the capital. His bulldog tenacity and reputation for antagonism made him a formidable opponent for any equally loyal Unionist to challenge. Indeed, the Wisconsin representative wasted little time in making his concerns about potential traitors in the government known. On the second day of proceedings, July 9, 1861, he made the resolution that the Speaker of the House appoint members to a committee to review the cases of those "who are known to entertain sentiments of hostility to the Government of the United States, and those who have refused to take the oath to support the Constitution of the United States." Along with the power to examine the cases, Potter requested that the committee also be able "to send for persons and papers" that would established the suspects' guilt or innocence. After a vote in the affirmative, Potter's committee formed.[5]

The appointed men who joined Potter were of varied backgrounds. Representative Sidney Edgerton of Ohio's 18th District had issued a crushing condemnation of slavery in an early 1861 address, stating, "[If] the minority can dictate what shall be the peculiar views of a presidential candidate on the subject of slavery or any other subject, then we are slaves; and if we submit to such dictation, we ought to be slaves."[6] Representative Edward Haight of New York's 9th District was a War Democrat who had only just begun his service in March 1861. Representative Samuel Fessenden of Maine's 3rd District was also a newcomer to the House, although he was a Republican. Together they formed the Committee on the Loyalty of Clerks and Other Persons Employed by the Government, but the group's unofficial title of the Potter Committee spoke volumes about who was the driving force behind the effort.

Potter lived up to his reputation in the committee's early days. A week after organizing the committee, Potter approached the House for the assignment of a clerk to assist in the organization of evidence that daily arrived at their doorstep. The Wisconsin representative's request concerned Ohio representative Clement Vallandigham, a Peace Democrat, who asserted that the committee's investigation should only "be confined to the present session." "Before the present session closes," Potter assured him, "it will be necessary that a resolution shall be introduced here authorizing the committee to sit during recess." The number of reports that the committee received was supposedly so numerous that it would "be utterly impossible for [the committee] to close their labors before the close of the present session." A rewording of the resolution was suggested, and Potter's request was granted.[7]

Potter's report to the House on July 30, 1861, demonstrated his commitment to his work. After noting the great attention that the committee had given to the reports it had received, Potter noted that the committee members had "as yet scarcely advanced beyond its threshold." He stated, however, that the committee's existence was easily validated only one week into its work. The testimony demonstrated that there were numerous disloyal persons in the clerkships of the US government. The committee was "astonished at the number and aggravation of the well-authenticated cases of disloyalty" and expressed its outrage that some of the first round of the accused continued to hold their positions even after their superiors had been approached with the charges made against them. "That such [accused] persons should be retained in office," Potter exclaimed, "and *in some instances retained where the facts have been brought to the knowledge of those who have the power of removal,* must be the occasion of profound grief and humiliation to every patriotic and loyal heart." Potter believed that the news should stir anger within his fellow representatives; indeed, it might "well excite the honest indignation of the country."[8]

The battle to stir indignation against any department head who failed to immediately dismiss a suspected employee had begun. After securing the necessities to move forward with the investigation during the congressional recess, Potter's committee followed a simple method for uncovering disloyal employees. Informants were urged to come forward, with the assurance that the men whom they accused would not be able to refute them in the presence of the committee. Indeed, the accused were not made aware of the claims against them, and thus the committee collected its evidence with few voices raised against its proceedings.

For several contemporaries, who reflected on the methods of the committee after its official report was released in January 1862, the proceedings seemed to challenge the Sixth Amendment of the Constitution, particularly on the point that "the accused shall enjoy the right . . . to be confronted with the witnesses against him."[9] The Potter Committee maintained both during and after the investigation, however, that no rights were violated, as the accused were not on trial but merely being investigated by members of Congress. Still, it was clear that by December 1861, not all of the executive departments were willing to cooperate so readily with the committee's demands for response. Along with the secretaries of the Treasury and the interior, Abraham Lincoln found himself the target of the committee's displeasure as a result of his perceived inaction in response to the news of traitors within his own home.

THE ACCUSED WITHIN THE WHITE HOUSE

The investigation into Lincoln's White House staff was well under way by September 1861. Indeed, by the twelfth of that month, John Potter was prepared to confront Lincoln about suspected disloyalty within the Executive Mansion grounds. He sent a letter to the president that day, along with the evidence he had collected about Lincoln's gardener, messenger, and doorkeepers. While simple and to the point, Potter's note to Lincoln also sent two very clear messages. First, Potter clearly conveyed that Lincoln's gardener should be the president's chief concern, as out of the four suspects, only John Watt was named within the letter. Thomas Stackpole, Edward McManus, and Thomas Burns were merely listed as "others" within the introduction. Second, Potter concluded with a reminder that Lincoln's handling of this matter would be viewed in the public eye. After noting that he was doing his work "from a sense of public duty," Potter reminded Lincoln, "As this evidence will be laid before the House of Representatives, the committee deem it proper and respectful to submit the same to you, in order that you may take such action in the premises as in your judgment you may deem proper."[10] The caution was subtle, but Potter was indicating the first signs of his willingness to test presidential power with a flexing of congressional authority.

We cannot be certain exactly what evidence the president first received from Potter, as those records do not remain in any collected works of Abraham Lincoln's life, but from the eventual publication of the committee's findings, the presented evidence emerged. Of John Watt, whom Potter was particularly careful to name to the president, a little over a page appeared in the official report. By the time the news reached the public, Watt had been promoted to a lieutenant in the US Army, a fact that Potter found particularly disturbing. Four witnesses spoke against the man, and one of them was the postmaster for

Washington, DC. Two merely said that Watt's secessionist proclivities were well known, and another witness claimed to have heard Watt speak against the Union's soldiers as "cowards." While in Philadelphia's St. Lawrence Hotel, Watt supposedly voiced his belief "'that the southern confederacy must be acknowledged. That the United States could never conquer the south.'" Additionally, the Philadelphia witness said that he heard Watt denigrate the capabilities of the army's officers and praise Jefferson Davis as "'the best and bravest man in America.'" Another witness claimed to have heard similar from Watt in Philadelphia while the gardener was there and that Watt and his friends "'were much elated at the result of the battle of Bull Run, and were very free in expressing their feelings.'"[11]

Even more witnesses stepped forward to accuse messenger Thomas Stackpole. No fewer than six witnesses condemned Stackpole for traitorous behavior. Most of the accusers condemned him for visiting with "'one of the most bitter secessionists in the city,'" named Bill Spaulding. Most damningly, a guard at the White House had reported that in April 1861, he saw Stackpole leave the White House "through the little gate on the side into the street, and [he] appeared to be in conversation with some person." That person, he later determined, was Bill Spaulding. A visitor had just entered the White House, and Stackpole appeared to come "out from the President's House nearly every time that any one passed in, to make report of the situation inside." As Stackpole had to retrieve a pass from the guard every time he left, the guard supposedly kept a running total of Stackpole's leavings and figured the number to be "at least eight times." Purportedly, the guard became so agitated that he threatened to shoot Stackpole, saying, "'If Jeff. Davis comes here to-night I will put a pill through you.' Stackpole replied, 'you would not do that would you?'" The only other condemning evidence the committee could offer was a conversation that Stackpole had conducted with another witness in which the messenger said "'that he was still a Breckinridge democrat, and that they couldn't get along without him at the President's House.'"[12]

Only one witness named the two other accused servants. While on the grounds of the Executive Mansion, a Charles F. Anderson claimed to have eavesdropped on two men. One of those men was identified within the report only as "Edwards." In reality, this was Edward McManus, the doorkeeper of the White House's north entrance. McManus, claimed Anderson, had bitterly complained to his companions about the movement of troops to nearby Alexandria. "It was wrong to send the troops over there," McManus supposedly said, since "it all came from the black republican abolitionists of the north; and that it was a misfortune that they ever had anything to do with the government." While this could be viewed as a complaint about the politics of his employer, the most damning words of the supposed exchange followed. The witness testified that after one of McManus's associates assured the doorkeeper, "'Never mind, Jeff. Davis will be in power here within three months,'" instead of rebuking his companion, McManus supposedly responded with "'the sooner the better'" and embellished the statement by adding "'that Jeff. Davis was the finest man that ever was in the White House.'"[13]

Caught up in this supposed exchange was another White House doorkeeper, Thomas Burns. Noting the doorkeeper as "an Irishman" in the report, the witness failed to link any substantial words to Burns. However, the Potter Committee apparently believed the report that Burns "'seemed to agree with all they said'" was significant enough evidence, as the doorkeeper's "'manner and expression of countenance strongly indicated that he agreed with them in their sentiment.'" In this instance, clearly, Potter's committee deviated from its commitment to engage only those witnesses "who have associated with the accused for months or years" or whose words were without "mere partisan or personal feeling."[14]

The charges against McManus and Burns were flimsy at best and, like many of the reports made to the Potter Committee, based primarily on hearsay. Both men were also of Irish origin. Though the majority of the domestic staff within the White House had been of a foreign origin since the Buchanan administration (Thomas Stackpole being the exception), it was possible that a touch of xenophobia was at play against the two doormen. Certainly, a part of the testimony against the two men played on stereotypes of servants, particularly Irish-American ones, during the time period. Every employer's worst fear about his servants, beyond the suspicion that they were stealing the silverware or cheating their employer of quality hours, was that they would tarnish the reputation of the family.[15] In the witness's testimony against McManus, the doorkeeper's words ended with the flourish "that Mr. and Mrs. Lincoln were low, mean people, and that they did not know how to act as gentlemen and ladies." McManus's supposed speech was as perfectly crafted in its social implications as it was in its political ones.[16]

Indeed, there was ample evidence from within the White House that the protection of the First Family's image was of the utmost importance to Edward McManus. In one of his many published accounts of Lincoln, former secretary William Stoddard noted that McManus, whom he referred to by the affectionate title "Old Edward" in consideration of his many years as a White House doorkeeper, took great pride in any action, be it social or political, that magnified his employer in a positive way. "Anything," Stoddard emphasized, "to the glory of the President met [Old Edward's] gratified approval as though he himself participated in such sanction."[17] It stood to reason that any action to the detriment of the president affected McManus and the rest of the staff as well. Likewise, Lincoln's secretary John Hay spoke positively of both the older doorkeeper and Thomas Burns to Charles G. Halpine in 1863, describing McManus as a "chatty old greyhaired gentleman" and Burns as a man who had "outlived the storm of two reigns."[18]

Lincoln was aware of such service as he reviewed the evidence brought before him by Potter. Indeed, the president even had fond memories of his doorkeeper as, according to Stoddard, McManus was "said to have been the first man met in the White House by Mr. Lincoln who succeeded in making him laugh."[19] The president's initial thoughts on the charges against his household staff do not exist in any surviving correspondence, but his initial reactions from the writings of others can be tracked. In response to the charges of disloyalty in his home, Lincoln moved quickly to gather evidence and hear personal testimony from the accused. His reaction to the evidence presented, however, was not rash. In falling back on his training as a lawyer and by taking his time to consider the evidence presented against his staff, Lincoln proceeded far more slowly than pleased John Potter.

THE PRESIDENT'S INVESTIGATION

According to Lincoln's former law partner William Herndon, Lincoln once told him, "When I have a particular case in hand, I have that motive and feel an interest in the case, feel an interest in ferreting out the questions to the bottom, love to dig up the question by the roots and hold it up and dry it before the fires of the mind."[20] Lincoln displayed a similar "interest in ferreting out" and digging into the claims made against his employees. A day after Potter wrote his note to Lincoln, the president showed up on the doorstep of Commissioner of Public Buildings Benjamin Brown French. Lincoln had appointed him to the position only six days earlier. As commissioner of public buildings, French was in charge of appointing the staff for many of the public buildings, and he shared oversight of the White House servants alongside the Lincolns. French had just penned in his diary, "There never was so still a time in Washington," when the Lincolns' carriage pulled up with both the president and the First

Lady. Lincoln entered French's home and the two men "had a talk about the charges preferred vs. Watt, Stackpole, etc., at the White House."[21] The initial briefing complete, Lincoln instructed French to visit the White House at 8:30 the next morning for further discussion. French's involvement in the Potter investigation had only just begun.

Showing up promptly at the president's doorstep at the appointed time, French immediately became familiar with the charges brought against Lincoln's household. "The President handed me the communication from Mr. Potter," French noted, and soon the commissioner was brought up-to-date on the charges of disloyalty "in which Maj. Watt, Mr. Stackpole & Edward McManus, are all implicated." Lincoln then asked Watt to make his case against the committee's charges. French listened attentively while Watt presented his "testimony *per contra*, which, considering it goes to prove a negative," said French, "is very strong." French decided that Watt was not guilty of the charges brought against him. Lincoln's reaction was unknown, but given that all of the accused retained their positions, it was likely along similar lines. The president sent French home with the charges against the other accused, for which there was not yet firm evidence. French did not appear terribly concerned over the charges, however, as he merely noted that he would simply look it over on Sunday "as a matter of curiosity."[22]

A month passed without any reactionary response from Lincoln concerning disloyalty within his home. Midway through October, however, Lincoln sent French a note asking the commissioner for an update on Thomas Stackpole. French's October 15 response assured the president that he had produced "nothing definite against Stackpole except what is contained in Mr. Potter's report." "As a matter of course," French noted, "all sorts of stories, based, probably, on [the Potter] report, are brought to me, but I put no faith in any thing I hear unless it be substantiated by 'proof as strong as Holy Writ.'" French's letter to Lincoln conveyed his personal desire to remove no one from his position within the White House. The note carried another warning, however, that Lincoln likely would not have missed even without French's conclusion. The committee's investigation into the White House servants was public knowledge; indeed, French acknowledged to Lincoln that "such a general outcry has been made against some of the employees at your house, that I did not know but it might be expedient to try to get rid of the clamor by the removal or resignation of some of them."[23] To do anything but immediately react to the issue was to invite public criticism.

Lincoln, however, refused to react without evidence stronger than hearsay. In fact, he merely attempted to move Watt from outside the White House and into "his proper place in Regiment" between September 1861 and January 1862.[24] Stackpole, McManus, and Burns continued to work in the Lincoln White House when the committee's report was released in January 1862. Indeed, not long after Potter's letter reached Lincoln's desk in September, Lincoln endorsed Watt to become a lieutenant in the Union army. Thomas Stackpole remained in the White House until after Lincoln's death and was one of only two people to whom Lincoln ever extended a personal loan while he was president. The president made the $380 loan to Stackpole on November 8, 1861, only a month after he quizzed French on the commissioner's thoughts about Stackpole's loyalty.[25]

That the final decision fell to Lincoln to keep the accused employed was evidenced by French's closing assertion to Lincoln that he would not interfere without word from the president. Perhaps Lincoln viewed the situation in the same manner that French did, believing that if they removed the accused, in French's words, "it would turn out about the same as the fable of the fox and swarm of flies—a new swarm, hungrier than the old, would come!"[26] Or perhaps, as suggested by Lincoln's loan to Stackpole, the president simply trusted the men who worked for him. At any rate, intimidating hints from Potter that the public would not be happy to learn of his perceived inaction did not sway Lincoln. The president's own investigation into the White House's supposedly "disloyal" employees had not resulted in incriminatory evidence concerning treason. As such, the accused remained, even though this would have provided the perfect opportunity for Lincoln to remove gardener John Watt, whom he personally disliked, from his home.

That Lincoln harbored suspicions of untrustworthiness against Watt was evident in a letter between Lincoln's personal secretaries. Two days after Lincoln made his loan to Stackpole, John Hay wrote to a traveling John Nicolay, "Hell is to pay about Watt's affairs. I think the Tycoon begins to suspect him." No love was lost between the president's personal secretary and Watt (indeed, Hay hoped that Watt "could be struck with lighting"), but the secretary's ire with the gardener had to do with finances—both Hay and Nicolay suspected Watt of assisting Mrs. Lincoln in dubious financial affairs. They were entirely correct in this suspicion, as Watt had assisted the First Lady in covering up some of her expenses. Even at that moment, Watt was traveling with Mrs. Lincoln in New York, assisting the First Lady on one of her shopping trips to the city. In November, however, Lincoln's secretaries could only continue to monitor the gardener's and the First Lady's monetary interests. Watt "has his eye peeled for a pop at me," believed Hay, "because I wont let Madame have our stationery fund."[27]

The Potter investigation into Watt likely pleased Hay, who undoubtedly was thrilled that Lincoln was beginning to reach the end of his patience with the gardener. Covering excess spending and influencing Mary Lincoln, however, was not the sort of treason that Potter's committee targeted. Still, Hay's words suggested that Lincoln held an unfavorable opinion of Watt in the fall of 1861. This was perhaps further supported by the fact that Lincoln sent a letter on November 16, 1861, to Lorenzo Thomas, letting him know that while Watt "had been detailed to do service about the White-House," he was no longer "needed for that purpose" and Thomas should "assign him to his proper place in Regiment."[28]

Mary Lincoln believed that Watt's name appeared before the Potter Committee because of one William Wood, and she put pen to paper the day after Potter's note arrived at the Executive Mansion in September 1861 to share her thoughts on the accusations with the congressman. Wood and Mary were connected to one another in both public and private gossip during the Lincolns' early days in Washington, and Wood used his budding relationship with the First Lady in his attempt to secure the nomination and appointment as commissioner of public buildings. At some point prior to September 1861, however, the two had a falling out. Wood's dream of being commissioner was dead. Mary Lincoln wrote to Potter that Wood "supposes Watts [sic], was one of the means of his removal—and employs men, to bring false charges against him."[29] The First Lady also claimed to recognize the name of one of Watt's accusers as a man she knew to be an associate of Wood's.

Mary's difficulties with both Woods and Watt stemmed from allowing these men into her confidence. In his attempt to win her favor, however, Wood fell afoul of Mary Lincoln. His attempt to bring the Potter Committee's investigation to the White House was one that he undoubtedly knew would cause both Watt and Mary Lincoln great grief and hand wringing. They could not have anyone looking into Watt's dealings too closely, or Mary's own financial indiscretions might be uncovered. Two weeks after Potter launched his investigation, Watt received a commission to the lieutenancy of the US Army. Why did Abraham Lincoln meet this request? Supposedly, Mary refused to share sleeping quarters with her husband until Watt's request was met.[30] She did not simply lobby her husband over the matter of Watt's innocence, either. A week before Potter wrote to Lincoln, on September 8, Mary had already written to Secretary Caleb Smith about Wood's accusations and promised him that "Major French, who has long known Mr Watts [*sic*], will bear testimony to his good name."[31] Likewise, she wrote to Simon Cameron on September 12, instructing him to speak to Watt directly if he had any concerns about the "false charges" Wood had made against Watt.[32]

Exactly what Lincoln knew of the situation prior to Potter's letter on his desk is unknown. What is certain, however, is that Lincoln had become increasingly impatient with Watt as November passed. The president thus attempted to re-move Watt from everyday contact with Mary yet allowed him to remain in the army. Had he believed that the gardener was guilty of treason, he could have easily removed Watt thanks to the accusations made in the Potter Committee report. But with a lack of firm evidence concerning treason, Lincoln remained unwilling to use the committee to remove the troubling Watt from his household.

By January, however, Lincoln likely knew that real damage could be caused by Watt's promotion; Potter had begun to aim for higher targets than clerks. On Potter's part, this development seemed to come not from any personal animosity, but from frustration that suspected disloyal individuals remained a threat to the Union. Only a month before the official report was to be released to the public, Potter once again returned to the House floor to request assistance in urging the executive departments into action. Particularly, a resolution requesting cooperation singled out the secretaries of the Treasury and the interior, Salmon Chase and Caleb Smith. When asked by Kentucky representative Charles A. Wickliffe "for the character of the information called for," Potter reported that neither Chase nor Smith had provided communication that would assist the committee in determining "whether the departments have removed those who have been reported to them as disloyal." The committee wished that "if such persons have not been removed, the departments by this call would have an opportunity to furnish the reasons."

Wickliffe's response signaled the unease that some members of the House felt at the committee's proceedings: while "he did not feel himself called upon to defend the departments named . . . he did not understand how far this House has the right to assume the executive powers of this government." However, after another representative voiced his concern that those who were "charged with disloyalty ought to have an opportunity of refuting the allegations which he had learned incidentally had been afforded them," Wickliffe asserted, "If we have heads of department who are not competent to judge of the qualifications or loyalty of their subordinates, we should strike and remove them." Further than that, he believed, "We should aim at higher game than mere clerks."[33]

The end result of the debate on the House floor was that "the resolution being objected to was not received for consideration."[34] Yet the aim of the committee was clear for all to see. Potter's committee was already challenging the president's cabinet members. In the *Report on the Loyalty of Government Employees*, Lincoln's perceived inaction concerning the White House staff, particularly John Watt, would be targeted and publicly made known as well.

LINCOLN AND EXECUTIVE OVERSIGHT

The report quickly cast its membership into the role of intercessor between the executive offices and the loyal Unionist audience that awaited its findings. Then the committee surreptitiously began its work to cast doubt on the decisions made by the executive branch by claiming that it was "the office of the committee to step in and supply a channel of communication between the people, who have for years known those disloyal men, and the distinguished gentlemen whose duty it becomes, upon proper evidence, to remove them from office." The people, of course, knew "that in a time of civil war, disloyal men will be constantly seeking the confidence of the government, in order to betray its secrets, and to enjoy its patronage." Likewise, "it would be strange" if such attempts "were not often successful." As such, it was "therefore in no spirit of distrust of those who have been called by the President to aid him in the execution of the laws and the administration of affairs that the committee ask for authority to continue their inquiries into the character of public servants."

This was war, in other words, and mistakes were bound to occur even under watchful executive eyes. The committee simply planned to add another set of eyes to make certain that no traitor went undetected. When framed in this manner, the explanation encouraged the audience to view executive oversight as a natural consequence of war. Lincoln and his cabinet could then be viewed as not *intentionally* failing in leadership but as simply needing the additional support and guidance of the legislative branch in a time of unprecedented circumstances. Indeed, Potter and his fellow committee members went on to acknowledge that "the position of President and heads of departments is not favorable to the receipt of information prejudicial to the loyalty of those employed under them." The damning evidence belonged to "fellow clerks and citizens of Washington, who find it difficult to gain access to those in power, amid the press of public business."[35]

In conducting its investigation, the Potter Committee asserted that, given the national crisis, it collected testimony in the best manner that it thought possible. Its defenses were many. The committee asserted that its task began "by calling such witnesses as the committee were led to believe, from the best information they could obtain, possessed the most reliable knowledge of the sentiments and views of the parties charged in relation to the present rebellion." To ensure the witnesses' honor, the committee noted that testimony by oath was required and that the majority of those who came forward with evidence were well qualified to testify, as they were fellow clerks who worked alongside the accused. The committee obviously realized that such witnesses would be called into question, as the report quickly assured that Potter and the others had "endeavored to avoid, as far as possible, all testimony founded in mere partisan or personal feeling." Likewise, while the committee sought to avoid such errors, some testimony "may not, in all cases, have escaped this source of misinformation," as it was a natural consequence of the times.[36]

Potter's committee seemed to find it likely that innocent men had been caught up in their investigation. However, the committee's conclusions regarding the possibility that it pursued innocents was remarkably far removed from Lincoln's approach involving his own employees. "It may happen that loyal men have become the victims of unjust suspicion," the Potter Committee report conceded, "and the fact is to be regretted." The benefits of the removal of a few innocents, however, far outweighed the cost of undetected traitors, in the committee members' eyes. They believed that the innocent should not have felt betrayed; after all, "they cannot complain if the government should feel constrained to remove [the innocent] from public at a moment when its very existence is imperiled by treachery and violence." At any rate, the jobless could take comfort in the fact that "in no instances has any evil consequences followed to the individual other than the loss of the office." The innocents' patriotism would see them through the ordeal; due to their continued upstanding character, the public would have little doubt that only a misunderstanding had somehow occurred.[37]

Additionally, anyone who read the opening of the report might have been a little uneasy at the method the committee freely admitted to taking in ferreting out traitors. "As a general rule," Potter explained, "the parties charged were not examined by the committee; nor were they notified of the charges preferred against them with a view to the introduction of rebutting testimony." His explanation for the committee's actions was simple: the congressional committee did not function as executives of punishment. They could not cast final judgment, nor should anyone think that they had done so. Indeed, Potter likened his committee to "the grand jury, rather than to the court of justice." His report gave the impression that the committee's findings were merely relayed "to the President or to the heads of departments, with abstracts of the evidence in each case," and had little impact on the accused in the court of public opinion.[38]

Indeed, Potter made certain that everyone knew that the burden of judging the cases fell to the president and his men, on "whom the responsibility rests, and who may be supposed to feel the deepest interest in the matter, [since they] should be correctly informed as to the character of clerks and others, who stand in confidential relations to them and to the government." Whether or not the president and the heads of the departments trusted the evidence that Potter supplied, "the committee nevertheless believed that [the alert] might lead to further inquiries on the part of the head of the department, or other appointing power, to whom it was sent." The times were dangerous, and "the importance and the necessity for immediate action in the premises" meant that time could not be wasted.[39]

Yet within its report, the Potter Committee was clearly dismayed by the fact that it believed that time *was* being wasted. Throughout the report, the committee communicated its displeasure that certain heads of the departments were not moving with the haste it deemed necessary. Particularly, it reported unfavorably on Abraham Lincoln's failure to remove John Watt from service not only from within his home but also from his position as a lieutenant. The committee included its letter to Lincoln warning that Watt was being investigated, and it also carried Potter's warning to Lincoln that the House would be informed that Watt was being investigated. Potter had sent the letter to Lincoln as a courtesy, "in order that [he might] take such action in the premises as in [his] judgment [he might] deem proper." Lincoln had not only failed to heed Potter's warning but also advanced the gardener to the position of lieutenant in the US Army. The committee was not shy about pointing out this fact. "It is proper to state," the report noted, "that more than two weeks before the appointment of Mr. Watt as a lieutenant in the army the chairman informed the President that testimony had been taken before the committee gravely impeaching the loyalty of [Watt]." Because of this, Potter and his committee could "only add an expression of surprise that, in the face of such testimony, a man clearly disloyal, instead of being instantly removed, should have been elevated to a higher and more responsible position."[40]

PRESS COVERAGE OF THE POTTER
COMMITTEE'S REPORT

The report placed the president and his decision in a bad light in some circles, and in the most public of manner. The press was not going to let the incident pass, either. The *Alexandria (VA) Local News* rehashed the committee's critique of Lincoln's actions when it told its readers on January 29, 1862, that "Potter's Investigating Committee report unfavorably upon the case of John Watt, late a gardener at the President's House, and complain that notwithstanding they reported their charge of disloyalty to the President, so far from that individual's being dismissed, he was appointed a Lieutenant in the U.S. Army—at which 'the Committee express their surprise.'"[41] The *Cincinnati Daily Press* called for department heads who were "knowingly retaining clerks even suspected of disloyalty" to "be themselves shortened an official head."[42]

Another Ohio newspaper, the *Ashtabula Weekly Telegraph*, also seized on the fact that the president's gardener had been caught in the committee's net when it reported that "the late gardener of the President—subsequently promoted to a Lieutenant in the U.S army," had "devoted his leisure hours to the company of avowed Secessionists." Such information was an "unpleasant development," the newspaper noted, "but it [was] proper that the country should know of them in order that the proper remedy may be demanded." "Popular sentiment," the newspaper believed, would rightly allow Potter's committee to "continue until every Traitor has been dismissed from the confidence and pay of the Government."[43] These public calls for the executive branch to bow to the findings of a congressional committee were dangerous to both Lincoln and his department heads. Yet Lincoln had another public weapon at his disposal: the fear that the Potter Committee's procedure threatened the republic.

For all of the grief that the press coverage of the committee's report caused Lincoln, he was not without his defenders in the press. Through either their support or condemnation of the proceedings, national coverage of the investigation both justified and condemned the executive branch's leadership in dealing with the accused. The *Washington (DC) Evening Star* initiated a call for caution when reviewing the Potter Committee's findings, and one can deduce the varied attitudes toward the committee's proceedings in the responses to the newspaper's January 29, 1862, coverage of the report.

The *Evening Star* began its coverage in a familiar pattern. Like other publications, it acknowledged that little surprise should greet the fact that there were Southern enemies among them in this time of war in Washington. Indeed, the writer assumed that his readers knew that there "must be much disloyalty among some employed by the Government." However, the *Evening Star* made an interesting choice in describing the committee's efforts when it noted that, just as Potter and his fellow committee members had done their job of tracking down guilty individuals, the report "no less clearly proves that a portion of the testimony relied on by the committee in framing their bills of indictment against individuals, is of parties notoriously the personal enemies of those they seek to arraign." The *Evening Star* scathingly continued by noting that condemning testimony came from individuals "whose testimony in open court would not be regarded by any jury of their fellow citizens, as being worth a straw." It went on to decry the practice of accusing men who had not been allowed either to testify on their own behalf or to meet their accusers in the committee chamber. The *Evening Star* did not take the Potter Committee at its word that it had done its due diligence to check the trustworthiness of its informers, concluding that "no pains seems to have been taken by the committee to ascertain the animus of witnesses in volunteering their testimony."[44]

Thus in the *Evening Star*, Lincoln and the executive branch found a friend. The article explained that the "fact" that Potter's committee gathered ex parte evidence "accounts for the declension of the Executive officers of the Government in many cases to act upon the committee's representations concerning persons accused by it." In light of such actions that would endanger the Union's values, the executive's decision to keep men such as Watt, Stackpole, McManus, and Burns employed was the correct one. By allowing tainted testimony into the committee's chambers, Potter and his fellow committee members had "produced testimony overbalancing that secretly produced against them."[45]

In closing, the *Evening Star* still acknowledged that it "regard[ed] the report as demonstrating the necessity for ridding the public service of all who are not heartily loyal." At the same time, however, it closed by warning that the details of the report should encourage those in the future to "hereafter guar[d] against the possibility of doing injustice to individuals through star chamber trials, in which the accused are wholly deprived of the right of self-defence."[46]

By concluding with a comment about the "star chamber," the *Evening Star* dramatically ushered the nineteenth-century equivalent of the "legal freedoms" bogeyman into the room. With the ongoing war and suspension of habeas corpus, it was increasingly easy to make references to the fifteenth- and sixteenth-century Star Chamber courts of England. This early modern throwback was a product of the times: literature on the Tudor dynasty was popular, and books such as Agnes Strickland's *Lives of the Queens of England* and David Hume's behemoth *The History of England* enjoyed popularity throughout the nineteenth century. Particularly, readers were attentive to Hume's description of what was regarded as the Star Chamber's "dangerous" inquiry into the lives of English, and later, British, subjects. Even though such scholars as the British historian Lord Bacon had "extoll[ed] the utility of this court," Hume warned that "men began, even during the age of that historian, to feel that so arbitrary a jurisdiction was incompatible with liberty."[47] Certainly, Hume's *History of England* did little to improve the Star Chamber's reputation within the pages of his book, and Americans took note. They used it passionately in their newspaper pieces throughout the years, throughout both the North and South, to attack the president, cabinet secretaries, and Congress. It was regarded as one of the "dangerous instruments to play with" in politics and was pointed out to have "been odious for centuries, even under a monarchy which is now free, and in which the subject may write and say what he pleases."[48]

The words of the *Evening Star* were eagerly picked up around the nation. The *Alexandria Local News* quoted the *Star*'s assertion that the committee report showed "the necessity for ridding the public service of all who are not heartily loyal, and at the same time for hereafter guarding against the possibility of doing injustice to individuals through the star chamber trials, in which the accused are wholly deprived of the right of self-defence."[49] Not all agreed, however. An author who identified himself only as "Pro Patria" in the *National Republican* angrily seized upon the *Star*'s words, declaring, "Let the investigating committee persevere in the good work, even though partial success only crown their arduous labors. Traitors, or those included that way, say it is a *Star Chamber*, and *ex parte* proceeding. Let their efforts be vindicated by the Government and the country. 'Let justice be done, though the heavens fall!' 'Be just, and fear not.'"[50]

Yet some still did not think the committee's investigation was worth the price it would exact from the republic. The *Alexandria Local News* reprinted the *New York World*'s thoughts on the investigation: "It is a notorious fact that many of the cases narrated in [the report] have ere this been refuted by evidence proving loyalty, and stating that the committee has been the receptacle of evidence of rivals, enemies, and disappointed office-seekers."[51] Clearly, there were those who did not trust the evidence revealed by the committee, but could Lincoln rely on such assertions to justify his inaction toward those who were accused in his own household?

There was evidence from within the White House that the president valued the reporting on the committee's abuses by the *Evening Star*, the *Local News*, and the *World*. As historian Michael Burlingame has pointed out, Lincoln's secretary William Stoddard submitted newspaper articles that were friendly toward the president's policies and may have been written at the president's directive.[52] Stoddard initially covered the committee's work positively in the days before Potter's September letter to Lincoln. On June 24, Stoddard had lamented, "One of our most constant vexations is the consciousness that our city teems with spies."[53] On August 5, he happily noted, "The work of purging the Departments of secession employees, has gone on merrily the past week, and a number of valuable sources of information to the rebel leaders have been mercilessly dried up."[54] On September 5, only a week before Potter contacted Lincoln, Stoddard proclaimed, "The 'Potter Committee' has done and is doing a most important work, and have made themselves a terror to the swarming spies of Washington."[55]

Early February told a different story. Lincoln clearly felt the pressure of the public coverage of both his and his cabinet members' perceived inaction. The public did not know of the private steps he had taken to investigate his employees' loyalty, and his insistence on the existence of incriminating evidence could be taken as weakness by some. Thus, in Stoddard's nameless reporting, we find perhaps the fullest defense of Lincoln's actions:

> Speaking of the faithfulness of many of our leading men, do we not often forget, in our hot haste to denounce corruption, what a terrible thing is the injustice which deprives a man causelessly of that honor and reputation which is dearer than life? I have known cases, of men sent home in disgrace and ruin after long, severe and self-sacrificing public service, on the strength of accusation brought against them by personal and political enemies. There can be [no] doubt that every such fall weakens the republic dangerously. We should be careful of the honor of those in power, wary of believing aught to their discredit, even if we add to this a more vengeful bitterness in punishing the undeniably guilty.[56]

Potter might have argued that any of the accused who were truly loyal would be vindicated by actions over time, but Stoddard painted a picture of the stark reality. The accused's names were, even at that moment, being publicly tarnished. They had not been given the ability to challenge their accusers during testimony. The damage was done, and those who worked in the White House knew this. Not only that, but in what was labeled a dangerous threat to the republic, the committee was now damaging the names of the president and his cabinet members without respect to either their position or judgment. Suddenly, the enemy was not the men who worked within the halls of the White House; the enemy was those who made a stab at the heart of the republic's values.

Because enough of the public held strongly to such a belief, Lincoln was able to retain the accused within his household. The only exception was Watt, whose lieutenant appointment the Senate invalidated early in February 1862 and whose questionable dealings with the First Lady finally caught up with him.[57] For Lincoln, the entire affair was a lesson in the difficulties of managing life in a home where the domestic and political spheres were so intertwined. More significantly, however, the investigation the Potter Committee conducted into the loyalty of Lincoln's household staff allowed him to test the strength of his presidential position and justified his leadership style of steadily pursuing the truth. Lincoln recognized the fallacy of being guilty by association based on circumstantial or hearsay evidence. From his experience as a lawyer, he knew that the accusations against his employees would never be admitted in a court of law. All of the committee's actions—its choice of words to chastise both the president and the department heads in its official report, Potter's attempts on the House floor to whip up indignation against executive inaction, and the manner in which the committee's findings were made public in the press—were designed to challenge executive authority.

Fortunately for Lincoln, although the indignation stirred up by the report was high, his faith that the people would respect his honorable position was validated. Potter's committee did not find itself active beyond 1862. A committee from the House of Representatives, it seemed, could not hold the president hostage even in a time of great national fear. Nor could it fully intimidate a frightened public into believing that its safety should come at the cost of the accused being denied the right to confront their accusers. The people's belief that their legal rights had to be protected ultimately trumped the nation's massive fears about the accused who maintained their positions. Ultimately, Lincoln was able to stand his ground against those within Congress who made a power play to question his judgment. Through steady leadership and the values he held as a lawyer, he remained committed to republican values and was not swayed by evidence that did not produce a reasonable doubt about his employees.

Notes

1. Margaret Leech, *Reveille in Washington: 1860–1865* (New York: Grosset and Dunlap, 1941), 15.

2. "The Potter Investigating Committee and the Traitors: Their Abettors and Apologists," *National Republican* (Washington, DC), February 6, 1862.

3. January 9, 1861, entry, Horatio Nelson Taft, "The Papers of Horatio Nelson Taft," *American Memory from the Library of Congress*, accessed November 1, 2012, http://www.loc.gov/collection/diary-of-horatio-taft/.

4. William B. Hesseltine, "The Pryor-Potter Duel," *Wisconsin Magazine of History* 27, no. 4 (June 1944): 400–9.

5. Cong. Globe, 37th Cong., 1st sess. (1861), 26.

6. Sidney Edgerton, *State of the Union: Speech of Hon. Sidney Edgerton, of Ohio, Delivered in the House of Representatives, January 31, 1861* (Washington, DC: H. Polkinhorn, 1861), 1.

7. Cong. Globe, 37th Cong., 1st sess., 1861, 148.

8. Ibid., 357; emphasis added.

9. "Bill of Rights Transcript Text," *The Charters of Freedom*, accessed December 29, 2013, http://www.archives.gov/exhibits/charters/bill_of_rights_transcript.html.

10. "Loyalty of Clerks and Other Persons Employed by Government," in *Reports of Committees of the House of Representatives Made during the Second Session of the Thirty-Seventh Congress. 1861–'62, Printed by Order of the House of Representatives. In Four Volumes*, vol. 3, no. 16 (Washington, DC: Government Printing Office, 1862), 29.

11. Ibid.

12. Ibid., 84–85.

13. Ibid., 85.

14. Ibid., 85, 2.

15. For American views on servants, see Daniel E. Sutherland, *Americans and Their Servants: Domestic Service in the United States from 1800 to 1920* (Baton Rouge: Louisiana State University Press, 1981) and Margaret Lynch-Brennan, *The Irish Bridget: Irish Immigrant Women in Domestic Service in America, 1840–1930* (Syracuse, NY: Syracuse University Press, 2009).

16. "Loyalty of Clerks," 85.

17. William O. Stoddard, *Lincoln's Third Secretary: The Memoirs of William O. Stoddard* (New York: Exposition Press, 1955), 74.

18. John Hay to Charles G. Halpine, November 22, 1863, in *At Lincoln's Side: John Hay's Civil War Correspondence and Selected Writings*, ed. Michael Burlingame (Carbondale: Southern Illinois University Press, 2000), 68.

19. William O. Stoddard, *Inside the White House in War Times* (New York: Charles L. Webster & Co., 1890), 10.

20. Don E. Fehrenbacher and Virginia Fehrenbacher, eds., *Recollected Words of Abraham Lincoln* (Stanford, CA: Stanford University Press, 1996), 242.

21. September 13, 1861, in Benjamin Brown French, *Witness to the Young Republic: A Yankee's Journal 1828–1870* (Hanover, NH: University Press of New England, 1989), 375.

22. September 14, 1861, ibid., 376.

23. Benjamin B. French to Abraham Lincoln, October 15, 1861, Abraham Lincoln Papers, Library of Congress, American Memory, accessed September 10, 2013, http://memory.loc.gov/ammem/alhtml/malhome.html.

24. Abraham Lincoln to Lorenzo Thomas, November, 16, 1861, in *The Collected Works of Abraham Lincoln*, ed. Roy P. Basler et al. (New Brunswick, NJ: Rutgers University Press, 1953), 5:25.

25. Harry E. Pratt, *The Personal Finances of Abraham Lincoln*. (Springfield, IL: Abraham Lincoln Association, 1943), 82.

26. Benjamin B. French to Abraham Lincoln, October 15, 1861, Abraham Lincoln Papers.

27. John Hay to John George Nicolay, November 10, 1861, Burlingame, *At Lincoln's Side*, 14. See also ibid. 217n63, n64, n65.

28. Lincoln to Lorenzo Thomas, November 16, 1861, *Collected Works*, 5:25.

29. Mary Todd Lincoln to John F. Potter, September 13, 1861, in *Mary Todd Lincoln: Her Life and Letters*, ed. Justin G. Turner and Linda Levitt Turner (New York: Alfred A. Knopf, 1972), 103–4. See also Turner and Turner's words on Mary and Wood's relationship, ibid. 100.

30. Michael Burlingame, *Abraham Lincoln: A Life* (Baltimore: Johns Hopkins University Press, 2008), 2:267.

31. Mary Todd Lincoln to Caleb B. Smith, September 8, 1861, *Mary Todd Lincoln*, 101–2.

32. Mary Todd Lincoln to Simon Cameron, September 12, 1861, ibid., 103.

33. "By Telegraph: Congressional: House," *Wheeling (VA) Daily Intelligencer*, December 31, 1861.

34. Ibid.

35. "Loyalty of Clerks and Other Persons," vol. 3, no. 16, 2.

36. Ibid.

37. Ibid, 3.

38. Ibid.

39. Ibid.

40. Ibid., 29.

41. "General News," *Alexandria (VA) Local News*, January 29, 1862.

42. "Treason in High Places," *Cincinnati Daily Press*, January 24, 1862.

43. "The Potter Investigating Committee," *Ashtabula (OH) Weekly Telegraph*, February 8, 1862.

44. "The Report of the Potter Investigating Committee," *Washington (DC) Evening Star*, January 29, 1862.

45. Ibid.

46. Ibid.

47. David Hume, *The History of England: From the Invasion of Julius Caesar to the Revolution in 1688 A.D.* (London: George Bell, 1854) 3:70.

48. George Gould, "Judge Gould to Mr. Lincoln," *Holmes County Farmer* (Millersburg, OH), December 31, 1862; "Depotism Overleaping Itself," *Nashville Union and American*, June 9, 1861.

49. "General News," *Alexandria (VA) Local News*, January 30, 1862.

50. "The Potter Investigating Committee and the Traitors: Their Abettors and Apologists," *National Republican* (Washington, DC), February 6, 1862.

51. "General News," *Alexandria (VA) Local News*, January 30, 1862.

52. Michael Burlingame, *Dispatches from Lincoln's White House: The Anonymous Civil War Journalism of Presidential Secretary William O. Stoddard* (Lincoln: University of Nebraska Press, 2002), xix.

53. "Spies in Washington," ibid., 12.

54. "Cleaning Out the Departments," ibid., 17.

55. "The Cleaning-Out Committee," ibid., 24.

56. "Unjust Denunciation," ibid., 55–56.

57. See Burlingame, *Abraham Lincoln*, 2:276–80.

EQUALITY, STATESMANSHIP, AND THE LINCOLN IMAGE IN PROGRESSIVE PRESIDENTIAL RHETORIC

Jason R. Jividen

In February 2007, just two days before Abraham Lincoln's birthday, Barack Obama announced his candidacy for the US presidency in front of the old Illinois state capitol—the site of Lincoln's famed "House Divided" speech. Obama's declared purpose was to fulfill the "promise" of America, and he tied this promise specifically to the Lincoln legacy. Obama offered myriad reforms supposedly necessary to live up to that legacy: reshaping the economy to provide for greater equality of opportunity; higher standards for education; better pay for teachers; affordable college tuition; increased funding for scientific research; broadband lines in both city and countryside; better benefits and retirement plans for workers; the abolition of poverty in the United States; universal health care; energy independence; the defeat of terrorism; an end to the Iraq war; improved benefits for veterans; and a rebuilding of the US military.[1]

For the two years leading up to Obama's presidential inauguration, academics, journalists, and Obama himself frequently made the ubiquitous Obama-Lincoln connection.[2] Obama chose "A New Birth of Freedom" as the theme for his inaugural ceremonies, traveling the same route Lincoln took to the White House and even taking the oath of office on the same Bible Lincoln had used. However, the most serious and thoughtful of Obama's appeals to the Lincoln image came earlier, in his 2006 best-seller *The Audacity of Hope*. Here Obama claimed that Lincoln's political thought was central to his own understanding of the purposes and practice of American democracy. He reminded his readers of Lincoln's support for federal investment in railroads, canals, and other internal improvements; land grant colleges; the Homestead Act; and science

Our loved hero of yesterday, great emancipator of an oppressed people.
Our loved hero of to-day, staunch defender of all who are oppressed.
GREAT IN THEIR SIMPLICITY-SIMPLE IN THEIR GREATNESS · ALIKE IN ORIGINALITY-STRENGTH OF CONVICTION-AND FEARLESSNESS·
ALIKE IN SYMPATHY FOR HUMAN NEEDS-ALIKE IN ABILITY TO SEE AND SEIZE THE HOUR'S DEMAND-AND
ALIKE IN THEIR HOLD UPON THE HEARTS OF THE PEOPLE·

Theodore Roosevelt and Abraham Lincoln, emancipator and defender of the oppressed. Courtesy of the Library of Congress, LC-DIG-ppmsca-36104.

and technology. Such investments helped integrate the national economy and extend "the ladders of opportunity downward to reach more and more people." Obama suggested that for Lincoln, "the resources and power of the national government can facilitate, rather than supplant, a vibrant free market."[3]

Obama suggested that while Lincoln had laid "the groundwork for a fully integrated national economy" during the Civil War, it was only "during the stock market crash of 1929 and the subsequent Depression that the government's vital role in regulating the marketplace became fully apparent."[4] As Thomas Krannawitter observed, for Obama, it seemed that Lincoln had somehow envisioned the principles of the New Deal years before Franklin Roosevelt first put them into practice.[5] Obama claimed Lincoln as the progenitor of his own Progressive liberalism. Yet such appeals to Lincoln were nothing new in American politics. Rather, Obama's use of Lincoln was merely a more recent variation on a preexisting theme, a stock Progressive appeal to Lincoln repackaged for a new audience.

In his seminal book, *Lincoln Reconsidered*, David Donald discussed the American political tradition's attempt to "get right" with Lincoln. Until the turn of the twentieth century, the claim to Lincoln's political inheritance had predominantly been in the possession of the Republican Party. However, in the Progressive Era, the claim to the Lincoln inheritance became a partisan issue in the 1912 presidential election. William Howard Taft, Theodore Roosevelt, and Woodrow Wilson all publicly claimed to follow in the Lincolnian tradition. Likewise, in 1932, as part of their heated debate over what could and should be done to address the challenges of the Great Depression, Hebert Hoover and Franklin Roosevelt engaged in a similar disagreement about just who could plausibly claim to follow in Lincoln's footsteps. The claim to the Lincoln inheritance had become a major component of presidential rhetoric.[6]

American presidents' attempts to appropriate the Lincoln image have often turned on an appeal to the American promise of equality, said to be proclaimed in the Declaration of Independence, vindicated in the Civil War and the Reconstruction Amendments, and developed through the Progressive Era, the New Deal, the Great Society, the civil rights movement, and beyond. Central to these debates were the meaning and influence of Lincoln's claim that we were a nation "dedicated to the proposition that all men are created equal."[7]

Arguing against the institution of slavery and defending the idea of free labor, Lincoln sought to secure individuals' equal liberty to exercise diverse and necessarily unequal talents in pursuit of their interests, under the rule of law, while expecting an inequality of results or outcomes among individuals in that pursuit. Lincoln understood that this pursuit of equality was moderated by the limited government constitutionalism that followed from the premise that all men were equally endowed with natural and inalienable rights. Lincoln's pursuit of equality was very different from the modern egalitarianism often espoused by modern-day politicians, both in principle and practice. This modern pursuit of equality was said to focus not on securing the formal equality of individuals before the law or equality of opportunity, but rather on equalizing substantive outcomes among both individuals and groups. Generally, this pursuit called for the presence of a strong, centralized national government to pursue such ends. Its proponents often sought to alter or abolish fundamental constitutional structures and procedures (e.g., various aspects of federalism, representation, separation of powers) thought to be antidemocratic or reactionary obstacles to the goal of greater equality in American society.[8]

Beginning in the Progressive Era, American presidents sometimes neverthe-less looked to Lincoln's rhetoric of equality to articulate and justify modern egal-itarian claims and proposals, severing Lincoln's understanding of equality and statesmanship from its grounding in the constitutionalism and natural rights thinking of the American Founding Fathers. Clearly, an exhaustive account of such rhetorical claims to Lincoln is not possible in the space of this chapter, but it focuses briefly on the most far-reaching and significant examples. The heavy lifting in this effort took place in the speeches of Teddy Roosevelt, Woodrow Wilson, and Franklin Roosevelt. By abstracting away from the natural rights basis of Lincoln's equality, these presidents separated the pursuit of equality from any principled limits, divorcing it from the principles and institutions Lincoln thought fundamental to healthy republican government. In so doing, they offered up a version of Lincoln that served as an empty vessel into which later rhetoricians poured principles and policies that departed significantly from Lincoln's own understanding of American democracy.

LINCOLN AND THE PRINCIPLE OF EQUALITY

Our key sources for understanding Lincoln's thoughts on the principle of equal-ity are his speeches on the slavery crisis of the 1850s. While it is certainly too strong to say that Lincoln did not think about the equality principle prior to the 1850s, he did not often speak about it as an abstract principle of natural right prior to 1854. Some, such as political theorist James Ceaser, suggest that this might be due in part to a Whiggish ambivalence about appeals to ab-stract principles as opposed to history, tradition, and custom. As Ceaser notes, however, Lincoln saw the events of the 1850s as requiring a serious consideration of the idea of natural equality and its moral and theoretical centrality to American democracy. With the spread of slavery into the western territories, the Kansas-Nebraska Act and the repeal of the Missouri Compromise, Senator Stephen A. Douglas's "popular sovereignty" doctrine, and the *Dred Scott* decision, Lincoln came out of political retirement to argue that the slave interest had abandoned the Founders' intention to keep slavery on the path of ultimate extinction. Rather, the slave interest had either declared moral indifference to the institution (Douglas's popular sovereignty) or declared slavery a good for both slave and master (Calhoun's "positive good" thesis). In his 1854 speech on the Kansas-Nebraska Act and the Lincoln-Douglas debates, Lincoln turned to the principle of equality to explain the moral foundations, and moral limitations, of majority rule and popular government.[9]

There is perhaps no better example to help us understand Lincoln's notion of the principle of equality here than his speech on the *Dred Scott* decision. Chief Justice Roger B. Taney infamously argued that given the existence and toleration of slavery at the time of the nation's founding, the authors of the Declaration of Independence could not have intended black people to be included in the phrase "all men are created equal." Lincoln responded with the following:

> I think the authors of that notable instrument intended to include *all* men, but they did not intend to declare all men equal *in all respects.* They did not mean to say all were equal in color, size, intellect, moral developments, or social capacity. They defined with tolerable distinctness, in what respects they did consider all men created equal—equal in "certain inalienable rights, among which are life, liberty, and the pursuit of happiness." This they said, and this meant. They did not mean to assert the obvious untruth, that all were then actually enjoying that equality, nor yet, that they were about to confer it immediately upon them. In fact they had no power to confer such a boon. They meant simply to declare the *right,* so that the *enforcement* of it might follow as fast as circumstances should permit. They meant to set up a standard maxim for free society, which should be familiar to all, and revered by all; constantly looked to, constantly labored for, and even though never perfectly attained, constantly approximated, and thereby constantly spreading and deepening its influence, and augmenting the happiness and value of life to all people of all colors everywhere.[10]

To truly understand the idea of the standard maxim, one should note that Lincoln here drew a clear distinction between equality of rights, on the one hand, and equality of personal attributes, abilities, and talents, on the other. Following the political theory of the Declaration, Lincoln held that human beings possessed natural equality. That is, according to the laws of nature and of nature's God, all human beings were equally endowed with natural and "inalienable rights, among which are life, liberty, and the pursuit of happiness." In Lincoln's view, no human being had a claim by nature to rule over any other human being without his consent.[11] Hence governments derived their just powers by the consent of the governed. "No man," Lincoln claimed, "is good enough to govern another man, without the other's consent. I say this is the leading principle—the sheet anchor of American republicanism." According to Lincoln, as evidenced in his speeches against the Kansas-Nebraska Act and Douglas's popular sovereignty, the fugitive slave codes, and *Dred Scott*, by denying the principle of natural equality, the slave interest had undercut any principled, objective argument for government by consent of the governed.[12]

For Lincoln, according to nature, individuals ought to have equal liberty to pursue their own interests under the rule of law. Lincoln's understanding of equal liberty was captured in his many statements on natural rights and free labor. Lincoln argued that a human being ought to be able to eat the bread that he has earned by the sweat of his own brow.[13] While there was no clear indication that he had read John Locke's *Second Treatise of Government*, Lincoln held to the Lockean view that the origin of private property consisted in the natural and equal right that every human being had to his body, to the labor of that body, and to the fruits of his labor.[14] Lincoln's views here were consistent with those of the American Founders. Madison famously offered this understanding of equality in his tenth Federalist essay. The first object of government, Madison argued, was the protection of the "different and unequal faculties of acquiring and possessing property."[15]

Lincoln expressed this sentiment most clearly in his metaphor of the race of life. In his July 4, 1861, message to Congress, Lincoln characterized the war as a struggle "to elevate the condition of men—to lift artificial weights from all shoulders—to clear the paths of laudable pursuit for all—to afford all, an unfettered start, and a fair chance, in the race of life. Yielding to partial, and temporary departures, from necessity, this is the leading object of the government for whose existence we contend."[16] Lincoln thus characterized the pursuit of equality as an effort to secure individual equality of opportunity, under the rule of law, to exercise diverse and necessarily unequal talents and abilities.[17] Even in this most fundamental and limited formulation, in the right to pursue one's interests under the rule of law, Lincoln's pursuit of equality was subject to inherent limitations.[18]

Lincoln's idea of equality was necessarily intertwined with a statesmanlike appreciation for the rule of law and the limitations of political practice. Take, for example, Lincoln's handling of the slavery problem both before and during the war. In this case, the pursuit of equality was necessarily inhibited by the constitutional structure established by the consent of the governed and by the practical limitations to emancipation. Although Lincoln believed slavery to be an affront to the principles of the Declaration, he rejected the notion that national authority could legitimately be used to abolish slavery in the states where it already existed. As the political theorist Joseph Fornieri has noted, Lincoln rightly understood that the slavery question was necessarily wrapped up in different jurisdictions of authority; that is, he distinguished legally among slavery as a local, state, and national institution. Lincoln believed that, constitutionally, the federal division of power prohibited the national government from interfering with slavery where it already existed, but the territories, being under federal authority, were a different matter. It had been assumed, at least as far back as the Northwest Ordinance, that Congress had the power to legislate with respect to slavery in the territories. Thus the federal government could make a reasonable case for the restriction of slavery in the western territories. Before the Civil War and the passage of the Reconstruction Amendments, to have argued that the general government possessed the right to interfere with slavery where it already existed would have been understood as unconstitutional and seen as a usurpation of state and local authority.[19]

Lincoln's efforts to restrict the spread of slavery into the territories, and his ultimate handling of emancipation, illustrated both the principled and practical limitations of his pursuit of equality. As an imperative of the standard maxim, Lincoln sought to return slavery to the path of ultimate extinction through established political and constitutional means, especially elections and regular legislation. Given his constitutional reservations about the power of the federal government to interfere with slavery where it already existed absent a constitutional amendment, Lincoln believed that emancipation was constitutionally defensible only as a war measure. Emancipation was a necessary means to impair the South's war effort by confiscating slave property, under the commander-in-chief power accorded to the president under Article II of the US Constitution. Emancipation, of course, would be incomplete without an amendment to the Constitution itself;

that is, emancipation in its fullest sense could be accomplished only through the constitutionally structured consent of the governed.

Many have wondered why Lincoln did not free slaves in states that were not in open rebellion against the US government.[20] One must understand this in light of the requirements of the rule of law and government by consent of the governed that guided Lincoln's pursuit of equality. According to Lincoln's reasoning, it would have been unconstitutional to free slaves in states not in open rebellion against the United States without the consent of those states. One must not forget that, as was the case in the Preliminary Emancipation Proclamation, Lincoln offered the border states compensated, consensual emancipation, and Southern states were offered compensated emancipation should they return to the Union. Lincoln's refusal to free slaves in the border states with the Emancipation Proclamation only reinforced the fact that he understood the pursuit of the standard maxim to flow through government by consent of the governed and the rule of law.[21]

With the coming of the Progressive Era, however, this fundamental element of Lincoln's pursuit of equality began to disappear in presidential rhetoric. The pursuit of equality was unmoored from its theoretical grounding in limited government, natural rights principles and thus was separated from the rule of law and government by consent as those things were understood by Lincoln. As both an intellectual and a political movement, Progressivism contributed lasting changes to American political development. Broadly stated, the Progressives sought a reinterpretation of the American political order by giving the people more direct power over all levels of government and, in turn, by giving government—particularly the federal government—more power to regulate the economy. The Progressive Era was the first major period in American political development to feature as its central, defining characteristic an open and direct criticism of the principles of the Declaration of Independence and the US Constitution.[22] According to the Progressives, these founding documents were merely the products of the dead hand of the past. The eighteenth-century political thought that gave rise to them had proven incorrect in light of modern circumstances. Institutions built on these ideas were deemed incapable of solving the problems of modern industrial society at the dawn of the twentieth century.

The Progressives understood that the Constitution set up a general government of limited powers. Such things were explicit and persistent obstacles to implementing Progressive policies aimed at the regulation of certain sectors of the economy and the redistribution of wealth and private property in the name of social and industrial justice. These policies, many Progressives argued, would not be enacted as long as the political process was dominated by powerful special interests and as long as the Constitution held supposedly antidemocratic obstacles to majority rule (e.g., indirect representation, a difficult method of constitutional amendment, federalism, and a cumbersome legislative process). So, in order to secure greater social, political, and economic equality, the people needed more direct control over their representatives and their Constitution. In addition, to articulate the ends and means of a growing national administrative state, people needed leadership in the form of a powerful, rhetorical president. The Progressives' frequent rhetorical appeals to the Lincoln image and Lincoln's rhetoric of equality became central to this transformation.

THEODORE ROOSEVELT'S LINCOLN:
EQUALITY AND DIRECT DEMOCRACY

Perhaps more than any other American president, Teddy Roosevelt frequently invoked Lincoln's name in support of his political opinions and policies. Roosevelt's speeches and writings abound with references to Lincoln. After reading Progressive journalist Herbert Croly's book *The Promise of American Life* in 1909, Theodore Roosevelt was convinced that the Founders' political science had become obsolete in light of changing historical and economic circumstances. With Croly, Roosevelt came to argue that the progress of history had led to the necessity of a stronger, more efficient national government, unhampered by institutional mechanisms like federalism and separation of powers.[23]

When he broke with the Republicans in 1912, Roosevelt repeatedly argued that the Bull Moose Progressives alone were the rightful political and spiritual heirs of Abraham Lincoln. He argued that, like Lincoln, the Progressive Party believed that the purpose of American democracy was "to elevate the condition of men—to lift artificial weights from all shoulders—to clear the paths of laudable pursuit for all—to afford all, an unfettered start, and a fair chance, in the race of life."[24] Roosevelt situated this claim within the proposition that there can be no "genuine" democracy without "economic democracy," wherein men were given the equal opportunity to become intellectually, morally, and materially fit to be their own masters.[25]

In modern industrial America, where men were increasingly tied not to the land, but to the factory, the national government had to increase its efforts to secure equality of opportunity by reining in special interests, providing for labor legislation, industrial safety, and increased regulation of the national economy, among other policies. This would not happen, Roosevelt believed, unless the people were given increased and more direct control over their elected representatives, court decisions, and the Constitution.

At first glance, Roosevelt's economic democracy sounded like Lincoln's understanding of equal liberty. Seemingly, Roosevelt suggested that individuals should have the equal right to pursue their interests by exercising their own talents and abilities. However, those familiar with the "New Nationalism" speech at Osawatomie should seriously question Roosevelt's claim to have been led by Lincoln's principles. Here Roosevelt bluntly explained what his pursuit of his economic democracy entailed for property rights:

> We grudge no man a fortune in civil life if it is honorably obtained and well used. It is not even enough that it should have been gained without doing damage to the community. We should permit it to be gained only so long as the gaining represents benefit to the community. This, I know, implies a policy of a far more active governmental interference with social and economic conditions in this country than we have yet had, but I think we have got to face the fact that such an increase in governmental control is now necessary.[26]

Note that, for Roosevelt, the general government must be empowered to determine the acceptable use of property, and it must respect property rights only insofar as it is socially useful to do so.[27] Roosevelt denied the very foundation of Lincoln's notion of equality—that by nature, nothing should come between a man's hand and his mouth. For Lincoln, this meant that, insofar as it was possible, government should exalt and protect the rights of private property. The unstated premise beneath Roosevelt redistributionism was that majority tyranny was impossible under current economic conditions and the progress of history.[28]

Roosevelt's pursuit of equality thus rested on very different foundations than Lincoln's equality, and as such, it implied different and expanded means to secure its end. Roosevelt's pursuit of equality necessitated an overcoming of the institutions that Lincoln believed fostered a healthy republican government. For Lincoln, the pursuit of equality, rightly understood, would recognize the worth of the constitutional forms and institutions that helped structure and shape a measured and sober popular government. Yet, calling for an end run around the institutions of the Founders' Constitution, Roosevelt claimed that if the people were to achieve equality of opportunity in modern America, they needed increased and more direct means of controlling their government. Throughout his political speeches of 1912 and 1913, Roosevelt appealed to the authority of Lincoln to defend Progressive demands for initiative, referendum, and the recall of public officials and judicial decisions by referenda. Lincoln, however, never argued for such devices, nor did he ever say anything to suggest that his support for the sovereignty of the people might require these. Lincoln did support the right of people to control all their public servants, but as suggested by his political approach to slave interest, he thought they must do so through established political channels and constitutionally structured modes of consent.

Lincoln seemed to understand that the political science beneath the Founders' Constitution was rooted in the belief in an unchanging human nature, capable of both the greatest goods and the greatest ills. Accordingly, the Founders sought to control the effects of factions by constructing political institutions in such a way as to moderate the political demands of the majority faction.[29] Representation, separation of powers, and other supposedly antidemocratic devices such as the amendment process were designed to allow the "cool and deliberate sense" of the community to find expression, as opposed to "every sudden breeze of passion" or "transient impulse" of the moment.[30] Roosevelt's embrace of direct democracy and redistributionism illustrated how far he really strayed from Lincoln and the Founders' understanding of American government. Roosevelt sometimes compared his opponents to Stephen Douglas, but it was actually Roosevelt that resembled Douglas. Lincoln vehemently opposed Douglas's popular sovereignty, because it placed no objective moral or constitutional limits on the will of the majority. Like Douglas, Roosevelt denied the very possibility of majority tyranny. Any reading of the Lincoln-Douglas debates would demonstrate that there was surely no better critic of Roosevelt's dismissal of majority tyranny than Lincoln himself.

Despite his rhetorical claims to the Lincoln legacy, Roosevelt rejected Lincoln's principles. Roosevelt insisted that any interest that did not actively and consciously serve the public good was a "special interest" that must be "driven out of politics."[31] Lincoln surely believed that self-interest could not serve as the sole standard of right action, but he understood that self-interest could not be expunged from the human soul and hence could not be driven out of political life. Just as the Founders believed that the latent causes were sown in the nature of man, Lincoln too held that human nature did not change. For Lincoln, we shall always have men "as weak, and as strong; as silly and as wise;

as bad and good"; thus the danger of majority tyranny cannot be transcended. Lincoln appreciated that our selfishness and our love of justice stood in "eternal antagonism."[32] According to Lincoln, the task of statesmanship and institutions was to mitigate that antagonism as far as possible, but to contend that either side of this fundamental tension could be abolished from the human condition was to expect the impossible.

WOODROW WILSON'S LINCOLN: PROGRESS AND PRESIDENTIAL LEADERSHIP

Woodrow Wilson also frequently appealed to Lincoln on the campaign trail to advocate for greater economic equality and a new understanding of the American political order. Wilson openly rejected and sought to overcome the natural rights–based political theory and limited government constitutionalism of the American Founders. Inspired by Hegel's philosophy of history, Wilson insisted that the idea that there might be transhistorical truths that applied to all men at all times was mistaken. Wilson's project required a direct engagement with the principles and institutions of the American founding, which were constructed on the basis of such transhistorical standards: a belief in an imperfect and enduring human nature and belief in natural and inalienable rights belonging to all human beings, everywhere and always.[33]

Key to Wilson's analysis of the Founders' Constitution was a critique of separation of powers, what he referred to as the spirit of "checks and balances." In Hegelian fashion, Wilson argued that every generation perceived the world in terms of the dominant thought of its age. The Founders, Wilson claimed, designed their institutions in light of the principles of Newtonian physics applied to politics. Under such manner of thinking, the Founders saw their Constitution as embodying counterbalanced forces mutually held in check like the parts of the solar system.[34] According to Wilson, a constitution read in the eighteenth-century spirit of checks and balances unnecessarily inhibited and restricted energetic, active government.[35] New economic problems in industrial twentieth-century America required new political formulas; Americans had to overcome the spirit of checks and balances if they were to keep pace with the times. "Living political constitutions," Wilson argued, "must be Darwinian in structure and in practice. Society is a living organism and must obey the laws of life, not of mechanics; it must develop."[36]

Above all, Wilson claimed, our understanding of the Constitution tended to inhibit the emergence of competent and energetic political leadership to

solve social and economic problems. Wilson endeavored to craft a new notion
of statesmanship for the twentieth century, a vision of leadership for a new
age. He used Lincoln as a model on which to build Progressive leadership for
the twentieth century.[37] According to Wilson, Lincoln had attained a level of
intellectual and moral insight higher than that of the generality of men. As a
true leader of men, Lincoln possessed a kind of oracle into history, able to discern the way in which historical progress was tending, to see "horizons which
[the people] are too submerged to see." As a moral-rhetorical leader, Lincoln
was able to interpret seemingly inchoate public opinion, synthesize it into a
coherent vision, and articulate it back to the people in understandable form.[38]
For Wilson, such leadership is crucial in overcoming the spirit of checks and
balances and in opening the nation to the progress of history.

The constitutional presidency of the American Founders assumed that while
executive authority was ultimately derived from the sovereignty of the people,
in civil society that authority is defined, structured, and limited by the people's
Constitution as fundamental law.[39] For Wilson, institutional limitations on government were on the wrong side of history. Insofar as human nature evolved and
developed over time—as Wilson's historicism posited—institutions designed
in light of an assumption of a necessarily imperfect and unchanging human
nature were obsolete and stood in the way of progress. Constitutionally limited
and balanced government must be overcome through proper leadership to meet
the demands of the current day. For Wilson, the real power of the executive
came not from the Constitution, but from a mandate conferred directly by the
people themselves, expressed in election results and public opinion. Wilson's
Lincoln, as the man of the people, became the guiding example in our political
history of this interpreter-leader of the modern American administrative state.[40]

Ultimately, as Herman Belz claimed, one saw traces of this idea in Clinton Rossiter's, James Randall's, and Gottfried Dietze's variations on the "Lin-
coln-as-dictator" thesis, which mistakenly divorced Lincoln from the political
science of the Founders, making him the "prototype of twentieth-century presidential government, ruling through rhetorical leadership of public opinion rather
than adherence to the texts and forms of the Constitution."[41] Whether and how
the Lincoln presidency contributed to this transformation of the presidency has
long been a source of debate. The constitutionality, and the implications, of many
of Lincoln's actions in response to the firing on Sumter remained controversial.

In his July 4, 1861, message to Congress, understanding the controversial
nature of his actions, Lincoln suggested that his measures, "whether strictly

legal or not, were ventured upon, under what appeared to be a *popular demand*, and a *public necessity*; trusting, then as now, that Congress would readily ratify them."[42] It was often observed that Lincoln made a claim here reminiscent of Locke's argument for executive prerogative in his Second Treatise. To invoke Lockean prerogative based on popular demand, the American president could appeal outside the Constitution and directly to the people, as the source and judge of executive power. Yet, as Benjamin Kleinerman noted, Lincoln's use of the "popular demand" argument to justify his actions appeared only early in the war. In fact, it seemed to be an anomaly in Lincoln's political rhetoric. More frequently, Lincoln explained and defended his actions on constitutional grounds, particularly appealing to the president's unique constitutional duty to take care that the laws be faithfully executed and the presidential oath of office to preserve, protect, and defend the US Constitution. The constitutional duty to preserve the Union through constitutional means became the defining feature of Lincoln's arguments on discretionary executive authority.[43]

One ought not to lose sight of the fact that Wilson's embrace of Lincoln's statesmanship was premised fundamentally on a desire to release statesmen from the fundamental law of the Founders' Constitution. Yet Lincoln repeatedly suggested, as he did in his 1838 Lyceum Address, that the success of American democracy required our unwavering dedication to that fundamental law.[44] As such, it seemed difficult to conclude that Lincoln was the best model for Woodrow Wilson's plebiscitary presidency; however, here we must briefly consider a related but still more fundamental difference between Wilson and Lincoln.

The spirit of checks and balances, of which Wilson was so critical, arose in the effort to secure natural and inalienable rights. For Wilson, the notion of natural and inalienable rights was as much an obstacle to progress as the spirit of checks and balances.[45] Given that the notion of natural and inalienable rights depended on the possibility that there were abstract, enduring truths applicable to all human beings, Wilson's Hegelianism denied the very possibility of such rights. Lincoln once declared, "All honor to Jefferson, to the man who, in the concrete pressure of a struggle for national independence by a single people, had the coolness, forecast, and capacity to introduce into a merely revolutionary document, an abstract truth, applicable to all men and all times."[46] Wilson, on the other hand, attempted to divorce Lincoln from the idea of abstract truth altogether, having once strangely praised Lincoln as a man without "any theories at all," who did not seek to "tie you up in the meshes of any theory."[47] For Wilson, the American tradition ought not to be understood in terms of a dedication to abstract natural rights principles but must be discussed as an organic, intensely practical tradition, in which government evolved and adapted to ever-changing circumstances.[48]

According to Wilson, although the Declaration "names as among the 'inalienable rights' of man the right to life, liberty and the pursuit of happiness, it expressly leaves to each generation of men the determination of what they will do with their lives, what they will prefer as the form and object to their liberty, in what they will seek their happiness."[49] Liberty thus was no longer understood with any reference to natural and inalienable rights, but rather was the continually changing, procedural, conventional result of a deal between the government and the governed. As the result of conventional agreement, and devoid of any basis in nature, the objects of our consent were not subject to any limitations or guidelines save the will of the parties at the time of that agreement. Wilson's reading of the Declaration ripped the theoretical ground from beneath the very notion of limited government and, with it, any enduring, objective defense of limited government.[50] As Lincoln's arguments regarding the slavery issue repeatedly indicated, the natural rights principles of the Declaration placed transhistorical limits on what men consented to and continued to guide our understanding of liberty, equality, and self-government. Despite Wilson's claim to follow Lincoln, his political thought departed sharply from that of the sixteenth president.

FRANKLIN ROOSEVELT'S LINCOLN: STATESMANSHIP AS THE REDEFINITION OF RIGHTS

One finds a similar problem in Franklin Roosevelt's frequent appeals to Lincoln's legacy of equality in the rhetoric of the New Deal. Despite the Progressives' efforts to appropriate Lincoln, the Republicans still clung firmly to their own claim to Lincoln's legacy into the 1930s. It was well documented by historians that FDR self-consciously sought to remedy this. As early as 1929, the appeal to Lincoln's legacy became a staple in Roosevelt's political rhetoric. With regard to the New Deal, this appeal hit its peak from 1936 to 1938. Above all, FDR sought to associate the Lincoln legacy with a new and expanded understanding of the scope of the national government in addressing the challenges of the Great Depression.[51] Echoing Wilson, Roosevelt claimed that the old political ideas, at least as they were currently understood, were incapable of securing equality of opportunity in contemporary historical and economic circumstances. Reliance on the old liberalism of the American founding, and the limited-government constitutionalism framed in light of such principles, proved disastrous. FDR claimed that new circumstances required new ideas, new political formulas, and above all, a new understanding of visionary statesmanship aimed at securing economic equality through presidential leadership of public opinion and a growing national administrative bureaucracy. Wilson's plans for the presidency, and the place of the Lincoln example in it, found a home in the New Deal.

Roosevelt routinely looked to Lincoln as an exemplar of this kind of visionary statesmanship. In January 1936, Roosevelt wrote a birthday tribute to Lincoln to be read in Cleveland, Ohio, where he summed up his understanding of Lincoln most succinctly as "a character destined to *transfuse with new meaning the concepts of our constitutional fathers* and to assure a Government having for its broad purpose the promotion of the life, liberty, and happiness of all the people."[52] As Sidney Milkis observed, Roosevelt here offered a window into his own understanding of democratic statesmanship.[53] In asserting that Lincoln "transfused" the concepts of our constitutional fathers with "new meaning" (presumably referring to emancipation), FDR associated Lincoln with a notion of Progressive leadership similar to that of Woodrow Wilson. In suggesting that Lincoln gave "new meaning" to the concepts of the American Founders, FDR readopted, but also redirected, the Lincoln image as a model of Progressive leadership, which he claimed required the "re-definition" of rights "in terms of a growing and changing social order."[54] Lincoln repeatedly argued in the face of the slave interest that he was reiterating rather than improving on the Founders' understanding of equality.[55] Nevertheless, Roosevelt used his Lincoln as a precursor to a new understanding of equality and a new kind of liberalism— Progressivism repackaged in the language of individual rights and liberalism.

On this note, Robert Eden usefully characterized New Deal thought as a variant of "pragmatic liberalism," as opposed to formal or classical liberalism. Pragmatic liberalism, Eden explained, was a "strain of modern or postmodern politics that does not stand upon liberal forms and constitutional formalities; that is in principle always willing (if not eager) to strike down the formalities upheld by classical liberalism, in favor of results, consequences, and programs that promise to actualize liberalism in its fundamental purposes."[56] According to Eden, the old, formal liberalism rested on the Lockean proposal (here we might say the Lincolnian proposal) "that reasonable men might turn to nature to discern the essential purposes of civil society and of government." Pragmatic liberalism, on the other hand, rested on the Progressive pragmatism of John Dewey and repudiated rationalistic, natural rights thinking as metaphysics "in favor of an essentially historical mode of critical thinking; there are no self-evident truths; the Declaration of Independence has no epistemic significance."[57]

Yet the success of the New Deal required Roosevelt, the rhetorician, to frame innovation in familiar terms and recognizable themes. It often required (at least, it still required in the 1930s and early 1940s) that the beginnings of a new tradition be couched in the language of the old tradition. Roosevelt closely followed Wilson's Progressive rendering of the Declaration and the Constitution, while placing greater emphasis on the traditional language of individual rights than his predecessors.

For Roosevelt, the progress of economic history demonstrated the need for government to aid in securing equality of opportunity by establishing and promoting new and primarily economic "rights," in which the state became the guarantor of individual well-being and security.[58] This idea lay beneath two of FDR's most famous addresses, his 1932 Commonwealth Club Address and his 1944 State of the Union Address. FDR suggested at the Commonwealth Club that the American pursuit of equality, defined under modern circumstances, required the type of statesmanship he attributed to Lincoln—that is, a statesmanship that transfused the principles of American republicanism with new meaning. Indeed, according to Roosevelt, *the very task of statesmanship* was (and has always been) to redefine our most essential rights in light of changing circumstances and historical progress. For Roosevelt, statesmen, acting as Wilson's leaders of men, were to continually redefine our rights, pitch that redefinition to the people, and have the people judge the choice-worthiness of the redefinition in their plebiscitary capacity, through public opinion and elections.

Specifically, this new task required a new understanding of the Declaration of Independence—identical, in fact, to that of Woodrow Wilson. According to FDR, we had to redefine the terms of the social contract, in which our rights had no basis in nature but were merely conventional and the result of deals struck between the government and the governed. Again, nothing could be further from the express terms of the Declaration or from Lincoln's exaltation of natural, prepolitical inalienable rights. However, FDR added something new to the equation: a redefinition of rights and equality to encompass what many refer to today as entitlements—that is, a new declaration of economic rights that included a right to employment, health care, social security, and so on. In short, rights to freedom from fear and freedom from want.[59]

Despite FDR's efforts to incorporate Lincoln into his political rhetoric, the New Deal theory of equality should be distinguished from the guiding principles of Lincoln's political thought. Lincoln sought, insofar as it was possible and prudent, to secure equality of opportunity in light of transhistorical standards rooted in nature. Our natural equality not only suggested that the legitimate powers of government were derived from the consent of the governed but also implied that there were limits as to what things the governed might rightfully consent to. Like Wilson, FDR appeared to deny the natural standards and the principled limits that guided Lincoln's pursuit of equality. For FDR, there seemed to be no ground on which to posit theoretical limitations on our pursuit of equality, or on any other perceived end, extrinsic to our will under a given set of circumstances.

FDR sometimes suggested that the New Deal theory of government was expressed by Lincoln when he said that "the legitimate object of government is to do for a community of people whatever they need to have done, but cannot do at all, or cannot do so well for themselves, in their separate and individual capacities."[60] Surely, Lincoln and Roosevelt would agree that things like employment, decent wages, adequate shelter, and medical care were highly desirable goods. People simply needed food, shelter, and medical care to survive, and government, according to the political theory of the Founders, was instituted among men to first secure the right to life.

As Harry Jaffa suggested, according to the political principles that informed both Lincoln and the Founders, there was no a priori rule in such matters. To simply characterize such intermediate goods as fundamental rights ran the risk of conflating means with ends. The end of government in securing natural and inalienable rights was not subject to deliberation, but rather was held to be an inference from the laws of nature and of nature's God, principles deemed true everywhere and always. Yet the manner in which such things were to be done, whether privately or publicly, whether by local governments, state governments, or the general government, was a matter of deliberation and prudence. Simply stated, the determination of just what the people could or could not do as well, or not so well, for themselves was open to debate. This was because such things were not properly regarded as the ends of government—that is, not as fundamental rights in and of themselves—but rather were counted as among the means by which we sought to secure natural and inalienable rights to life, liberty, and the pursuit of happiness. Lincoln did not characterize such public goods and services as a necessary imperative of equality or simply as a matter of right in themselves. To suggest that Lincoln somehow believed that one's rights were being secured only insofar as certain means or results in the exercise of those rights were equalized was surely incorrect.[61]

MODERN APPROPRIATIONS OF LINCOLN

Franklin Roosevelt's economic declaration of rights helped introduce a new rhetoric of rights in American political discourse, in which the distinction between our fundamental rights and the results of our exercising those rights has become increasingly blurred in presidential rhetoric. This helped us understand the ease with which President Obama invoked the authority of Lincoln in arguing for the Affordable Care Act, nationwide Internet access, educational reform, and energy independence. All of these goods, Obama suggested, were an imperative of Lincoln's unfinished work, of his challenge to future generations to fulfill the American promise of equality. Obama's Lincoln thus was prepared by those who came before him. The Progressives and FDR redefined Lincoln, recast him in the Progressive mold, and offered a version of Lincoln well suited for Obama's use. Once Lincoln's importance was severed from the defining features of his political thought, then the Lincoln example was potentially capable of meaning whatever we wanted it to mean. One must wonder, of course, how far this idea can be stretched before the Lincoln example is rendered essentially meaningless, before it becomes merely an empty vessel into which we might pour varied, unrelated, and contradictory interpretations of equality, however much they comport with Lincoln's words and deeds.

To the extent that we accept that equality is a goal to be secured through statesmanship and politics, then the character and content of that equality are of great importance, for the manner in which we understand equality helps us understand the legitimate political means by which that equality ought to be secured.[62] Lincoln, Teddy Roosevelt, Woodrow Wilson, and FDR all wrestled with fundamental problems and questions that cut to the heart of our core assumptions about what American democracy is and what it ought to be. Despite their claims to the Lincoln legacy, however, the Progressive and modern liberal appropriation of the Lincoln image began with a rejection of the first principles of Lincoln's political thought. Progressivism and modern liberalism's rejection of modern natural rights thinking and its indifference to constitutionalism, separation of powers, and limited government were necessarily related. The choice-worthiness of such institutional arrangements followed from the assumption that there was an enduring and necessarily imperfect human nature that we comprehended through human reason.

Our reason tells us that all men are born with inalienable rights, that the purpose of government is to secure those rights, and that these rights, by definition, place limits on the objects of our consent. Moreover, given the imperfections of human nature, our reason suggests that political power ought to be constitutionally balanced, limited, and held accountable by representation and structured modes of popular consent. Lincoln understood that this is not in spite of the principle of equality, but because of it.

Insofar as these principles are rejected in light of historical progress and economic change, then limited constitutional government is likely to be deemed obsolete. The modern pursuit of equality is likely to be severed from the Lincolnian idea that, rightly understood, the pursuit of equality is necessarily limited and tempered by these principles. The denial of an enduring and imperfect human nature, the rejection of the principle that all human beings are equally endowed with natural and inalienable rights, the radicalization of the pursuit of equality, and the willingness to alter constitutional forms and structures under the guise of Progressive statesmanship are all intimately related.

Notes

This chapter is adapted from portions of Jason R. Jividen, *Claiming Lincoln: Progressivism, Equality and the Battle for Lincoln's Legacy in Presidential Rhetoric* (DeKalb: Northern Illinois University Press, 2011). Jividen thanks Northern Illinois University Press for its permission to draw on that work here.

1. Barack Obama, "Campaign Speech at Springfield, Illinois," February 10, 2007, accessed September 1, 2013, http://www.theguardian.com/world/2007/feb/10/barackobama.

2. See, for example, Barack Obama, "What I See in Lincoln's Eyes," *Time*, June 26, 2005; cf. Peggy Noonan, "Conceit of Government: Why Are Our Politicians So Full of Themselves?," *Wall Street Journal*, June 29, 2005.

3. Barack Obama, *The Audacity of Hope: Thoughts on Reclaiming the American Dream* (New York: Three Rivers Press, 2006), 152.

4. Ibid., 152–53, 159.

5. Thomas L. Krannawitter, *Vindicating Lincoln: Defending the Politics of Our Greatest President* (Lanham, MD: Rowman and Littlefield, 2008), 293–94, 308.

6. David Herbert Donald, *Lincoln Reconsidered* (1955; repr., New York: Vintage Books, 1961), 3–18.

7. Abraham Lincoln, Address Delivered at the Dedication of the Cemetery at Gettysburg, November 19, 1863, in *The Collected Works of Abraham Lincoln*, ed. Roy P. Basler et al. (New Brunswick, NJ: Rutgers University Press, 1953), 7:23.

8. On modern egalitarianism, see Martin Diamond, *As Far as Republican Principles Will Admit: Essays by Martin Diamond*, ed. William A. Schambra (Washington, DC: American Enterprise Institute Press, 1992), 241–57, 326–29; Harry

V. Jaffa, *How to Think about the American Revolution: A Bicentennial Cerebration* (Durham, NC: Carolina Academic Press, 1978), 13–48; Thomas Sowell, *A Conflict of Visions* (New York: Basic Books, 2002), 129–50.

9. James W. Ceaser, *Nature and History in American Political Development: A Debate* (Cambridge, MA: Harvard University Press, 2006), 50–52. On the equality principle and Lincoln's thoughts on free labor and the self-made man, see Gabor S. Boritt, *Lincoln and the Economics of the American Dream* (Memphis, TN: Memphis State University Press, 1978).

10. Lincoln, Speech at Springfield, Illinois, June 26, 1857, *Collected Works*, 2:405–6.

11. See John Locke, *Second Treatise of Government*, ed. C. B. Macpherson (Indianapolis: Hackett, 1980); see esp. § 54. See also Thomas Jefferson to Roger C. Weightman, June 24, 1826, in *Thomas Jefferson: Writings*, ed. Merrill D. Peterson (New York: Library of America, 1984), 1516–17.

12. Lincoln, Speech at Peoria, Illinois, October 16, 1854, *Collected Works*, 2:266; Lincoln, Speech at Chicago, Illinois, July 10, 1858, ibid., 2:499. See Harry V. Jaffa, *A New Birth of Freedom: Abraham Lincoln and the Coming of the Civil War* (Lanham, MD: Rowman and Littlefield, 2000), 300.

13. Lincoln, Speech at Springfield, Illinois, July 17, 1858, *Collected Works*, 2:520; Lincoln, Reply: First Debate with Stephen A. Douglas at Ottawa, Illinois, August 21, 1858, ibid., 3:16; Lincoln, Speech at Hartford, Connecticut, March 5, 1860, ibid., 4:9.

14. George Anastaplo, *Abraham Lincoln: A Constitutional Biography* (Lanham, MD: Rowman and Littlefield Publishers, 1999), 234, 330n473; Jaffa, *How to Think about the American Revolution*, 45. See Locke, *Second Treatise*, 18–29. Lincoln's understanding of equality and the principle that all men are created equal appears to have been shaped, at least in part, by a combination of influences. In addition to his reading many of the speeches, writings, and documents of the American Founders (especially. Jefferson), Lincoln drew on the writings of Euclid, the speeches of Henry Clay, and of course, the Bible (especially Gen. 1:27, Gen. 3:19, and Matt. 7:12). See, for example, Lincoln, Fourth Debate with Stephen A. Douglas, September 18, 1858, *Collected Works*, 3:186; Lincoln to Henry L. Pierce and Others, April 6, 1859, ibid., 3:376; Lincoln, Reply: Seventh and Last Debate with Stephen A. Douglas at Alton, Illinois, October 15, 1858, ibid., 3:303; Lincoln, Fragment on Slavery, July 1, 1854, ibid., 2:222–23; Lincoln, Speech at Lewistown, Illinois, August 17, 1858, ibid., 2:546; Lincoln to George B. Ide, James R. Doolittle, and A. Hubbell, May 30, 1864, ibid., 7:368; cf. Lincoln, Speech at Peoria, Illinois, October 16, 1854, ibid., 2:264–65.

15. James Madison, "Federalist 10," in Alexander Hamilton, James Madison, and John Jay, *The Federalist*, ed. Jacob E. Cooke (Hanover: Wesleyan University Press, 1982), 58.

16. Lincoln, Message to Congress in Special Session, July 4, 1861, *Collected Works*, 4:438.

17. Jaffa, *How to Think about the American Revolution*, 148–49. Also see Krannawitter, *Vindicating Lincoln*, 311–12; Diamond, *As Far as Republican Principles*, 255–57.

18. Anastaplo, *Abraham Lincoln*, 234, 330n473.

19. Joseph Fornieri, "Lincoln and the Emancipation Proclamation: A Model of Prudent Leadership," in *Tempered Strength: Studies in the Nature and Scope of Prudential Leadership*, ed. Ethan Fishman (Lanham, MD: Lexington Books, 2002), 130–31, 139.

20. Consider Richard J. Hofstadter, The *American Political Tradition and the Men Who Made It* (New York: Knopf, 1954), 93–137; Lerone J. Bennett Jr., "Was Abe Lincoln a White Supremacist?" *Ebony* 23 (February 1968): 35–42; Lerone J. Bennett Jr., *Forced into Glory: Abraham Lincoln's White Dream* (Chicago: Johnson Publishing, 2000); Thomas J. DiLorenzo, *The Real Lincoln: A New Look at Abraham Lincoln, His Agenda, and an Unnecessary War* (New York: Three Rivers Press, 2002), 10–32; Michael Lind, *What Lincoln Believed: The Values and Convictions of America's Greatest President* (New York: Doubleday, 2004), 1–27, 191–232.

21. On the prudential, legal, and political difficulties surrounding emancipation and the border states, see Fornieri, "Lincoln and the Emancipation Proclamation," 139–43; Krannawitter, *Vindicating Lincoln*, 271–82; Eric Foner, *The Fiery Trial: Abraham Lincoln and American Slavery* (New York: W. W. Norton and Company, 2010), chap. 7, esp. 240–47; Allen C. Guelzo, *Lincoln's Emancipation Proclamation: The End of Slavery in America* (New York: Simon and Schuster, 2004), 8–9, 134, 173, 201.

22. See John Marini and Ken Masugi, eds., *The Progressive Revolution in Politics and Political Science* (Lanham, MD: Rowman and Littlefield, 2005); Ronald J. Pestritto and William J. Atto, eds., *American Progressivism: A Reader* (Lanham, MD: Lexington Books, 2008), 1–32; Bradley C. S. Watson, *Living Constitution, Dying Faith: Progressivism and the New Science of Jurisprudence* (Wilmington, DE: ISI Books, 2009).

23. Jean M. Yarbrough, "Theodore Roosevelt and the Stewardship of the American Presidency," in *History of American Political Thought*, ed. Bryan-Paul Frost and Jeffrey Sikkenga (Lanham, MD: Lexington Books, 2003), 537, 542. See Theodore Roosevelt, "The New Nationalism," Speech at Osawatomie, Kansas, August 31, 1910, in *The Works of Theodore Roosevelt*, National Edition, ed. Hermann Hagedorn (New York: Charles Scribner's Sons, 1926), 17:5–22; Roosevelt, "Limitation of Governmental Power," Address at the Coliseum, San Francisco, September 14, 1912, ibid., 17:306–14.

24. Roosevelt, "The Heirs of Abraham Lincoln," Speech at the Lincoln Day Banquet, New York City, February 12, 1913, *Works*, 17:364; cf. Lincoln, Message to Congress in Special Session, July 4, 1861, *Collected Works*, 4:438.

25. Roosevelt, "Progressive Democracy," a review of Herbert Croly's *Progressive Democracy* and Walter Lippmann's *Drift and Mastery*, November 18, 1914, *Works*, 12:232–39.

26. Roosevelt, "New Nationalism," 13–14.

27. Ibid., 9. See Yarbrough, "Theodore Roosevelt," 545.

28. On this point, Roosevelt often cited James Bryce, *The American Commonwealth* (London: MacMillan and Company, 1888), 3:143.

29. Madison, "Federalist 10" and "Federalist 51," *Federalist*, 56–65, 347–53.

30. In Hamilton's formulation, it is a "just observation" that the people "commonly *intend* the PUBLIC GOOD. . . . But their good sense would despise the adulator, who should pretend that they always *reason right* about the *means* of promoting it." Hamilton, "Federalist 71," *Federalist*, 482. Also see "Federalist 63," ibid., 424–25.

31. Yarbrough, "Theodore Roosevelt," 548. See Roosevelt, "New Nationalism," 5–22.

32. Lincoln, Response to a Serenade, November 10, 1864, *Collected Works*, 101; Lincoln, Speech at Peoria, Illinois, October 16, 1854, ibid., 271.

33. On Wilson's historicism and the principles of the American founding, see Ronald J. Pestritto, *Woodrow Wilson and the Roots of Modern Liberalism* (Lanham, MD: Rowman and Littlefield, 2005), esp. chaps. 1–2.

34. Woodrow Wilson, *Constitutional Government in the United States* (1908; repr., New York: Columbia University Press, 1961), 57. Also see Woodrow Wilson, *The New Freedom: A Call for the Emancipation of the Generous Energies of a People* (1913; repr., Englewood Cliffs, NJ: Prentice-Hall, 1961), 19–20, 41.

35. Wilson, *New Freedom*, 19–20.

36. Ibid., 42. See also Wilson, *Constitutional Government*, 56–57.

37. See, for example, Woodrow Wilson, "'Abraham Lincoln: A Man of the People,' An Address in Chicago on Lincoln's Birthday," February 12, 1909, in *The Papers of Woodrow Wilson*, ed. Arthur S. Link (Princeton, NJ: Princeton University Press, 1966), 19:33–46; Woodrow Wilson, "An Address in Chicago to Democrats on Lincoln's Birthday," February 12, 1912, ibid., 24:152–53; Woodrow Wilson, "Address in the Williams Grove Auditorium, Williams Grove, Pennsylvania," August 29, 1912, in *A Crossroads of Freedom: The 1912 Campaign Speeches of Woodrow Wilson*, ed. John Wells Davidson (New Haven, CT: Yale University Press, 1956), 52–61. Woodrow Wilson, "Lessons from Lincoln," address delivered at the Coliseum, State Fair Grounds, Springfield, Illinois, October 9, 1912, in *Crossroads*, 394–98. Also see Woodrow Wilson, "Leaders of Men," June 17, 1890, *Papers*, 6:644–71.

38. Wilson, "'Abraham Lincoln,'" 40–41.

39. James W. Ceaser, *Presidential Selection: Theory and Development* (Princeton, NJ: Princeton University Press, 1979), esp. 192–97; Jeffrey K. Tulis, *The Rhetorical Presidency* (Princeton, NJ: Princeton University Press, 1987), 117–44.

40. Wilson, *Constitutional Government*, 54–81. See Pestritto, *Woodrow Wilson*, 209–10. Also see Krannawitter, *Vindicating Lincoln*, 299–301.

41. Herman Belz, *Abraham Lincoln, Constitutionalism, and Equal Rights in the Civil War Era* (New York: Fordham University Press, 1998), 19, 28. See Clinton Rossiter, *Constitutional Dictatorship: Crisis Government in the Modern Democracies* (Princeton, NJ: Princeton University Press, 1948), 212, 224; James G. Randall, *Constitutional Problems under Lincoln*, rev. ed. (Urbana: University of Illinois Press, 1951), 30–47; Gottfried Dietze, *America's Political Dilemma* (Baltimore: Johns Hopkins University Press, 1968), 57–58, and see also 185–90 and 175–205 more generally.

42. Lincoln, Message to Congress in Special Session, July 4, 1861, *Collected Works*, 4:429.

43. Benjamin A. Kleinerman, "Lincoln's Example: Executive Power and the Survival of Constitutionalism," *Perspectives on Politics* 3, no. 4 (December 2005): 805–8.

44. Lincoln, "The Perpetuation of Our Political Institutions": Address before the Young Men's Lyceum of Springfield, Illinois, January 27, 1838, *Collected Works*, 1:112–15.

45. Charles R. Kesler, "Woodrow Wilson and the Statesmanship of Progress," in *Natural Right and Political Right: Essays in Honor of Harry V. Jaffa*, ed. Thomas B. Silver and Peter W. Schramm (Durham, NC: Carolina Academic Press, 1984), 115–18; Charles R. Kesler, "The Public Philosophy of the New Freedom and the New Deal," in *The New Deal and Its Legacy: Critique and Reappraisal*, ed. Robert Eden (New York: Greenwood Press, 1989), 157–58.

46. Lincoln to Henry L. Pierce and Others, April 6, 1859, *Collected Works*, 3:376.

47. Wilson, "'Abraham Lincoln,'" 39. See Pestritto, *Woodrow Wilson*, 57.

48. Pestritto, *Woodrow Wilson*, 57; Woodrow Wilson, "A Calendar of Great Americans," February 1894, *Papers*, 8:373–74.

49. Wilson, *Constitutional Government*, 4; Wilson, *New Freedom*, 42–43.

50. Kesler, "Woodrow Wilson," 115–18; Kesler, "Public Philosophy," 157–58.

51. See Ronald D. Rietveld, "Franklin D. Roosevelt's Abraham Lincoln," in *Franklin D. Roosevelt and Abraham Lincoln: Competing Perspectives on Two Great Presidencies*, ed. William D. Pederson and Frank J. Williams (Armonk, NY: M. E. Sharpe, 2003), 10–60; Alfred Haworth Jones, *Roosevelt's Image Brokers: Poets, Playwrights, and the Use of the Lincoln Symbol* (Port Washington, NY: Kennikat Press, 1974).

52. Franklin D. Roosevelt, "'A Tribute to Abraham Lincoln,' to Be Read on His Birthday," Letter to the Lincoln Association of Cleveland, Ohio, January 25, 1936, in *The Public Papers and Addresses of Franklin D. Roosevelt*, ed. Samuel I. Rosenman (New York: Random House, 1938), 5:68; emphasis added.

53. Sidney M. Milkis, "Franklin D. Roosevelt, the Economic Constitutional Order, and the New Politics of Presidential Leadership," in *The New Deal and the Triumph of Liberalism*, ed. Sidney M. Milkis and Jerome M. Mileur (Amherst: University of Massachusetts Press, 2002), 34–35.

54. Franklin D. Roosevelt, "New Conditions Impose New Requirements upon Government and Those Who Conduct Government," Campaign Address on Progressive Government at the Commonwealth Club, San Francisco, California, September 23, 1932, *Public Papers*, 1:753.

55. See, for example, Lincoln, Speech at Springfield, Illinois, June 26, 1857, *Collected Works*, 398–410; Lincoln, Reply: Fifth Debate with Stephen A. Douglas, at Galesburg, Illinois, October 7, 1858, ibid., 3:220.

56. Robert Eden, "On the Origins of the Regime of Pragmatic Liberalism: John Dewey, Adolf A. Berle, and FDR's Commonwealth Club Address of 1932," *Studies in American Political Development* 7 (Spring 1993): 76–77. Harvey C. Mansfield Jr., *America's Constitutional Soul* (Baltimore: Johns Hopkins University Press, 1991), 1–17, 193–208.

57. Eden, "Regime of Pragmatic Liberalism," 77. On the criticism and redefinition of liberalism, see John Dewey, *Liberalism Old and New* (New York: Milton, Balch and Company, 1930).

58. See Milkis, "Franklin D. Roosevelt," 37–40.

59. Franklin D. Roosevelt, "New Conditions Impose New Requirements upon Government and Those Who Conduct Government," Campaign Address on Progressive Government at the Commonwealth Club, San Francisco, California, September 23, 1932, *Public Papers*, 1:742–56; Franklin D. Roosevelt, "Unless There Is Security at Home, There Cannot Be Lasting Peace in the World," Message to the Congress on the State of the Union, January 11, 1944, ibid., 13:32–44.

60. Franklin D. Roosevelt, "Introduction" to the 1938 Volume of *Public Papers*, 7:xxviii–xxxi; cf. Lincoln, "Fragment on Government," [July 1, 1854?], *Collected Works*, 2:220–22.

61. See Harry V. Jaffa et al., *Original Intent and the Framers of the Constitution: A Disputed Question* (Washington, DC: Regnery Gateway, 1994), 261–62, and see also 28–29, 122–23; Krannawitter, *Vindicating Lincoln*, 310–11.

62. Here I follow Mansfield, *America's Constitutional Soul*, 56–59. See also 31–34, 93–95, 185–86, 196–200.

CONTRIBUTORS

Burrus M. Carnahan is the author of *Act of Justice: Lincoln's Emancipation Proclamation and the Law of War* (2007), *Lincoln on Trial: Southern Civilians and the Law of War* (2010), and numerous articles about Abraham Lincoln, international law, and the law of war. A former associate professor of law at the US Air Force Academy in Colorado, he is currently a professorial lecturer in law at the George Washington University, Washington, DC, and a foreign affairs officer at the Department of State. He was a member of the scholarly advisory group for President Lincoln's Cottage in Washington, DC, for 2012–14 and serves on the board of advisors for the Lincoln Forum.

Charles M. Hubbard is a professor of history and the executive director of the Abraham Lincoln Institute for the Study of Leadership and Public Policy at Lincoln Memorial University in Harrogate, Tennessee. He has served on the Tennessee Historical Commission and the board of advisors of the Lincoln Bicentennial Commission. He is a founding board member of the Abraham Lincoln Institute of the Mid-Atlantic. Dr. Hubbard is a former director of the Abraham Lincoln Library Museum and a former managing editor of the *Lincoln Herald*. He is a Senior Fulbright scholar and a Mellon Foundation recipient. He received the Lincoln Diploma of Honor for contributions to the field of Lincoln studies. He received a special Abraham Lincoln Bicentennial edition of the Order of Lincoln in 2009. He has contributed numerous articles about Lincoln and Civil War diplomacy to scholarly journals. His written and edited books include *The Many Faces of Lincoln* (1997), *The Burden of Confederate Diplomacy* (1998), *Lincoln and His Contemporaries* (1999), *Historic*

Reflection on U.S. Governance and Civil Society (2001), and *Corregidor in War in Peace* (2006).

Jason R. Jividen is an associate professor of politics at Saint Vincent College, where he also serves as a fellow in civic and constitutional affairs for the Center for Political and Economic Thought and as director of the Aurelius Scholars Program in Western Civilization. Dr. Jividen has delivered numerous invited lectures and conference papers on topics in ancient and modern political philosophy, the principles of American founding, Lincoln's political thought, American Progressivism, and civic education. His recent peer-reviewed publications include *Claiming Lincoln: Progressivism, Equality, and the Battle for Lincoln's Legacy in Presidential Rhetoric* (2011); *Statesmanship and Progressive Reform: An Assessment of Herbert Croly's Abraham Lincoln* (with J. David Alvis, 2013); "American Democracy and Liberal Education in an Era of Relevance," in *Higher Education in an Era of Relevance*, edited by Timothy L. Simpson (2013); "American Progressivism and the Legacy of Abraham Lincoln" (with Ronald J. Pestritto, 2014) in *Lincoln and Liberty: Wisdom for the Ages*, edited by Lucas Morel; and "Presidential Statesmanship as Civic Education," in *Expositions: Interdisciplinary Studies in the Humanities* 8, no. 2 (2014).

Edna Greene Medford is a professor and the chairperson of the Department of History at Howard University, where she has taught for twenty-eight years. She specializes in nineteenth-century US history, with an emphasis on slavery, the Civil War, and Reconstruction. Dr. Medford serves on several advisory boards, including the Lincoln Forum (executive committee), the Ulysses S. Grant Association, *Washington History* magazine, the Abraham Lincoln Bicentennial Foundation, and the Lincoln Studies Center (Knox College). Her publications include studies of the Lincoln presidency and the African American transition from slavery to freedom. She lectures regularly on a number of topics, including African American responses to Abraham Lincoln's wartime policies. She is the author of *Lincoln and Emancipation*, a coauthor of *The Emancipation Proclamation: Three Views* (2006) and the introductory author of *The Price of Freedom: Slavery and the Civil War*, volumes 1 and 2.

Ron Soodalter is an independent scholar and a freelance journalist. In addition to his two current books, *Hanging Captain Gordon* and *The Slave Next Door*, Soodalter's publications include articles in magazines and journals. He has written for several publications, including the *New York Times*, *Smithsonian*, *Civil War Times*, *Military History*, *New York Archives*, and *True West*, and has been a featured columnist for *America's Civil War*. Soodalter's primary focus is in the area of popular cultural history and material culture. He is the recipient of the International Regional Magazine Association's 2010 Gold Award and the 2014 Award of Merit for History. Soodalter currently serves on the board of directors of the Abraham Lincoln Institute and the advisory board of the SS *Columbia* Project.

Mark E. Steiner is an American legal historian, having received both a JD and a PhD from the University of Houston. He has served as an associate editor of the Legal Papers of Abraham Lincoln project, based in Springfield, Illinois. He is now Godwin Lewis PC Research Professor and a professor of law at the South Texas College of Law in Houston, where he teaches American legal history, as well as consumer law and Texas civil procedure. He is the author of *An Honest Calling: The Law Practice of Abraham Lincoln* (2006).

Daniel W. Stowell is the director and editor of the Papers of Abraham Lincoln, a project of the Abraham Lincoln Presidential Library and Museum. Prior to holding this position, he was the director and editor of the Lincoln Legal Papers. He is the author or editor of six books, several booklets and articles, and a half dozen electronic publications, such as *The Lincoln Log: A Daily Chronology of the Life of Abraham Lincoln*. His editorial work includes *The Papers of Abraham Lincoln: Legal Documents and Cases*, 4 vols. (2008).

Natalie Sweet is a research fellow at the Abraham Lincoln Institute for the Study of Leadership and Public Policy as well as an adjunct in the history department at Lincoln Memorial University. She was a 2007 History Scholar Finalist in the Gilder Lehrman Institute of American History's History Scholar Program and a past recipient of the James Still Fellowship at the University of Kentucky, where she received her MA in history in 2010. In 2012, she was awarded a research fellowship from the White House Historical Association to study the domestic staff that worked in the Lincoln White House. Her articles have appeared in both the *Lincoln Herald* and the *Journal of the Abraham Lincoln Association*.

Frank J. Williams, chief justice (retired) of the Rhode Island Supreme Court, has served as president of the Lincoln Group of Boston and of the Abraham Lincoln Association. From 2001 to 2010, he served on the US Abraham Lincoln Bicentennial Commission. He has presented various lectures and numerous articles about Lincoln over the years and is the literary editor of the *Lincoln Herald*, in which he surveys the field of Lincolniana. His books include *Abraham Lincoln: Sources and Styles of Leadership* (1994), *Abraham Lincoln Contemporary: An American Legacy* (1995), *Judging Lincoln* (2007), and *Lincoln as Hero* (2012).

INDEX

Italicized page numbers indicate figures.

abolitionist movement, 56, 57. *See also* emancipation *entries*
Adams, John, 62
African Americans. *See* black Americans
Albany Evening Journal, 81
Alexandria (VA) Local News, 168, 170
American exceptionalism perspective, 32, 34
American Republican Party, 39
Anderson, Charles F., 158–59
Anderson, Robert, 21
Annual Messages, 42, 100
anti-Catholicism, 32, 35–36, 39–41, 159
Article II, US Constitution, 108
Ashley, James, 102–3
Ashtabula Weekly Telegraph, 168
Atlas & Argus, 79, 82
Audacity of Hope, The (Obama), 176, 178

Baker, Edward D., 16
Bale, Abraham, 10–11
Bates, Edward: on citizenship ambiguities, 32; habeas corpus dispute, 76; in "law firm cabinet," 19; and Lincoln's clemency approach, 110; prisoner-related issues, 24, 134; West Virginia statehood question, 22
Beall, John Yates, 121–24
Belz, Herman, 45, 188

Bissell, William H., 10
black Americans: citizenship debate, 38, 42–49; military service, 23–24, *33*, 46–49, 101, 118–21; and peace negotiations, 102
Black Hawk War, 8, 90, 139
Blair, Montgomery, 19, 21, 22, 24, 122, 144
blockade imposition, 68, 74, 132, 133, 145n1
Booth, John Wilkes, 49
Bradford, Augustus, 144
Bromwell, Henry, 113, 117, 124
Brooks, Preston, 154
Browning, Orville H., 95–96, 122
Buchanan, James, 57
Burlingame, Michael, 171
Burns, Thomas, 157, 159, 160, 162
Burnside, Ambrose, 77–78
Butler, Benjamin F., 95
Butler, William, 17

cabinet, Lincoln's management style, 7, 19, 21–25
Cadwalader, George, 76
Caledonian, 118–19
Cameron, Simon, 19, 164
Campbell, David B., 15
Canisius, Theodore, 37, 41
Carnahan, Burrus M., 2